DESCENDANTS OF CYRUS

DESCENDANTS OF CYRUS

Travels through Everyday Iran | *Christopher Thornton*

POTOMAC BOOKS | *An imprint of the University of Nebraska Press*

Library of Congress Cataloging-in-Publication Data
Names: Thornton, Christopher, author.
Title: Descendants of Cyrus: travels through everyday Iran /
Christopher Thornton.
Description: Lincoln: Potomac Books, an imprint of the
University of Nebraska Press [2019].
Identifiers: LCCN 2019009201
ISBN 9781640120372 (cloth: alk. paper)   ISBN 9781640122710 (mobi)
ISBN 9781640122703 (epub)   ISBN 9781640122727 (pdf)
Subjects: LCSH: Iran—Description and travel. |
Thornton, Christopher—Travel—Iran.
Classification: LCC DS259.2 .T48 2019 | DDC 955—dc23
LC record available at https://lccn.loc.gov/2019009201

Set in Arno Pro by Mikala R. Kolander.

I am an Iranian. A descendant of Cyrus the Great. The very emperor who proclaimed at the pinnacle of power 2,500 years ago that "he would not reign over the people if they did not wish it." And [he] promised not to force any person to change his religion and faith and guaranteed freedom for all.

—SHIRIN EBADI,
Nobel Peace Prize acceptance speech, 2003

CONTENTS

ACKNOWLEDGMENTS

First of all, I'd like to express great appreciation to all of my Iranian friends for the enthusiasm, support, and advice they offered from the start of this project. This also includes the people of Iran, whose warmth and hospitality I was so fortunate to receive on my three trips to the country, and all of whom I consider friends-at-large. They convinced me of the merits of this book and its message—that there is another side of Iranian history, culture, and society that the world outside of Iran needs to be aware of, in order to bring greater understanding to the political differences of today. Then there is the editorial staff at Potomac Books—Tom Swanson, Ann Baker, and the rest of the team—who also recognized the merits of the book and had the necessary experience and professionalism to see it through to completion. This includes Virginia Perrin, the copy editor, who toiled over the manuscript with the meticulous care needed to catch slight inconsistencies in spellings and terminology that my glazed eyes could no longer identify. A very special thanks goes to my Iranian content editor, who supplied invaluable suggestions and corrections to the fine points of Persian history, culture, and language. Finally, let me not forget my agent, Erik Hane, the catalyst for this entire effort. Had he not recognized the value of the book and relentlessly gone about finding a publisher, none of the rest of us would have had much to do these past many months.

Editorial note: Transliterations from languages that don't use the Latin alphabet can often be messy, and Farsi, particularly, poses special challenges. With that in mind, every effort was made to settle on Latin spellings that most closely represent the original Farsi terms and pronunciations. If any of these cause an affront to Persian linguists, I can only express my sincerest regrets.

DESCENDANTS OF CYRUS

1 | Tehran

There is not a single school or town that is excluded from the happiness of the holy defense of the nation, from drinking the exquisite elixir of martyrdom, or from the sweet death of the martyr, who dies in order to live forever in paradise.
—*Etalaat* newspaper, in the aftermath of the Iran-Iraq War

In a scene near the beginning of the film *Argo*, about the rescue of the U.S. diplomats held hostage at the beginning of the Islamic Revolution, there is a shot of the Tehran skyline with a backdrop of the snow-capped Alborz Mountains. It is reminiscent of similar shots of Boulder, Colorado, set against the panorama of the American Rockies. Like the Rockies, the Alborz are suffused with mythology, which would be expected of any natural feature in an ancient land. According to Indian philosophy, all of the continents were connected by a single mountain range. Ancient Persian thinkers took this a step further, believing that the Earth's mountains rose from a round, flat plain, and beneath the surface they were linked together like plants joined at their roots, and this union formed a unifying force. Above ground the mountains were drawn together by a single peak. In the case of the Alborz this would be Mount Damavand, at 15,312 feet the highest in the Middle East. Some historians believe that this line of thinking paved the way for Zoroastrianism and the concept of monotheism.

The shot from *Argo*, and any of Tehran that feature the backdrop of the Alborz, as most do, is an apt metaphor of life in Iran today. One only needs to imagine the mountains as the Islamic regime: It is a looming fact of daily life, always present and never to be ignored. At times it may seem to disappear, just as the mountains are occasionally shrouded by the Tehran smog, but always it returns, as fixed and immobile as the mountains themselves.

The mountains have been a fixture of the landscape longer than the city they tower over. Tehran is not one of the great capitals of the Middle East, like Cairo, Damascus, and Baghdad. As Middle Eastern cities go, Tehran is an upstart. Until the end of the first millennium the dominant city south of the Caspian Sea was Rey, or Raghes in its ancient form. But Rey was not meant to last. It was attacked, destroyed, and rebuilt after invasions by the Arabs in the seventh century and the Turks in the eleventh. In the thirteenth century the Mongols provided the death blow, razing the city and slaughtering most of the residents. Nearby Tehran, previously known only for agricultural production, primarily pomegranates, became a convenient alternative for urban settlement. It slowly grew into a small city, and by the sixteenth century it became an important administrative center of the Safavid dynasty. In 1796 Agha Mohammad Khan Qajar chose to make it his capital.

To say that Persian rulers have been fickle in their choice of capitals is an understatement. Tehran is the thirty-second in the history of the empire. Agha Mohammad Khan's reasoning, like that of his predecessors, was strategic. Tehran was close to the Caucasus region, then under Persian rule but threatened by imperial Russia, and it was a safe distance from an aggressive Ottoman Empire to the northwest. Also, by choosing Tehran as his capital he stayed clear of the regional rivalries in Shiraz and Esfahan and local leaders who might rebel against him. Tehran was, in many ways, a safe pick.

In 1850 the city had only eighty thousand inhabitants, but in 1878 a new plan expanded the city walls, and in the 1920s and 1930s Reza Shah Pahlavi rebuilt the city in quasi-European style, cutting wide boulevards through dense neighborhoods and laying out streets in the grid pattern copied from the Europeans. New buildings combined Western and traditional Persian designs, as Iran began to look westward for cultural influence. The modernization trend accelerated under Pahlavi's son, Mohammad Reza Shah, who aimed to tilt Iran further westward. New universities and research centers opened, again mimicking European architectural styles but with a hint of Persian classicism. Tehran became the capital of not only the Iranian government but a thriving cultural scene. The population swelled.

This is the Tehran that greets visitors today—along with the backdrop of the Alborz Mountains. The circumstances of my first visit were unique. It was June 2009, a few days after the contested election that saw firebrand hardliner Mahmoud Ahmadinejad returned to power through what many still believe were rigged voting results. Within hours of hearing the election results protestors poured into the broad avenues and squares that Reza Shah had built, waving placards that demanded, "Where is my vote?" Forces of the Revolutionary Guard and riot police were dispatched to intimidate dissenters, but the dissenters were not to be intimidated.

A little background on travel to Iran: Americans, Canadians, and citizens of the United Kingdom are not allowed to wander freely in the country. They must be accompanied by a licensed tour guide, and their visas and itineraries must be approved by a special office within the foreign ministry. New arrivals are met at the airport by their assigned guide, and I was greeted by mine—Sohrab—who had driven up to Tehran from his home in Shiraz the day before. But he almost didn't make it. He spent most of the night at a police station, after being stopped at a checkpoint that had been set up to keep the ranks of protestors from growing. Once he produced the documents proving that he had been appointed as my guide for the next two weeks he was allowed to leave, but only after these were verified by the foreign ministry, when the office opened in the morning.

Sohrab was a self-described "cool guy" who had a wife and two sons, but "I play around," he acknowledged, with casual bravado. He had lived in the U.S. for ten years, first in Florida, where he earned degrees in business and computer technology, and then in San Jose, California, working in the IT industry and riding his Harley-Davidson through the hills of Silicon Valley. "Illegal" CDs—*John Coltrane, Chet Baker in Tokyo*—rattled in the side-door pocket of his Volvo sedan.

He asked: Did I want to go straight to my hotel, or was I ready to start sightseeing? The question was a nonstarter. I wanted to plunge right in, and so we did. Our first stop was the most significant symbol of cultural, social, and political life in Iran today. It was the shrine of Ayatollah Khomeini, conveniently situated, for arriving visitors, on the highway that connects Imam Khomeini International Airport with the center of Tehran. At night the brilliantly lit, garish green dome is the brightest beacon on the road, a draw for the Shiite faithful and those who still revere Khomeini as their spiritual guide and political prophet, one sent by God to guide the Iranian nation back onto a heavenly path and away from the more secular-minded rule of Mohammad Reza Shah.

Khomeini's true believers are regular visitors to the shrine, and their cars nearly filled the parking lot when we pulled in. A mural-size painting of Khomeini and current supreme leader Ayatollah Khamenei stretched across the entrance. We passed through a series of brightly lit prayer halls with pilgrims lounging, while others sat cross-legged on the thick carpets as they flipped through dog-eared Qurans. Others drowsed in the sleepy hours of midafternoon, combining their midday nap with a moment of spiritual reverie. Finally we reached the room that contained the bier of Khomeini. It was brightly lit but far more modest than I expected, just a single bier elevated a few inches from the ground and draped with a gold and green cloth.

The faithful, sitting propped against the wall and sprawled on the carpet, paid no attention to me, which was deeply satisfying. I didn't want to be a spectacle, just another invisible visitor passing through, as thousands did each day. A few restless eyes were directed my way, but they soon returned to the Qurans spread across their laps or the bier of Khomeini. What was surprising was that there was no buildup, no air of ceremonial suspense in the approach to the final resting place of arguably the most influential Shiite leader of modern times. Politics aside, the small room represented the common touch that enabled Khomeini to connect with the common people. After a few minutes Sohrab and I wound our way back through the prayer halls and back to the entrance that led to the parking lot and twenty-first-century Tehran.

Sohrab asked again, Did I want to head to the hotel? He was not prodding or pushing, just expressing classic Persian hospitality. Still, again my answer was no—better to see the city in full swing, protests or not. It might take a little doing, Sohrab said, to wind our way around the streets and squares where demonstrations were taking place, which may or may not be blocked. And there was no way to know what was the easiest path through the city because the internet and mobile phone network had been cut. We'll find a way, I told him, and we did, first to the Abgineh Museum, housed in a nineteenth-century villa on Tir Street. Also known as the glass museum, the Abgineh could become a tragic mountain of shattered shards if a major earthquake were to strike this part of Tehran. Fortunately, this has yet to happen, so the collection of glasswork and ceramic ware, with some items dating back nearly a thousand years, stands secure on shelves and shielded within protective display cases for visitors to ogle. After gazing at the glass, there is the building itself, where a red-carpeted circular staircase connects the floors where former salons and reception rooms have been converted into exhibition halls. After touring the interior of the building one can wander in the surrounding garden, which offers no radiant glasswork or nineteenth-century décor but neatly kept lawns and towering greenery that create a rustic retreat in the center of the city.

Next was the National Jewels Museum—if we could get there, Sohrab said—and we did, after being rerouted a few times to keep us away from political trouble, or potential trouble. This meant being stuck in a traffic jam or two, but that is the smoothest of smooth driving in downtown Tehran.

Adjacent to the Central Bank of Iran, the Jewels Museum is a bomb-proof, heavily armed, guarded vault that contains more emeralds and sapphires, rubies and diamonds, than any single pair of eyes has ever seen, piled in pyramids within bulletproof display cases. Nowhere in Iran is the wealth of the Persian Empire more ostentatiously displayed, and nowhere is the contradiction between the Iranian past and present so vividly on display. The visitors—Iranian, Western, Asian, and others— pause to gape at the piles of jewels and the wealth they represent, but the message is a mixed one. From one perspective they stand for the enormous wealth that the empire accumulated all the way through the final Pahlavi dynasty. From another they illustrate the material self-indulgence of the monarchies that culminated in the Pahlavi dynasty, which the Islamic Revolution aimed to end, to return Iran to "the path to God." These included thirty diamond-studded tiaras, shields and swords encrusted with jewels, and the showpiece of the collection, the Koh-i Noor diamond, one of the largest in the world. It was Mohammad Reza Shah who brought them to the attention of the world by trotting them out at state functions and other formal ceremonies, raising the question of whether they were meant to reflect the glory of the Iranian nation or the monarch himself. And it was this creeping perception of megalomania that contributed to his downfall.

With all the commotion out on the street, it was a day for museum hopping. On our way north we had stopped at the Museum of Reza Abbassi. On display were ceramics and metalwork, tiles and silver coins from the ancient Achaemenid period, textiles and jewelry, a golden rhyton from the seventh-century dynasty—in other words, the trea-sure trove of an attic labeled "Persian history," dusted off, and scattered through the museum's floors. But the galleries had few visitors. The locals were trying to catch what bits of news they could, and most of the tourists who had not fled the country were staying close to their hotels. Sohrab and I had almost free run of the place, until an itchy guard appeared to tell us that the museum was closing—early.

It was edging past midafternoon but time enough for another stop, if we could zigzag around the blocked-off streets. We did, and pulled up in front of the National Carpet Museum, with enough time for a peak before closing. Sohrab dropped me off at the entrance, and I began wandering through the two floors of kilims and *gabbehs, soumaks,* and *souzanis,* some recently woven, others hundreds of years old, classic works whose age only added to their value.

Probably no craft art is more associated with Iran than the production of carpets, and a finely woven Persian carpet will fit more snugly into the category of art than craft. The best take not weeks or months but years to produce, and families purchase them not only to provide decoration for the house but to serve as investments that will appreciate in value if they are well looked after. I was getting a short course in the history of carpet making just by reading the display cards propped around the museum: about the variety of knots that go into the weaving; the source of the colors that produce the natural dyes; the many styles of carpets that result, from *ghali* to *ghalitcheh, zaronim* to *sedjadeh, kelleghi* to *kenareh;* and the regions of Iran that have developed their own patterns—Kerman and Khuzestan, Tabriz, Mashhad, and Esfahan, Shiraz, Kashan, and Qom—much like wine regions of France that have cultivated their own vintages. But then the visit was cut short.

Suddenly a guard was making the rounds, announcing that it was closing time. But it was only 4:15—forty-five minutes should have been left for stragglers to wander. Still, he was fidgety, nervous, insistent, and when I stepped outside I found out why. The corner of Fatemi and Karegar Avenues was shrouded in tear gas. The shouts of protestors could be heard on the other side of the bushes that separated the museum from the street. Police vans filled the intersection. Protestors were being thrown inside.

Sohrab appeared, holding a plastic trash bag.

"Take this—put it over your face."

We threaded through knots of protestors, their eyes red and faces running with tears. In the middle of the street an old woman in a black chador was shouting in a frenzy.

"What's she saying?" I asked.

"She's cursing the government," Sohrab replied.

"But what's she saying?"

"'Fucking bastards, beating your own people!'"

We reached the car and zigged and zagged in the direction of the hotel wherever the path was clear. Tehranis not battling with riot police were heading home from work, hailing taxis, and descending the steps of metro stations, maintaining an appearance of calm, even if the pace was brisker.

My hotel was the Kosar, off Vali Asr Square. Outside a crowd of protestors filled the narrow street, sprouting green streamers, green wristbands, green T-shirts, green bandanas—waving the color of the antigovernment green movement. One of the desk clerks had emerged from the reception area to watch, then motioned for me to stand back under the cover of the parking area, out of range of snipers who might be planted on the rooftops. Without warning, a team of *basij* militiamen raced the length of the block on motorbikes, clubs raised.

Shortly after the Islamic Revolution, Ayatollah Khomeini saw that the regime could hold on to power only by maintaining an army of grassroots enforcers to quell dissent and to serve as riot police should protests erupt. So he formed the basij, or "guardians of the revolution." Today their forces number over a million, spread over the entire country. Its ranks, both men and women, are drawn almost exclusively from the marginalized working class and others without a clear path to advance in Iranian society. For their service they are rewarded with perks such as preferences in hiring, job promotions, and admission to universities. These were the young men now revving their engines and waving their truncheons, challenging the crowd. Some, no doubt, were true believers in the Islamic regime, others little more than hired guns but using the moment to make the most of their show of force.

The crowd gathered in front of the Kosar and headed toward Vali Asr Square, where several hundred riot police had massed. A column of Revolutionary Guard troops were marching down Vali Asr Street, while several dozen *basiji* swirled into the roundabout on motorbikes, weaving defiantly in and out of the rush-hour traffic. Around the square people had gathered on sidewalks and squeezed between the parked cars to watch the militiamen on the other side, waiting for—neither knew what.

Stretching thirty miles, from the southern suburbs to the apron of the Alborz Mountains to the north, Vali Asr Street is Tehran's main artery and political mileage marker. Running as straight as a compass arrow, it cuts through the conservative, working-class neighborhoods, bypasses the Tehran bazaar, and then begins a long, sleepy climb toward the mountains and North Tehran, de facto headquarters of the reformist movement and all that rankles the government. To travel the length of Vali Asr Street is to experience the many facets of Iranian society that the media lens usually overlooks.

"If they make a move, get out of the way," a man beside me said. "They show no mercy."

Almost on cue, a team of basiji rounded the corner, riot shields raised. Their commander—a bullish, pudgy man with razor-sharp eyes set in a taut face—had given the order to break up the thickets of onlookers, and so they charged up onto the sidewalk astride their motorbikes as the spectators cleared out, retreating to the side streets.

There were a lot of sparks but no fire. I began walking up Vali Asr Street, and soon—all too soon—an odd sense of normalcy returned. Pedestrians filled the sidewalk and shopkeepers were sitting on stoops, absorbing the late-afternoon sun. But a few blocks later the traffic stopped. Horns began blowing, at first only a few, but others soon joined in. Near the intersection of Beheshti Street a young woman pulled me aside. Her eyes were bloodshot and swollen.

"They're spraying tear gas ahead," she said in fluent English. "Be careful."

She paused, and in her voice was the certainty of uncertainty, of being sure only of what one does not know.

"They took my sister and my parents away. They were shouting with their fists in the air when the police came. I don't know where they are."

She paused again.

"I don't know what to say," she said. "I apologize for my country . . ."

I would hear this many times over the next few days: "I'm so sorry . . ." and "I apologize for my country." Always I brushed these off—"Don't worry about it" . . . "It's not *your* fault"—as though a violent insurrection was no more an inconvenience than street litter, and any individual could be responsible for either. But one afternoon I heard it again— "I'm so sorry"—and this time the apologist gave the reason for his sympathy: Michael Jackson had died.

Around the intersection the sweet, acrid mist of tear gas still hung thick in the air. By the time I reached Sae'e Park I felt like an actor who had wandered off the stage and out of the theater entirely. Couples sat on benches in the dusk of the summer evening, and the vendors did a brisk business selling ice cream cones and cotton candy to giggling children.

My destination was Bix, an upscale restaurant advertising California-Mediterranean cuisine in the Gandhi Street Shopping Center, which was more of a center for trendy restaurants and cafés than any retail trade. When I arrived almost all the tables were empty, but in a little while the patrons began filing in—women in pressed jeans, colorful headscarves, and form-fitting manteaux, the thigh-length jacket worn by most Iranian women. Men wore European-cut shirts and polished shoes. These were classic "North Tehran elites," upper-class profession-als able to obtain Western visas to escape Iran for holidays abroad, and until recently their higher incomes allowed them to escape the financial strains brought by years of economic sanctions. But no more. Galloping inflation and a plummeting rial now had even the formerly financially insulated complaining about the price of pistachios.

I was about to dig into my roasted vegetable pizza when Parviz and Raha, a couple seated at the table across from me asked what I was doing in Iran—under the circumstances. It was an understandable question—under the circumstances—and one that deserved an hon-est answer: I had been planning the trip for more than a month, the time it took for my visa to be approved, and I saw no reason to cancel it because of the circumstances. Then I had a question for them, one that they might choose not to answer, or one they might, here in the bastion of the green movement and the "North Tehran elites." What did they think of the election results? The candidates?

"Same shit, different shade," Parviz was quick to reply.

I asked him to explain.

"All of them—they've all served the same rotten system."

Parviz's "same shit" referred to Hossein Mousavi and Mehdi Karroubi, the reformist candidates preferred by reformist-minded Iranians like Parviz and Raha, but four years later the "same shit" label would have applied to current president Hassan Rouhani. Like Mousavi and Karroubi, Rouhani had been nurtured by the same political system that had produced Khamenei, Ahmadinejad, and the other hardest of the hardliners, Ayatollah Ahmad Janati, chairman of the Assembly of Experts, and Ali Larijani, former nuclear negotiator and secretary of the National Security Council. Since candidates must prove their ideological stripes to be allowed to run in any race, liberal voters are always left with the choice of the least bad.

In Parviz's view, the outcome of the election, no matter how it was tilted or fudged, mattered little. Hardliner, reformist—both meant the perpetuation of "the same rotten system." So, I asked, was nothing gained? Was there no point to the people taking to the streets?

Parviz forced a thin smile. "The people have finally seen that there's nothing inside these leaders," he said. "And the leaders have learned that the people are willing to fight them."

Raha cut in. "We deserve better," she said. "All this talk of nuclear power and arguments with the West are just ways of keeping the people distracted. They're not what the people really care about. We want to see much more attention paid to the problems in our own country."

I asked her—if the government were to collapse what would the people want?

"I'm not sure. I'm not really sure what I want. There would be a lot of confusion. For many of us this is all we've ever known, but we do know we don't want all this religion in politics."

I finished my pizza and then had a pot of tea at the Café de France, which, like Bix, was on the second floor of the complex. A brick fireplace and a set of floor-to-ceiling bookcases gave it a cozy, homey feel. A vintage poster for the 1960s western *A Fistful of Dollars* starring Clint Eastwood was tacked to the atrium-like ceiling, which made the small room feel much larger than it was. Flamenco guitar pumped from a CD playing behind the serving counter. A scan of the bookshelves showed a sincere interest in American culture, even if the titles could provide only the smallest of peepholes into a sprawling, complex subject. There was *The Anatomy Lesson*, by Philip Roth, and Ralph Nader's *The Big Boys: Power and Position in American Business.* Not all young Iranians were battling the basiji out on the streets. The Café de France and the other coffee shops on the second floor had their share of customers. Were these late-night café loungers apolitical, apathetic? No, not at all. A revolutionary movement is like an army, its ranks filled with various specialists. Some rebels will resist the regime by circulating news via Facebook posts and tweets. Others ask provocative questions in the university classrooms. Both men and women will push the boundaries of the Islamic dress code. And then there are those who will shout, "Where is my vote?!" in the streets.

Witnessing a society in chaos is like watching a windshield splinter after a pebble has hit it. One never knows where the cracks will spread, which areas will be left untouched, or how extensive the damage will be.

I stayed at the café until closing time and chose to forgo a taxi, preferring to walk back to the hotel the same way I came, along Vali Asr Street. Tehran looked like any city about to shut its eyes for the night. Metal gates had been pulled down over the storefronts, though the lights of the occasional pizza shop or juice bar still glowed. Then the chanting started.

"Allahu Akbar! Death to the dictator! Allahu Akbar! Death to the dictator!" sounded across the rooftops from somewhere in the shadows of the dim side streets. After about fifteen minutes the street was lined with basiji, standing in pairs about thirty feet apart, their helmets hanging from the handlebars of their motorbikes, riot shields propped against the trees. Further along, in the small square at the intersection of Vali Asr and Jamal Od-Din about fifty young men had gathered under a street lamp. One held a pipe and another a long stick of wood. One of the men climbed on top of a road barrier and spoke while the rest gathered to listen. His speech finished, they restarted their bikes and rode off into the night. Minutes later, a fleet of fire trucks raced toward Vali Asr Square, followed by a column of troop transporters packed with riot policemen.

Back at the Kosar, there was no point in trying to find out what was happening. The internet connection had been slowed to a speed that rendered it useless, and every TV channel besides the state-run networks had been blocked, or reception was fitful. Word of mouth was the only way news traveled, and the night desk clerk told me that along Enqelab Avenue two buses and a bus shelter had been set ablaze.

The next morning Sohrab picked me up after breakfast for a tour of the sights of Tehran, or those we could get to depending on whatever demonstrations might pop up. Our first stop was Golestan Palace, not far from the hotel. It was still midmorning, so things were quiet out on the streets, but when we reached the access road that led to the palace entrance we hit an impasse. The road ran alongside the building housing the Ministry of Justice, and the police had blocked it. Tensions were simmering, and nervous leaders do not take risks. I thought Sohrab was going to return to Nasser Khosro Street, but no. He tapped the horn for the guard to move, as gentle a tap as a horn tap can be, but a honk of the horn nonetheless. The guard shouted that we could go no further and waved us back toward Nasser Khosro. Sohrab grabbed a manila envelope from under his seat and held it out the window.

"We're from the foreign ministry!" he shouted.

The guard shouted back and waved us back to Nasser Khosro.

No horn tap this time, but we didn't move. Sohrab waved the guard over to the car and showed him the envelope. He didn't open it, just displayed the seal identifying it, as he said, from the foreign ministry. It contained nothing more than the papers certifying his role as my guide during my stay in Iran, but it was enough to prod the guard to draw the barrier aside, and we proceeded to the palace.

I had to ask him how he had managed to get us in.

"Simple," he said. "They push, you push back. Don't take their shit."

We parked and passed through the entrance, which had not been closed, despite the barrier and the presence of the obtrusive guard.

We had the grounds to ourselves. As we stood in the grand courtyard, Sohrab was more animated by the troubles of the present than the glories of the past.

"Everything that has happened in the past thirty years is alien to our society," he said. "We haven't always had good leaders and political freedom, but at least we had social freedom. That son-of-a-bitch back there," he said. "Nothing in our culture tells us to accept that. Look at the words of our poets. They tell us that the people are supposed to guide society, not the rulers. We're not the kind of people to do what we're told just because someone says so. Our challenge now is to get back to the true character of our society."

This reminded me of my own characterization of revolutionary Iran: Think of it as a third-grade classroom run by a strict schoolmaster whose students just *won't* behave. They may pretend to when he stands in front of them, but as soon as his back is turned they make faces and hurl spitballs, and worst of all they don't take him seriously.

"In Iran religion isn't a cultural unifier like it is in the Arab world," Sohrab continued, "and it isn't as central to the Iranian identity. When the Arabs brought Islam here we took from it what we wanted, and things that ran counter to the Persian culture we ignored. It became more of a philosophy of life, not the kind of rules associated with religion."

What I was getting was part tour-guide talk, part political science lecture, but the circumstances could not have been better for a fusion of the two. Evidence for Sohrab's claim appeared on the palace walls, which were arrayed with blue-and-yellow tile paintings portraying elegant peacocks and hunting scenes in swirling rococo curves. Such images were common in Persian art but unthinkable in traditional Islamic painting, which forbids the portrayal of any living creature.

Sohrab wasn't so distracted by the guard at the gate, and the political reality he represented, that he neglected to fill me in on the history of Golestan and what it signified in Persian history. He told me that the palace became the seat of the royal household in the mid-eighteenth century under the rule of Agha Mohammad Khan Qajar. Most important, it was during the nineteenth century that Iran absorbed many cultural influences from the West, primarily central Europe. Consequently, the many grand halls would feel right at home in the Balkan peninsula, so meticulously do they mimic the decorative style of nineteenth-century southeastern Europe, with Persian touches. Chandeliers brightened the interiors, which were given the illusion of even greater grandeur by the ceiling-high mirrors that filled the rooms. Polished wooden tables and velvet seat covers replaced the hopelessly out-of-fashion sofas and bolster cushions. A special hall was added to show off Golestan's chinaware, some of it presented as gifts by European royalty. The message, expressed in the design of the palace, was clear: Iran was eager to shed its Asian identity. Another hall features Iranian and European paintings. And then there is the tilework.

The interiors of Golestan Palace may be magnificent in their seamless blending of Persian and European design, but it is the tilework that steals the show. The walls of the courtyard are decorated with elaborately painted hunting scenes, depictions of court princes, wild animals, and exotic birds, all painted on square tiles in brilliant blue and yellow, with accents in green, white, and pink. Throughout the courtyard tapered palm trees stand at attention like a distinguished honor guard, and tall, delicate archways connect the courtyards to the halls inside.

The beauty of the place had a soothing effect even on Sohrab, who dropped his political gripes to lead me over to the Edifice of the Sun, two towers that were added to give anyone who climbed to the top a bird's-eye view of the city. And he showed me the private retreat of Nasser ad-Din Shah, a small terrace with a marble throne, dubbed "the nook" (*kherbrat*), which once had a fountain and small pool. It was here that the shah preferred to spend his quiet time, to allow the affairs of state to be washed away by the water from the fountain.

An urban island, Golestan Palace is as serene today as it was in the nineteenth century, even in the midst of the postelection turmoil and the chants of antigovernment demonstrators. If there were protests going on in the streets nearby, we didn't hear them. If tear gas was being sprayed on the protestors, none of it drifted our way. Unfortunately, Reza Shah Pahlavi saw the palace as an eyesore, and a symbol of Iran's outdated (Asian) past. He was particularly offended by, and destroyed, the section where Nasser ad-Din Shah stashed his many women and enjoyed his many affairs. Some opposed the move, arguing that, morality and modernism aside, the wing represented a valuable part of Persian history. Despite these arguments, it came down. Yet neither Reza Shah, nor his son Mohammad, could completely sever themselves from this symbol of the glory of Persian history. Both held their coronation ceremonies in Golestan Palace and used it for state ceremonies.

Considering the geography of Tehran, built on the southern slope of a mountain range, it would make sense that the city would expand north, where cooler air would substitute for air conditioning in the pre-electrical era, and all through the summer water would cascade down from snowmelt at the higher elevations. Both of the Pahlavis followed the masses, or led them, building summer palaces within the forest land of Saad Abad, on the northern edge of Tehran. In the heyday of the monarchy Saad Abad was a royal preserve, off limits to the common folk. After the Islamic Revolution it became a vast museum complex covering over one hundred hectares of gardens and walking paths that lead into the Alborz Mountains, where panoramic viewpoints look down with superior remove on the seething, traffic-clogged city. No longer the Pahlavis' playground, today Saad Abad is the place where Tehranis come to stroll, and picnic, and smoke water pipes, and sip tea over endless games of backgammon on weekends.

One of the largest buildings of the complex was refitted as the Museum of Fine Arts, to display works by well-known Iranian artists as well as Western masters, such as the Spanish surrealist Salvador Dali and the Russian landscape painter Ivanovich Shishkin. As fine a painter as he was, none of Shishkin's forest scenes ever rivaled the view from the windows of the museum. Stately groves of birch trees arch over the roadways and walking paths that wind from museum to museum and often nowhere, the best direction of all.

After the fine arts museum I had plenty of time to take in the rest of Saad Abad's prime sights—the simply but aptly named White Palace and Green Palace—unless they, too, were going to close early. Which first?

Seniority ruled the day. I chose the Green Palace, because it was older and closer, in case it, too, shut its doors before closing time. Closing or not, I took my time getting over there, absorbing the beauty of the woods and the brightness of the sun as it passed through the summer leaves. This was the Tehran I had grown to enjoy—a city with ample oases of green to escape the maddening traffic that could paralyze the streets almost any time of day, and the needs, anguish, and activity of fourteen million souls, some of whom had recently spilled out onto the streets. Parks could be found in every part of town, but Saad Abad was the envy of them all, and on this day many Tehranis were taking advantage of it, treading the footpaths to avoid not only the traffic but the political chaos that added to it.

The Green Palace is so named both because of the plant life that climbs its exterior walls, imported from the northwest region of Zanjan, and the green stones from which it was built. Even though the Green Palace predates the Pahlavi period, the Pahlavis put it to good use, holding receptions and receiving important guests to show off its main attraction—the Mirror Hall, a room bedazzled with enough—yes—mirrors to turn a flickering candle into a sparkling light display. I wasn't wowed by the bling. It was the view from the rear terrace overlooking the city that was far more satisfying to the eyes. And it was a bold reminder of the sweep of Persian history, for the moment making the postelection tumult almost insignificant, a single discolored tile within a mosaic comprising thousands.

Then there was the White Palace, actually more manor house than anything that could be called a palace. Reza Shah Pahlavi added it to Saad Abad in the 1930s, to give the historic compound a bit of modern posh. By far the most unusual feature is the giant pair of boots that stand at the entrance, all that remain of a monolithic statue of Reza himself that once welcomed visitors. In 1979 revolutionaries tore down the statue but could never get to the firmly planted boots. They may remain a visual oddity, but far more peculiar is the interior of the palace, which stands as a time capsule of prerevolutionary Iran. Little has changed since Reza's son Mohammad fled the country on January 17,

1979. The décor is 1970s chic, with a tiger pelt on the floor that reminds visitors of the shag carpeting craze of the tasteless decade, and the shah's liquor bottles are left where they stood, to remind visitors of the very "un-Islamic" decadence of the Pahlavi era.

We had time for one more stop. Heading south from Saad Abad, Sohrab and I swung west past graceful, aquiline Milad Tower, which stands like a giant flower with a gently tapered stem supporting a bulbous crown. The tower was another modernizing project of Mohammad Reza in the 1970s that was never realized until decades after his downfall. The shah intended it to be the centerpiece of a vast business complex to boost trade and make his country a hub for international commerce. Reminiscent of Seattle's Space Needle, Milad Tower was going to place Iran at the center of a modern global economy. It didn't work out that way. Construction began in 1975, but four years later the shah was deposed, and the tower wasn't finally opened until 2007, a little late to serve as a symbol of a modern international economy and not the vision that the shah embraced. Today it better represents the colossal contradictions of today's Iran. Its revolving restaurant and telecommunications infrastructure plants a foot in a world we call "modern," yet the theocratic regime that opened it has drawn Iran backward, to a collection of values that most in the modern world view as regressive and repressive, even medieval.

Milad Tower behind us, we sped along the highway toward Azadi Square and another symbol of Tehran and the shah's monarchial rule. Dominating the enormous roundabout is Azadi Tower, named the Shahyad Tower when it was completed in 1971 for a ceremony to commemorate the 2,500th anniversary of the founding of the Persian Empire. But the massive military parade the shah ordered for the occasion, along with the amount of money spent, had skeptics wondering if he was really honoring the empire, the monarchy—which he headed—or himself. A giant upside-down Y pointing skyward, the tower was meant to signify the optimism of an emerging nation on the global stage, buoyed by seemingly endless supplies of petroleum being exported to an oil-thirsty world. Azadi Tower was a gateway, the splayed legs white curtains fluttering in a refreshing breeze.

Less than ten years later the Islamic Revolution would bring not only theocratic rule but all its inevitable contradictions to Iranian society. The King's Tower was renamed Freedom Tower, just as a long list of restrictions imposed constraints on almost every aspect of Iranian life. Instead of experiencing greater openness, the country damaged its ties with traditional allies and never cultivated new ones in the Arab or greater Islamic world. In a piercing irony, Hossein Amanat, designer of the tower, is a member of the Baha'i faith, a religious minority severely persecuted under Islamic rule, and shortly after the Islamic Revolution he fled the country. He has never been back.

Again, the day done, Sohrab dropped me at the hotel, and we set a pickup time for the next morning. This time Vali Asr Square was empty of Revolutionary Guard troops and basiji, but the desk clerk told me he had heard of more protests going on along Enqelab Avenue, a ten-minute walk south. I headed down to have a look. A protest was definitely going on, but this time there were no scuffles or tear gas or truncheon-wielding basiji roaring around on souped-up motorbikes. Instead, a long column of people, men and women, young and old, were marching along the street in silence. There were no chants. Many carried candles, the tender flames protected from the evening breeze by the walls of paper cups. In another cruel irony, they were marching along Enqelab (Revolution) Avenue toward Azadi (Freedom) Tower. If the purpose of the revolution was to point Iran in the direction of greater social and political freedom, the message was lost in translation. If the protestors had chosen to give voice to their grievances, I imagine they would have recited the lines of the Sufi poet Rumi, which expressed the freedom of the truly liberated spirit:

> Be like the sun for grace and mercy.
> Be like the night to cover others' faults.
> Be like running water for generosity.

Be like death for rage and anger.
Be like the Earth for modesty.
Appear as you are.
Be as you appear.

≈

It would be four years before I would return to Tehran, and in that time a political swing of the pendulum had rocked Iran. The chaotic presidency of Mahmoud Ahmadinejad had been replaced by that of liberal-minded pragmatist Hassan Rouhani. The hardliners had been pushed onto their back foot. Rouhani supporters celebrated in the streets on election night, honking horns and shouting cheers from car windows. In 2015 the nuclear agreement was signed, promising long-awaited relief from sanctions and the rebuilding of a long-ailing economy, which would be jump-started by massive foreign investment. Perennial optimists even talked of a "Persian Spring." Perennial cynics chose to watch and wait.

"They do this all the time," a friend told me who had voted for Rouhani, and it had been her first vote in a presidential election in decades because there was only a glimmer of hope that a vote would make a difference. "After hardline rule they'll let a reformer in to make us happy, but they won't let him really do anything." For days she was indecisive—wondering whether to give credibility to a "democracy" that many believed to be a sham, or to remain silent and have no reason to complain about the outcome.

Like Barack Obama in 2008, Rouhani rode a wave of youth support, a not insignificant voting block in Iran, considering that 60 percent of the population is under thirty and the voting age is sixteen. And Rouhani was reelected in 2017 with 57 percent of the vote, again driving supporters into the streets to celebrate, in Tehran and other cities. Prior to the election, there was apprehension in the air. Would the result be tampered with, as widely believed to have occurred in 2009? Iranian opinion was divided.

"They would never try that again," another Rouhani supporter told me. "Last time they were caught off guard. They thought the people would just accept whatever they said the outcome was. They never expected such resistance."

Rouhani took his victory as an opportunity to press for further social change. "It would be a misrepresentation and also an insult to the Iranian people to say they only had economic demands," he said. "People had economic, political, and social demands."

He threw even more red meat to his supporters: "We cannot pick a lifestyle and tell two generations after us to think like that. It is impossible. Their views about life and the world are different than ours."

Rouhani felt the wind at his back, the hardliners on the defensive: "People's access to social media should not be permanently restricted. We cannot be indifferent to people's lives and businesses," he went on. Hardliners cringed. It was social media sites that allowed protestors to plan demonstrations in 2009 when mobile phone service was cut, and it was social media that was largely credited with helping to drive former Egyptian president Hosni Mubarak from power in 2011—reason enough that Facebook, YouTube, Twitter, and the popular Telegram messaging service work fitfully, if at all, in Iran.

I wondered if Rouhani might prove to be Iran's Mikhail Gorbachev, the last chairman of the Communist Party and president of the Soviet Union—a well-intentioned leader who tried to reform a system whose internal rot had pushed it past the point of reform and ended up destroying it. I also wondered if his promising words had any trickle-down effect, if they would make any practical difference on the streets and in daily lives. To put this in American terms: "Where's the beef?"

No one expected Tehran to turn into the Sin City of the Middle East, as it was becoming in the days of the Mohammad Reza Shah, or for women to shed their headscarves to return to the city nightclubs, but Rouhani had apparently dented the forces of otherwise formidable hardline resistance.

"I like going back to Tehran now," a friend living outside the country told me. "So many new restaurants have opened up. Now there are lots of places to go at night. People play music on the streets, music that wasn't even allowed just a few years ago."

There had also been an explosion of coffee shops and late-night cafés, not only in Tehran but in any city of any size. A quick Google search of "coffee shops Tehran" yielded twenty-four hits for central Tehran alone. To his credit, Rouhani had expressed sympathy for the demands of Iran's young people, stating that Iranian society didn't offer them enough places to socialize and enjoy themselves—golden words to an entertainment-starved generation.

It was all too easy to become cynical in Tehran, and the cynics eyed Rouhani's words with customary suspicion: Perhaps it was a ploy to get young people off the streets and into cafés, where talk of insurrection, or even reform, would be cast into the wind by rushes of caffeine.

"This government doesn't give a shit about the people," another friend told me. "It only cares about one thing—staying in power. It doesn't do anything without thinking about its survival."

Whether survival was the motivating factor or not, Tehran had definitely "opened up"—by Iranian standards. On the grounds of the Iranian Artist's House, a complex of venues for art exhibits and film screenings, groups of musicians had gathered to play classic Persian tunes on modern instruments. One night I had dinner with a friend, back in Iran to look after her ailing mother, at a vegetarian restaurant with outside tables and a second-floor balcony overlooking the busy courtyard within Honarmandan Park. As a sign of Iran's newfound liberalism, social "safe zones" had developed, where the strictest codes of the Islamic regime could be suspended, or at least relaxed, but informally and unofficially, and always at the violator's risk.

When we met she leaned over the table, out of sight of the street, to give me a cursory hug. "Here it's okay," she assured me.

We shared a vegetarian pizza and a mammoth Mediterranean salad as middle-class families and members of Iran's creative underground filed through.

"Would you like anything else?" our waiter asked, once our plates had been cleared away.

"Can you bring me a glass of red wine?" my friend teased.

The waiter smirked. "Not now, but maybe if you come back in a few hours, after we're closed."

Each night I finished up at the Café UpArtMann, named for the apartment block where it occupied the ground and lower levels. The split-level gathering place is ground zero for disaffected, liberal-minded youth. The male baristas sport nose rings and dreadlocks, reasons for arrest for violating the codes of Islamic dress just a few years ago, and their female counterparts pay the most meager lip service to the hijab rule. The patrons follow suit, especially on the subterranean level, another step removed from the ubiquitous eyes of the regime, where women will allow their scarves to slip off the backs of their heads.

It was at the Café UpArtMann one night where I met Niloofar, a former journalist for a series of reformist newspapers. It was not by chance. The get-together had been arranged by my dinner partner at the Iranian Artist's House. I thought Niloofar would be interesting to talk to because she likely knew something about efforts toward free expression in Iran and the confrontations with the government they inevitably entailed.

Niloofar was young, in her early thirties, with a slight frame, bright face, and long, curly brown hair that hung below her drooping head-scarf. She had started working during the presidency of Mohammad Khatami, Ahmadinejad's predecessor, and like Rouhani a favorite of the liberal forces who had promised profound changes in Iranian society and who, like many reformers, came up far too short in their eyes.

"I had a lot of friends who were put in jail," Niloofar said, as we sipped chai teas and the background soundtrack played 1960s Brazilian bossa nova. "The government always had red lines, but we never knew what they were or where they were. A cartoon that was permitted the last month might be considered insulting or too critical the next. Or criticizing high government officials—if it was someone who was falling out of favor anyway this could be allowed, depending on what we wrote, but we could never be sure."

Niloofar's topics of interest edged close to red lines: gender issues, civil rights, free speech, and Iran's policies toward, and relationship with, the United States. Education was another favorite theme, as she saw many shortcomings in the Iranian system at all levels.

"In the history books there is so much mischaracterization of our past," she said. "All of the periods before the revolution are presented as dark, with a lot of emphasis on how the rule of the shahs harmed Iran."

I had to interject: "And then Ayatollah Khomeini came to power and returned Iran to its true—Islamic—path, and brought light to Iranian society."

She nodded.

This was curious. So much of what I had seen not only in Tehran but throughout the country did nothing to show the past periods as "dark." Persian culture, on the other hand, was loaded with artistic and architectural achievements, and they were trumpeted, not merely because they brought in badly needed tourist revenue, because the country didn't have the kind of tourist numbers to bring in any significant revenue. As in any ancient culture, they were a way of saying: This is what we accomplished. This is who we were. This is where we have been.

None of this is to discredit Niloofar's views on Iranian education. On the contrary—and Iranian society is replete with contradictions— they show the uneasy relationship the Iranian government has with its own past, its people, itself, and, above all, the Persian identity.

I recalled the comment of another friend, who told me how the love of wine expressed so profusely by the fourteenth-century poet Hafez was treated in classes on Persian literature: "We were told that Hafez was using wine symbolically, that when he talked about drunkenness he was really referring to his relationship with God. We all knew that was ridiculous. We laughed about it. We knew what Hafez was talking about."

Niloofar's complaints about the education system confronted issues that struck at the core of Persian society: "In the stories the students read in class men and women are presented in very traditional gender roles, and always there is the message that this is what society should be like. But these days everyone knows that it isn't like that at all and never will be. Some of the very conservative leaders would like women to go back to their traditional roles, but we know it's never going to happen. This creates such a contradiction. Everything we see in society tells us something else."

Higher education was not immune from criticism.

"So much of it is a monologue," Niloofar went on. "There should be a lot more exchange of ideas, a dialogue, going on in the classrooms. Students should be allowed to question what they're told, not necessarily to contradict it, but to ask critical questions about what they're learning."

These were the kinds of topics that flirted with the vague and ill-defined red lines—lines that were drawn and redrawn depending on which faction within the faction-ridden government was holding power. But the result was always the same—the newspaper was closed down. One day the entire staff would simply be told not to report for work. They were, in Niloofar's words, "fired."

"There was never any security," Niloofar continued. "We never knew how long we would be working or how long we would be out of work. It could be a month, six months, a year, even two years. In the end we would always get permission to open up again, because we applied under a different name. But we would have the same staff, or most of the same people. Some found other jobs, but it wasn't easy. We usually started the new paper with all or most of the same people."

The obscurity of red lines was a conscious strategy, I had heard before, from a couple of friends who had never worked as journalists for a reformist newspaper but had long experience navigating the dos and don'ts of the Islamic regime. They lived together, unmarried, illegal in Iran but unofficially "tolerated," or officially—the distinction is always intentionally vague. Called the "white marriage," the practice has become more popular in recent years, as economic hardship has prevented any long-term planning on matters such as marriage for so much of the population.

"It's a way to maintain control," the male half of the couple told me, "not to allow anyone to know clearly what is permitted and what isn't. That way there is always a level of fear in the people, and fear puts everyone on guard. It's the same not only with free speech but other aspects of society, like the Islamic dress code. At times it seems that the rules are loosening. There won't be any arrests for hijab violations, but then there will be a crackdown and many women will be arrested on charges of 'indecency.'"

Another friend of mine was caught up in one of those crackdowns, which typically take place at the beginning of summer, when lighter, looser clothing is more conducive to the punishing Persian heat. She was coming out of a supermarket when a police van in the parking lot was being loaded with women violating the government-imposed standards of modesty. All the way to the police station she berated the officers: "How long have you been trying to enforce this, tell us what to do, what to wear? You think we're ever going to listen to you?"

And so it went, all the way to the police station. The policemen ignored her, as they could, having been on the receiving end of such diatribes many times before. She had experience in this as well. This was her second arrest for "indecency." At the station she had to listen to a lecture from a mullah on proper Islamic behavior and sign a state-ment promising not to offend again. Her father had to appear with a proper hijab for her to wear before she was allowed to leave, and that was the end of it—until next time.

Imprisonment, arrest, persecution—all are tender themes to explore in Iran because they have a lengthy history. Northeast of central Tehran is a prison dating from the nineteenth century that once held not only common criminals but those who crossed the nineteenth-century red lines in their criticism of the ruling order—political prisoners in today's terminology. Today it is a museum, part of which recreates the prison conditions of nineteenth-century Iran in the original facility. Another section was a much more modern detention center that is also now a museum, paying homage to the prisoners held there in the final years of the rule of Mohammad Reza Pahlavi, whose authoritarian streak drove his reign into the depths of dictatorship.

In 1957, four years after the CIA-backed coup that toppled popular prime minister Mohammad Mosaddegh and threw open the door for the reign of the second Pahlavi, the American intelligence agency assisted the shah in setting up his own secret police and spy network. It went by the acronym SAVAK, which stood for Organization of National Intelligence and the Security of the Nation. It had sixty thousand members in its prime, and an administrative staff of several thousand more. The SAVAK was charged with ferreting out malcontents who might stoke rebellion against the ruling order, censoring the media and other forms of expression, and, as expected, "interrogating" prisoners. The means employed were drawn from the torture practices used by most authoritarian regimes, which led to the death or disappearance of many in custody. One specialty was the bastinado, beating the soles of the feet with a wooden stick, causing excruciating pain.

Iran's refuseniks were held in the newer addition to the nineteenth-century prison, now a museum showcasing the repression and brutality that the 1979 revolution sought to overturn. Inside the reception area the walls are covered with black-and-white photos of some of the inmates who passed through. One of them is Masoumeh Jazaveri, whom the SAVAK had caught with microfiche and recordings of speeches of Ayatollah Khomeini, then in exile. She was arrested while making a phone call to cancel a meeting because she feared, correctly, that SAVAK agents had been tailing her. At the time she was also carrying a stolen gun, which may not have been a proverbial "smoking gun" but did seal her conviction.

Masoumeh now works at the ticket desk, where she can eye her mugshot high up the wall on the other side of the room, and share stories of her incarceration with curious visitors. She displayed characteristic Persian hospitality, inviting me into her office for a cup of tea and a few minutes of reminiscences. She had bright eyes and was serene and confident, appearing perfectly at ease in her surroundings, in spite of what she had once endured within the same walls.

"We had no heat in the winter and no air-conditioning in the summer," Masoumeh began, describing the conditions at the prison. "There were five or six of us in every cell, and there was no toilet. Once in a while we would receive a little extra meat, and we would give it to the women who were weak or pregnant. Sometimes one of us would receive gifts, and they were always extra food along with necessary items like hygiene equipment we could never get in prison. Again, the food would be given to the weak women and those who were expecting children."

Then she added, almost impossibly: "I actually have very good memories of that time."

Masoumeh became one of the women on the receiving end of the others' charity. While in prison she gave birth to a son, now thirty-six years old and living in Tehran.

Soon enough came the chaos of the Islamic Revolution. One day the prison was quickly overrun with revolutionaries demonstrating against the rule of Mohammad Reza. Masoumeh was in one of the first cellblocks to be liberated. She fled to a medical clinic, where she was given a change of clothes so as not to be identified.

Masoumeh divorced her husband after hearing that he had been working as an informant for the SAVAK. He may have been the one to have turned her in, or it could have been one of his friends. She doesn't know. After prison she worked for a while as a teacher but was relocated far from home after word got out that she was supporting Mir Hossein Mousavi in the 2009 election. Behind her desk is a picture of herself with Zahra Rahnavard, the former candidate's wife.

In the end she was forced to take early retirement, which led to the job taking tickets at the prison museum reception desk.

I asked her what she thought of the leaders who had ruled Iran since the Islamic Revolution. Mohammad Khatami, another reformist cleric from the 1990s, she said, was a "nice man." I asked what she thought of America's leaders. At the mention of former president Barack Obama she became rhapsodic: "Nice man!" she exclaimed, throwing her hands across her chest.

What did she think of the current state of Iran? Was this the country she envisioned almost forty years after the revolution? With proper Persian obtuseness, she replied, "I never thought there would be this kind of criticism, so much fighting within the government."

And what kind of Iran would she like to see in the near future, ten or twenty years down the line?

With equal Persian brevity she had an answer for that too, and it was in tune with the times: "I'd like to see less corruption," she replied, "and I wish all of our intelligent young people wouldn't feel they had to leave Iran to find success in their careers."

Masoumeh's last wish was the most important, not only for the Iran of the present but any Iran of the future. The brain drain phenomenon had long been crippling the country, as university graduates in every discipline lined up at Western embassies in the hope of gaining residency, and a future, anywhere there was greater freedom and chances of a better life—economically, politically, socially—in other words, anywhere but Iran. Many university students chose their course of study based on the employment prospects it might offer outside Iran. English translation had become a popular major. A friend of mine earned a master's degree in foreign languages and found a pathway to migrate to Canada. Her brother was working on a PhD in abstract mathematics at the University of New Brunswick and did not plan to return to Iran.

No conversation on Iran-U.S. relations could conclude without mentioning the current American president, Donald J. Trump. Then Masoumeh dropped her characteristic Persian reserve and spoke with atypical Persian clarity: "He is *mad!* He knows nothing about the world!"

I thanked Masoumeh for the cup of tea and her stories and left to stroll for a while around the park-like grounds. Places that served as settings for the most reprehensible human horrors, like the Auschwitz compound in Poland, or the Khmer Rouge detention and torture center in Phnom Penh, had a way of dressing themselves up in the most everyday exteriors, which today only magnify, rather than conceal, the enormity of the crimes that took place hidden behind them. Around the prison, both the nineteenth-century blockhouse and Mohammad Reza's twentieth-century addition, leaf-littered pathways cut across well-kept lawns, and the streets that defined its borders were spared the nerve-straining traffic of central Tehran. Cars and delivery trucks trundled along with the casual ease of daily life.

To an outsider Tehran can feel like a city in a time capsule, one that experienced the tumultuous revolution in 1979 and appears, on the surface, to be caught in a phase of posttraumatic shock. Forty years have passed, but the chants of "Death to America!" still ring out at Friday prayers when global events call for a denunciation of the "Great Satan." But it has become a hollow, lifeless phrase, drained of the revolutionary fervor of 1979. The "Down with the USA" mural, accompanied by mockups of descending missiles on the American flag, still stretches the length of a high-rise tower in central Tehran, but it, too, is little more than a relic of an era and little more than another feature of the Tehran cityscape. And November 4, the anniversary of the takeover of the American embassy, is still commemorated outside the compound with the ritual burning of the American flag, but it has lost its meaning, as rituals do when they are repeated too often.

It has all gotten a little stale. The Great Satan of 1979 is not the Great Satan of 2019, and today's geopolitical realities are not what they were in 1979. Yet the revolutionary spirit, such as it exists, and its rhetoric, has not progressed much beyond 1979. A regime hardliner may argue that the geopolitical outlook of the Great Satan, and its methodologies, have also not changed since 1979, which may be true, from the hardliner's point of view, but revolutionary movements, like any political force, need to refresh themselves from time to time, to retune their message, to reshape their ideology to keep abreast of a changing world. The Islamic Revolution, like so many others, has become a spent force, saddled by the baggage of its own doctrines, political as well as social. After the overthrow of the shah they offered nothing to Iranian society, nothing that would improve life in Iran.

The result is that, despite the liberalizing trends fought for over the decades by counterrevolutionary forces, Iranian society has largely stagnated or, more correctly, been squelched. Iran has a lively contemporary art scene and its film industry is arguably the most accomplished in the Middle East, but the restrictions on all political, intellectual, and creative activity have mercilessly stifled what would otherwise be a thriving and vibrant society.

"This is dead country," a friend once told me, a remark that was a bit extreme, but it conveyed the acute sense of loss felt by many Iranians that the Islamic Revolution brought. Postrevolutionary Iran was another country, another society, another day-to-day reality from the Iran of the 1970s.

"My father liked to go to the Café Naderi," my dinner partner at the Iranian Artist's House told me. "It was where all the artists and intellectuals would hang out, talk about art and politics."

The Café Naderi was opened in 1927 by Khachik Madikians, an Armenian entrepreneur who also owned the hotel where it is housed. Throughout the twentieth century it became a focal point for artists, poets, and journalists. Today it prides itself on having preserved its original atmosphere by having retained the same tables and chairs, silverware, and décor, though framed photographs of Ayatollahs Khomeini and Khamenei now hang above the serving counter, where they compete with a nearby wall adorned with an array of photos that represent a who's who of prerevolutionary creative and intellectual life.

Behind a brick wall lining Taleqani Street stands perhaps the most poignant symbol of the Islamic Revolution. The former American embassy, renamed the U.S. Den of Espionage and now a museum, is dedicated to showing what hardliners would call American malfeasance and intrusion in Iranian affairs. It may be the starkest and most resonant time capsule in all of Iran. Little has changed since the mob of student demonstrators—the Muslim Student Followers of the Imam's Line—scaled the walls and took control of the compound on November 4, 1979. At the time, sixty diplomats and marine guards were still at work in the embassy and soon became bargaining chips in the longest hostage crisis in history. U.S.-Iran relations have been sucked into the same time capsule, where they have remained for forty years, stagnant except for regular spates of bristling acrimony.

The walls of the compound on Taleqani Street are decorated with anti-American murals, which must be refreshed from time to time, because they had changed slightly from when I first saw them in 2009. There was the Statue of Liberty with the face in the form of a human skull, the outline of a handgun filled with the Stars and Stripes, a lengthy quote of Ayatollah Khomeini denouncing American imperialism, and the ubiquitous "Down with the USA" stenciled in red, white, and blue. But like the building façade expressing the same sentiments a short distance away, these too have become an invisible part of the Tehran landscape. Pedestrians stroll past them without a notice, just as they ignore the government "news" put out over the state-sponsored networks.

"Prophet Mohammad is the true way," preached the English-language radio station I was able to listen to through the satellite TV connection in my hotel room. "The Islamic government has brought peace and justice," it trumpeted. It is hard to imagine who the audience is for this tripe, for the slice of the population with enough English ability to comprehend it is the better educated, Western-friendly class that deplores the regime and any radio messages it puts out. The target audience had to be foreign visitors in three-star hotel rooms like myself, in a half-hearted effort to make us believe that these pronouncements were the common sentiment on the "Persian street."

When I was there in 2009 the former embassy compound was still a headquarters for the security services operated by the Revolutionary Guard and therefore off-limits to visitors. Now it welcomed the public, even representatives of the American public, like myself, and with typical Persian hospitality.

"Welcome home," the ticket taker at the entrance said, after asking my nationality.

Passing through the entrance, I could have been stepping onto the set of *Argo*, or back into the far more surreal setting of 1979 Tehran. I had to give the movie's producers credit for coming up with a convincing location for shooting the embassy scenes at the beginning of the film. The actual embassy was designed in 1948 and modeled after American high schools of the 1940s. It was completed in 1951, two years before the CIA-sponsored coup that ousted Mohammad Mosaddegh. The cinematic replacement was the Veterans Affairs Medical Center in the San Fernando Valley, in suburban Los Angeles, which has become a treatment center for substance abuse.

The film also conveyed, quite accurately, the spasmodic revolutionary fervor that swept Iran. The stairways and offices have been left as
the diplomats abandoned them on November 4, 1979. One exhibit
features the shredder used to destroy reams of documents that the
Iranian government claimed were evidence of American crimes. After
the takeover, master rug weavers were employed by the Islamic government to piece together the thousands of strands of paper. In the hallway
that runs behind the banks of offices overlooking the courtyard, the
walls are covered by newspaper clippings reporting the events of that
day, accompanied by the same photos that have become iconic in the
West—blindfolded diplomats being led out of the main door among
mobs of students chanting anti-American slogans. At the far end of
the hall a cluster of rooms displays office machinery and electronic
equipment meant to serve as proof of spying and other acts of subterfuge going on in the "Den of Espionage." But for the routine visitor it
is hard to sort all this out, or to extend any degree of credibility. The
gadgetry may be little more than the usual collection of tech hardware,
circa 1979, that any large-scale embassy would have had on hand to
manage its daily duties.

On the day I had dropped in there were other visitors, all foreigners—a couple from Australia, three Indians, two students from China—
the same tourists one sees at religious and historic sites all over Iran.
But here there was a difference. At Golestan Palace or any of the major
mosques or shrines, the foreigners, myself included, will stand in awe,
gazing upward and outward at great expanses of space framed by architectural beauty rare in the world. In the drab corridors of the former U.S.
embassy the strongest sensation is one of claustrophobia, of physical
space as well as the history it represents. The rooms and hallways are tight
and cramped, the distance between the main building and the front gates
surprisingly short. The tension of the time can be sensed, like the aroma
of cigarette smoke that hangs in the air long after the butts have been
snuffed out. At other tourist sites, visitors usually have a good idea of what
they are expected to experience, and they perform to expectations—
awe, admiration, curiosity, maybe even a bit of perplexity. Here, visitors

walk the halls and look intently at the displays with an undefined sense of meaning. The museum is a snapshot in time but one without any clear context, only a prevailing impression of chaos and confusion, which is fitting for the events of 1979 but only adds to a feeling of unease.

Tehran has more museums that address its recent past, which has not been a happy one. On the north end of City Park, near the entrance that opens onto Fayaz Bakhsh Street, is a small building that houses the Tehran Peace Museum. It was opened in 2005 with an aim to "promote a culture of peace through raising awareness about the devastating consequences of war, with a focus on the health and environmental impacts of chemical weapons," according to its mission statement. I had found it by chance one evening while jogging through City Park, a short distance from my hotel. The simplicity of the name and the building itself, tied to its stated purpose, was intriguing—a museum for peace?—so I decided to have a look.

The emphasis on chemical weapons needs little explanation. During the eight-year Iran-Iraq War, from 1980 to 1988, Iran was on the receiving end of the first large-scale use of chemical weapons since their introduction in World War I. Mustard gas, tabun, sarin, and nerve gas rained down on both soldiers and civilians, primarily in the later years of the war. The numbers are sobering. In a single attack twenty thousand Iranian soldiers were killed immediately by nerve gas. In June 1988 five thousand people in the city of Sardasht were burned in a mustard gas attack. According to estimates by the CIA, at least fifty thousand of Iran's casualties in the war were the direct result of chemical weapons, but, as more have died from their effects in the succeeding years, that number has doubled. The weapons, and the materials used to make them, were supplied by companies in the United States, the Netherlands, West Germany, Australia, France, and Italy. The United States also provided the Iraqi air force with surveillance information with complete awareness that in the subsequent attacks chemical weapons would be used.

Reza Taghipoor, the director of the museum, was not a victim of a chemical attack. His legs were blown off when an Iraqi missile hit the ambulance that was transporting him away from the battlefield after he had been wounded by gunfire. He told me the story while giving me a tour of the museum, in his wheelchair. The use of child soldiers by Iran was widespread, particularly in the latter stages of the war. Reza was only fifteen in 1982 when he was caught up in one of the battles in Khoramshahr, one of the first cities to be captured by the Iraqis after their invasion but later retaken by the Iranians. Reza was struck by rifle fire but not severely. He managed to crawl to an ambulance and was loaded into it by combat medics, but before it could leave the battlefield, the missile struck. His legs had to be amputated just a few inches below his hips.

Most of the employees of the museum are veterans of the war, and many were victims of chemical attacks. Hassan Sadi suffered mustard gas exposure twice and is awaiting a lung transplant. Ahmad Salim has had corneal transplants, and Ahmad Zangiabadi worked as a volunteer guide until he died of collapsed lungs in 2014. All of the others have their own stories.

Word must have reached the museum that an American visitor was on the way, for the staff had a lunch buffet waiting when I arrived. Reza greeted me at the reception desk and started the tour with Elaheh, the museum's international relations officer, on hand to interpret. Reza is a large man, even in a wheelchair, yet his voice is soft and sober. He speaks in the matter-of-fact tone of someone who knows that war is nothing to be championed or spoken of in ringing tones. As he recounted the number of deaths and pointed to the graphic photos showing the effects of chemical weapons on the human body—skin lesions and eye damage—he remained remarkably demure, even droll, in his delivery.

Not all of the displays focus on the use of chemical weapons. Others recount violations of international law and crimes against humanity in other parts of the world—the civil war during the breakup of the former Yugoslavia, Israel's use of cluster bombs in the 2006 war with Lebanon, the Rwandan genocide of the 1990s. It was the kind of experience we should all have once in a lifetime—like a visit to the Hiroshima Peace Museum or the Auschwitz concentration camp—to remind us of the limits of human depravity, which evidence shows appear to be nonexistent.

Then our food was ready. Members of the staff had been unpacking delivery containers in the museum's combination conference room and lunchroom. Reza had other business to attend to and wheeled himself away to one of the inner offices while the rest of us gathered around the long multipurpose table to dig in. The aluminum trays were piled with dill rice, chicken and meat kebabs, and skewers of grilled vegetables. For once, I was glad not to be treated as a guest of honor. Elaheh and the other men seated at the table, all of whom bore the scars of war and had come face-to-face with its full horror, took turns filling their plates and pouring drinks with an ease that said that the message of the museum— the need to eliminate chemical weapons—was one that they had grown accustomed to. Unacknowledged was an uncomfortable truth: chemical weapons had also been used in the civil war in Syria by the regime of Bashar al-Assad, which the Iranian government backed. No mention was made of this, and most of the men in the room may not have been government supporters anyway, as few Iranians are. Consequently, the issue was one no one wanted to address, as it would have complicated the message of the museum as well as the lessons from their own experiences that they wanted to share with the museum's visitors.

While we dug in, and the aromas of Persian cooking filled the room, questions were tossed my way: What was my interest in coming to Iran? Where had I been? Where was I going next? These were, of course, coupled with the expected expressions of Persian politeness: "We appreciate having you. We don't get many American visitors." And I was showered with tourist tips: "You should really go to Esfahan." "Have you seen the gardens in Shiraz?" When we had had our fill there was a group photo shoot, the American visitor placed in the center and Reza wheeling himself back into the reception area to join, and then it was time to leave.

Curiosity about the Iran-Iraq War and the effect it had had on Iranian society had prompted my visit to the museum. All wars are choreographed barbarity: The rituals of organization and planning give them a veneer of respectability, but during the Iran-Iraq War this mindless slaughter reached new depths.

The two countries had engaged in petty border spats for centuries, but they seemed settled by the Treaty of Zuhab, signed in 1639. Three centuries later, the 1937 Treaty of Saad Abad reinforced what had already been tacitly observed—that the border ran along the Shatt Al-Arab waterway, which had become important for the export of both nations' oil. In the 1950s Iraq began encouraging the ethnic Arabs who had lived for centuries in the Iranian province of Khuzestan to secede, a campaign that gained momentum after the death of Egyptian president Gamal Abdul Nasser. Iraq's president, Saddam Hussein, fancied himself and his country becoming the new leaders of the Arab world. Iran's oil-rich Khuzestan Province, with its population of ethnic Arabs, became a prize to capture.

After the Islamic Revolution of 1979 Saddam saw his chance. The Iranian military had been decimated by the execution of dozens of senior military officers who had served under the shah, and the country was in chaos. He also counted on the ethnic Arabs of Khuzestan to abandon any allegiance to Iran and rally behind him. The late 1970s saw border skirmishes and territorial incursions as the two sides tested each other's mettle and supported potential rebels on the other side—for Iraq, the Arabs of Iran, and for Iran, the Kurdish minority in Iraq.

On September 22, 1980, Saddam Hussein launched a major invasion, and the Iraqi forces quickly took the city of Khoramshahr at a combined cost of fifteen thousand deaths. Saddam's rationale was to blunt any spread of the Shiite Islamic Revolution, which gained him favor in the West and the mainly Sunni Gulf countries that were caught between the two regional heavyweights. But the "flip" he expected of Iran's ethnic Arabs never occurred.

What followed was eight years of attacks and counterattacks, the firing of missiles at population centers, attacks on oil tankers and infrastructure, Iraqi attacks on military and civilian targets with chemical weapons, bellowing nationalistic and religious rhetoric, the kind of mano a mano trench warfare not seen since World War I, and the use of child soldiers to serve as "martyrs" for vaguely defined ideological causes. The Argentinian writer Jorge Luis Borges described the Falklands War as "two bald men fighting over a comb." The Iran-Iraq War could be described as a cockfight, the two sides thrashing each other to annihilation with little regard for what kind of societies would emerge, only who would survive as the dominant power in the Middle East. Nationalistic and religious fervor dominated. In April 1985 Ayatollah Khomeini would proclaim: "It is our belief that Saddam wishes to return Islam to blasphemy and polytheism. . . . The issue is one of Islam versus blasphemy, not Iran versus Iraq."

The war didn't have to go that way, or as badly, or last as long as it did. In 1982 Saddam Hussein offered Iran a truce, as it was apparent that the war was going nowhere, but Ayatollah Khomeini spurned it, as Iran was gaining ground and he saw the war as a way to whip up nationalist spirit and support for his Islamic Revolution.

"The propaganda was terrible," a friend of mine who had lived in Tehran at the time told me. "It was all about defending Islam and the new revolutionary government. They persuaded young kids to go to war, and they were told they would be martyrs if they died in battle. He even gave them keys that were meant to represent the keys to Paradise." By the end, more than 100,000 child soldiers were sacrificed as morale waned and younger recruits were needed to replenish the ranks due to battlefield deaths, draft dodging, and desertions.

Iran resorted to "human wave attacks" to overwhelm and disorient the Iraqi forces, raising the death toll. Masses of soldiers, primarily young conscripts and members of the loosely organized basij militia would be sent headlong against the Iraqi positions to pave the way for the regular army to continue the attack. In return, Saddam launched his "War of the Cities," bombarding Iranian population centers in the west, but also those as far away as Tehran. As many as one-third of city dwellers fled, fearing a massive chemical attack, which Saddam had threatened.

From 1984 to 1988, the last four years of the war, the conflict had become a stalemate. Neither side was able to make any significant progress. The Iranians threatened to close off the Strait of Hormuz to stifle the world's oil shipments. In July 1988 an Iran Air passenger airliner was shot down by the U.S. Navy cruiser *Vincennes*, killing all 290 passengers and crew members. Finally, on July 20, 1988, then speaker of the parliament Ali Akbar Hashemi Rafsanjani persuaded Ayatollah Khomeini to accept a ceasefire. The Iranian death toll was estimated at half a million, though some claim it was double that, or somewhere in between. In Iran, more than 100,000 children were orphaned. The border dispute that started the war remained unresolved and returned to the prewar status quo. Nothing was gained for either side.

One of the striking features of the war, which left a lasting impression on Iranian society, was the extreme imbalance in outside support. Almost all Western countries, including the Soviet Union, showered Iraq with weapons sales, intelligence information, financial aid, and, most important, chemical weapons or the ingredients to make them. Iran was isolated. Its only backer was Syria, too small and feeble in the face of much stronger global powers to help in any way.

I'd long thought that the experience of the Iran-Iraq War had had a stinging long-term impact on the collective Iranian psyche, which appears in current defense policies. Iran has no natural allies in the region. Aside from the arrival of Islam in 651 CE and the introduction of Arabic script, Iran has no substantial historic or cultural ties to the Arab world. For a few centuries the Silk Road established economic and cultural links between Iran and Central Asia, China, and Turkey, but Iran's distinctive history kept it a world apart. Therefore, when either regional or international conflicts boil over, there are no long-standing brothers-in-arms to rally to its defense. Although the United Nations named Iraq as the aggressor, throughout the war Iran received no international support. In a documentary film on Iran's recent history, former president Ali Akbar Hashemi Rafsanjani put it simply: "What can I say? We were all alone."

Another friend who remembers the missile attacks on Tehran and other cities told me: "We were *begging* for *one* anti-aircraft gun, and no one would give it to us."

In August 2018 Iran committed itself to investing in the development of new fighter jets, and the reasoning was again drawn from its experience in the Iran-Iraq War. "We learned that we cannot rely on anyone but ourselves. We saw that wherever we are vulnerable no one will have mercy on us," said the minister of defense, Amir Hatami.

The peace museum threw some light on the use of chemical weapons in the war, and the displays about other war crimes in recent memory only laid bare, once again, the depth of systematic barbarity that has become commonplace in the modern day. But it wasn't the end of the story. After a sincere thank you to Reza and Elaheh I headed back to North Tehran to another memorial of the war, the dubiously named Holy Defense Museum. It is more memorial than museum, but as either memorial or museum I took a particular dislike to its name. It was this kind of propaganda that compelled tens of thousands of young Iranians to swap their lives for a place in an illusory Paradise long after the war was deemed unwinnable. It framed the war as Aya-tollah Khomeini and his hardline clerics would like it to be seen, as a jihadist cause to defend the newly formed Islamic Republic from secular, Sunni, Baathist infidels, funded by Western imperialists, or any combination of these.

Fortunately, the interior of the museum is spared the revolutionary rhetoric. Instead, it resembles the kinds of war museums, or memo-rials, found wherever young men have sacrificed their lives for their nations, sometimes justifiably, sometimes as a result of nationalistic hubris, often a blending of both. Behind the glass display cases are the customary presentations of everyday objects found on the battlefield and in the possession of the dead. There are snapshots of dozens of victims—martyrs, in the Iranian context—framed by tongues of flame, each a miniature shrine to memorialize the lost as individuals rather than anonymous martyrs for a collective cause. As in almost every country that has seen war, there is a shrine for the unknowns, the true anonymous. And then there is the artwork.

This exhibit was the most moving. Radiating from the main entrance along a dimly lit hall was a line of paintings that depicted soldiers set against backgrounds drawn from another world—stylized landscapes, a heaven of stars or clouds, at times nothing but a backdrop of bold color. Each was meant to stand for a victim of the war removed from space and time, in the midst of their own onward journey. There was nothing heroic about the portraits. Many of the heads are bowed or turned away from the viewer. Aside from the military uniforms and occasional colors of the Iranian flag, nothing suggests the glory of war or the deaths that were the result. I walked the line of paintings, stopping before the most poignant to look a little more closely, hoping it might answer the question of the why of war, or offer a hint of its redeeming value, but the only sentiment to take away was the only appropriate one—of needless loss and sorrow.

This was enough gloom for one afternoon. Outside the winter sun was shining bright, and there was no Siberian air blowing down from the north carrying a frigid chill, so I left the museum to have a look at the latest addition to the Tehran cityscape. It was the Tabiat Bridge, more pedestrian walkway and urban social center than bridge, though to do justice to its name, it does connect Taleqani and Ab-va-Atash Parks on opposite sides of the Modarres Expressway that runs along the east side of Tehran.

The bridge was designed by Leila Araghian, and is a curving, swirling tetherwork of cables and suspension arcs propping up a two-level walkway that sports cafés and a food court in the middle of the 270-meter span. On a sunny afternoon it is one of the best places to admire the sweep of the city under glittering winter light. There were masses of Tehranis doing just that—absorbing the late-afternoon sun from the south-facing benches, sipping lattes and cappuccinos at the café tables, lingering along the high-rise sidewalk to enjoy the freedom of the open air and empty space, removed for a few moments from the burdens of past memories and the worries of the present. I, too, was able to let go of the images from the peace museum and the honors paid to the martyrs, at least for the moment. It was what Iranians have done for decades to sustain the promise of a brighter future, and I see the popularity of the Tabiat Bridge as representing this hope rendered into form. For brief moments, like a sunny winter afternoon, it is something not only to imagine but to experience.

Like my fellow walkers, I put the afternoon behind me.

2 | Tabriz

SEAT OF A REVOLUTION

No one can be summarily arrested, save *flagrante delicto* in the commission of some crime or misdemeanor, except on the written authority of the President of the Tribunal of Justice, given in conformity with the law. Even in such case the accused must immediately, or at latest in the course of the next twenty-four hours, be informed and notified of the nature of his offence.
—1906 Constitution of Iran

For a mega-metropolis of seventeen million, Tehran does not take long to escape. The day of departure I met my new guide, Aydin, in the breakfast room of the hotel before the last of the breakfast dishes had been cleared away. Tall, fresh-faced, bespectacled, Aydin better resembled an honor medical student than a professional tour guide. But he was prompt—even early—and ready to go.

We threw my bag in the trunk of his Saipa and zigzagged through the one-way streets until one dumped us onto Ferdowsi Street, and then we headed west along Enqelab Avenue. Luckily we were driving against the horrendous rush-hour traffic, and we had a last look at Azadi Tower before the rest of the city disappeared into the cocoon of smog that would envelope it for the rest of the day. We were going northwest, to Tabriz, with stops along the way that would take up the next four or five days. The first destination was Qazvin, one of the many former capitals of the Persian Empire but now the capital of only the Qazvin

Province. But as a former seat of the empire it had collected its share of gargantuan mosques and gaudy shrines and other must-see sights, enough to make it a must stop on the northern tourist trail.

Past the city of Karaj, a half an hour west of Tehran, factories and other industrial buildings began to appear beside the road—the depot of a trucking company, the reactor of a nuclear power station, a forest of electrical towers—first lining the highway and then stretching far from it, all the way to the foothills of the Alborz Mountains. Yet in spite of the congestion of industry the air was clear and the sun beamed brightly through a cloudless sky.

"Almost all of this is relatively new," Aydin said, as the tracts of industrial acreage sped past. "It's to keep the pressure off Tehran. No more industrial development can take place within a hundred kilometers of the city. Too many people are coming to the city for work and it just can't handle any more. This way people will also be able to live closer to their jobs."

It wasn't all smokestacks and docking ramps. There were housing developments too, bland, chockablock apartment complexes that had sprung up between the warehouses and shipping centers to minimize commute times for the newly citified and city dwellers eager to migrate out to these industrial exurbs. But fast-forward ten or twenty years and it is hard not to imagine these residential-cum-business tracts swallowed up by a swelling metropolis. Tehran is faced with the plight of many of the world's mega-cities—too many people for too few opportunities, too little space and infrastructure to bear the weight, and too little time to cope with the crisis. Expanding ever further beyond the city's limits seemed like a desperate attempt to buy time, hoping that a miracle cure for the problem of uber-urbanization would magically appear and make everything right.

But at the moment none of that was our concern. We had gotten out of the city before the daily traffic snarls could get the best of us and now had only Qazvin in our sights. After two hours of cruising the double-lane highway we rolled into town. It was early afternoon, time enough to see some of the sights of Qazvin before the day was done. Our first stop was the local laundromat—nineteenth-century style.

One hundred years ago, fresh water came to Qazvin from the natural springs found both within the town and the surrounding hills. Rather than scrub their laundry in open rivulets, the women of Qazvin brought their bundles of sheets and undergarments to the municipal wash house, where clear, cold water running through the *qanats*, or water channels, passed through what was in nineteenth-century terms the local laundry room. In the brightly lit, low-ceilinged hall the water bubbles along the blue-tiled qanats as local women, as costumed mannequins, prepare to load their wet bundles for the trek home.

On the way out I stopped at the ticket counter to ask if there was any information in English about the museum. The ticket taker slid me a brochure, with a nod that conveyed an odd mixture of acknowledgment and thank you, and then he made a request of his own: Did I have any coins? He collected coins from around the world, he explained, and had a habit of asking foreign visitors for any change they might spare.

I fished in my pocket but found nothing. But I wasn't done. I went back to the car, rummaged in my bag, and found two quarters, a dime, and a handful of pennies. Unfortunately, I had no nickel, but I didn't have the heart to tell him that. I returned to the counter and handed over the coins.

"American," I said.

His face brightened—without the nickel. He showed them to his boss, shuffling papers at a desk in the back of the room.

"Am-ra-ka-ei," he said, jangling the precious coins.

The boss ogled a quarter and held it up to the light to get a better look. Then he dug in a drawer and scooped out a handful of coins, brought them to the ticket window, and handed them over.

"Irani," he said. It was a cache of rials—one-thousand- and two-thousand- and five-thousand-denomination coins—rare because they are encountered so infrequently, and encountered so infrequently because, at an exchange rate of sixty thousand to the dollar, they are almost worthless. But it was the thought that mattered, so I scooped them up and expressed heartfelt thanks, which in Persian culture always carries currency.

Aydin and I hopped back in the car and headed over to the Shahzadeh Hossein shrine, where there was a funeral to attend. It wasn't planned that way. The Shahzadeh Hossein is the burial place of the son of Imam Reza, the eighth imam in the line of Shiite imams. The site is surrounded by a courtyard and shielded by a retaining wall. An elaborate façade done out in blue tile work with six minarets welcomes visitors. The tomb for the son of an imam is suitably grand.

Aydin and I had passed through the entrance gate when the funeral procession appeared. It had entered at the back of the complex, a dozen men carrying the bier that held the body. Many more paraded alongside, some wracked with emotion, wiping away tears. There were a few women too, old and young, treading along at the edge of the crowd, some carried away by emotion, others stone-faced. It was an insight into gender roles and gender expectations in the expression of emotion: either men or women may weep or remain consummately stoic. A man is no less a man for bursting into tears, and a woman no less a woman for refraining from doing so. Emotional expression knows no gender.

I asked Aydin if it was apropos to take photos. Sure, he replied, and so I snapped away as the cortege marched to the front of the shrine, where it stopped and the crowd gathered for a ritual recitation of prayers.

As the funeral procession paraded through the shrine the other visitors went about their business unperturbed, and the funeral marchers went about their business unperturbed by the presence of the visitors. It was the passage of life and death in a place meant to both honor the dead and acknowledge the honorariums extended by the living.

The funeral procession finished, we left the Shahzadeh Hossein. There was one more sight to see, if we could find it—the Cantor Church, also known as the Russian Church, built to serve the Russian engineers employed in road-building projects in the early twentieth century. Aydin had never heard of it, so he popped the name into his GPS, and we struck out, following wherever the GPS led us until it got us lost in the back streets of Qazvin. After a few twists and turns we were close, and find it we did, after soliciting help from a few Qazvinis strolling the back streets.

The Cantor Church is little more than a tiny redbrick building topped with a steeple that identifies it as a church. What had once been the diminutive nave has been converted into a gift shop selling postcards, icons, wooden crosses, and other Orthodox memorabilia to the few passing Christian faithful. It is more a museum to the Russian presence in Iran than Christianity itself, but still it remains, as a reminder of a complex period of Iranian history and the many invasions the country has borne.

The day was done. It was time to head to the hotel. And we found it without Aydin's GPS—a high-end five-star resort complex that had been designed to boost the country's tourist sector. It was modeled after multiperk resort complexes common to tourist destinations all over the world. It had a play area for children and a swimming pool and sauna—separate hours for men and women—and an onsite restaurant and café. The rooms were decorated in bland color schemes carefully chosen not to offend, with flat-screen TVs and toilet baskets brimming with shampoo bottles and other amenities. Of course there was no bar or nightclub, and none to be found anywhere in Qazvin, and therefore the effort to break into the international tourist market was doomed.

At the check-in desk I made a new friend. He had overheard my American-accented English while I was talking to the concierge and felt impelled to cut in. His name was Amir, and he had lived in New Jersey for about thirty years. For an Iranian American back in Iran, overhearing American-accented English, especially in Qazvin, was all the invitation he needed. As expected, questions poured out: Where was I from? How long was I in Iran? What was I doing here? Just traveling? What were my impressions?

Then Amir told me his story, or his woes. He was back in Iran to resolve a property dispute with the government, or, more accurately, an appallingly inefficient, disorganized, cumbersome bureaucracy. His case was exceptional, even by Iranian standards. Amir was trying to reclaim a parcel of land that had been seized by the government shortly after the Islamic Revolution.

"When it was all over they just took property if they wanted it," he said. "It happened a lot in the years of the war." For Iranians "the war" always meant the Iran-Iraq War. "If they had an eye on your property and there was an absentee owner, or if there was any confusion over its ownership, people from the government came snooping around, and they would come up with a reason to take it."

Frustrating, time-consuming, cash-draining, it sounded little different from any number of struggles with local government authorities, or trying to "fight city hall."

"I have two lawyers, but they're lazy and don't do anything. They don't know anything. I have to do all the work myself. But I still need them to represent me, so I have to pay them."

A gripe of this kind might resonate with frustrated citizens anywhere in the world, but Iran is forever Iran, and the social and judicial institutions don't quite work (or not work) like those in other parts of the world. I could see what Amir was up against—a deeply embedded culture of corruption, opportunism, stagnation, and passivity that had been implanted, nurtured, and allowed to spread through virtually all of Iranian society since the 1979 revolution. Yet, despite the odds, Amir was hopeful: "Finally, after coming back for the last couple of years, I have the title to the land back."

Anywhere in the world this would be a great coup, but this was Iran, where layers of administrative ambiguity and corruption run deep.

I asked, a bit naively—if he had the title to the land, wasn't that the end of it?

"Oh, no. There are more steps to go through, and more after that, and along the way everyone has their hand out. All of this is put in place so everyone who has something to do with it can get something out of it."

The land that Amir's family owned was in Rasht, about sixty miles to the north near the shore of the Caspian Sea, and because it was in Rasht it reminded me of a recent Iranian film I had seen—*A Man of Integrity*, by Mohammad Rasoulof. It deals with the dilemma of Reza, a disgruntled man from Tehran who owns a fish farm near Rasht, where he has lived a peaceful life with his wife and daughter until local commercial interests attempt a land grab by destroying his livelihood when he refuses to sell out. The film pointed an accusing finger at the endemic corruption and cronyism that has spread through all levels of Iranian society. Even Reza's wife, Hadis, the head teacher at the local high school, is dragged into the stew when she must confront the daughter of the powerful local tycoon behind the land grab.

Initially, and surprisingly, the film was allowed to be screened in Iran, but it was quickly pulled when its ripples roiled the political waters. The image of a principled individual battling a fatally corrupt system resonated too loudly with audiences, even though such a mythic theme would have spoken equally loudly to audiences far outside Iran.

A few days later I had a similar conversation in Zanjan, another regional city on the other side of the hills that rise from the Caspian Sea. I was sitting at a table in a late-night coffee shop frequented by frustrated and alienated Iranian youth. A group of young men had gathered around the TV on the other side of the room to watch a Real Madrid–Barcelona football match. Gathered at the other tables were young couples and small groups of liberal-leaning Iranians, indicated by the women's meticulously tailored hair styles, revealed by head-scarves that slipped off the back of their heads, and the natty jeans and unclipped beards worn by some of the young men.

A few eyes looked my way, and then one of the football fans wandered over to my table, extended a hand, and started a conversation. Or tried to. His English was rudimentary, though I understood that his name was Parviz and he had a degree in internet technology. Like many Iranian youth, he was unemployed. The next one to wander over was Hamed, another football fan. He shook my hand, welcomed me to Iran, asked where I was from, and then took a seat next to Parviz. Hamed had a degree in chemical engineering but had been working as the café's cook for the past five years because he couldn't find a professional job. Finally came Javad. Javad had a degree in civil engineering but was managing the café in the evenings until he could also find a more suitable job. Now all of Real Madrid's cheering section was gathered around my table, and I felt flattered that the on-field dazzle of Christian Renaldo could not compete with the novelty of a visiting American. As a visiting American my first obligation was to listen to their woes, for it was their rare opportunity to sound off to the most prime of sounding boards—a visiting American. Their gripes were much different than Amir's. They weren't trying to squeeze retribution out of a maddening, knotty bureaucracy.

But they did have deep frustrations to voice against a political and social system they saw as having failed them.

Of the three, all with degrees in areas that in many parts of the world could translate to career success, none were working in their chosen career paths.

"Unless you're religious, or your father was a martyr in the Iran-Iraq War, or you know someone high up in the government, it's impossible to get ahead in Iran," Javad moaned. He offered an abbreviated translation for the others. Heads nodded.

"All the stupid people, they go to the religious schools," he went on. "They can't get into the good universities. And while they're in school they're paid, and they don't have to do military service, and when they finish they get the good jobs. The rest of us, with degrees from the good universities, we get the lousy ones."

There was another translation. More nods of agreement. I offered a simple interpretation: "So everything is upside down. The smart people stay at the bottom unless they're religious or their fathers were martyred in the war or they have good connections, so the less capable people end up running the government."

Another translation. More nods of agreement.

"The problem is that there is way too much religion in Iran," Javad went on, seeking to strike at the core of the matter. "*Everything* goes back to religion—what we should eat, what we should buy in the stores, how the economy of the country should be run—'All this will lead to paradise!'—that's all we hear, but none of it works."

A translation. More nods.

"But it's all lies. Everything we've been told is lies. We were told the Prophet Mohammad divided the moon in half. This is the twenty-first century! How can anyone believe this? A lot of these stupid people who can't get into the good universities, they don't even believe in religion, they just see it as a way to get ahead, so they go along."

I asked him if there weren't students at the university who still considered themselves religious whether or not they supported the government. Javad was emphatic: "*No one* at my university believes in religion, or the government. Religion is something, but not everything. My father drinks and he believes in God, but he doesn't believe in the government."

Now there were amused nods of agreement. Parviz, the cook, added, "Half of Iranians don't believe in God anymore. Look at the Friday prayers. Almost no one goes to the mosque, not the young people."

I knew this was a slight exaggeration, and that the liberal class tended to overestimate their support as a form of wish fulfillment. Many Iranians were devout Muslims and believed in the tenets of the religion. But I also remembered a joke I had once heard, that the mosques in Saudi Arabia are crumbling piles of stone but filled on Fridays. The mosques in Iran are magnificent works of art but empty on Fridays. And there was some truth to this. Decades of government-enforced religious principles in what had long been a quasi-secular society had driven even the semi-faithful away not only from Islam but religion entirely. "It's a *shit* religion! It's *shit!*" Sahar, another friend, told me. But there were still hangers-on, those who hadn't allowed the notorious hypocrisy and dictums of the regime to dent their beliefs. Still, the comments of Javad and Parviz reflected the depth of alienation that many of the youth felt, and, with the Iranian population heavily tipped toward its younger generation, this meant widespread, critical, profound alienation, and this needed no translation.

"I would like to live in America," Parviz cut in. "How can I get a visa? We've heard that if you have a relative there it is much easier."

Or impossible, I wanted to add. For State Department interviewers of Iranian visa applicants, having relatives in the U.S. could translate to having accomplices willing to shelter relatives seeking to stay beyond the terms of their visa. Or it might not. It was all up to the whim of the interviewer.

This got their attention; their eyes fixed on me.

"Visa rules are being reviewed all the time and could change at any moment," I said, feeling wretched for fanning a flame of hope that could so easily be blown out, and probably would be. It was always like this when listening to Iranians longing to go to the U.S., study in the U.S., work in the U.S., or—an unimaginable fantasy—spend the rest of their lives as naturalized, tried-and-true American citizens. Against all my better instincts, I wanted to restore at least a thread of hope that a life in the U.S. might be possible.

"One of the best ways is to be accepted for graduate study at a top-notch university," I told them, feeling a bit like an employment counselor or student advisor. "Or, if you have a solid background in an area where the U.S. needs more skilled workers, you could apply for a job and then for a work visa."

Again, I knew that these options were the longest of long shots, but this group was in dire need of empathy and support, no matter how fanciful. And it was easy to see why a group of overeducated, unemployed, politically and religiously incorrect, stymied young men would find their confidence deflated, their optimism withered. Part of the reason lay in the everyday reminders of past grandeur and the achievements of the generations that had preceded them.

Earlier in the day Aydin and I had stopped at the Dome of Soltaniyeh, a massive block of stone topped with the third-largest dome in the world, after Istanbul's Aya Sofya and the Cathedral of Santa Maria del Fiore in Florence. Built at the beginning of the fourteenth century by Sultan Mohammad Khodabandeh, the building was meant to house the remains of the Shiite holy men Imam Ali and Imam Hossein, but that never came to pass, and so it was left to be the resting place of only Sultan Mohammad himself. The cavernous interior features blue tile mosaics and elaborate swirling stucco designs that cover the alcoves and ascend the pillars that support the massive dome, changing patterns as they rise into the distant gloom overhead. A stone spiral staircase leads to an external balcony that circles the building, and from there one can look out on the town of Soltaniyeh, once a Mongol capital, and the wide plain that surrounds it.

Then there are the Shiite shrines and burial places of other lumi-
naries in Iranian history. The architecture of the massive shrines, their
towering arched portals decorated in brilliant blue tile work, would
have impressed Cyrus himself. Within the burial chambers visitors
pay their respects by touching the metal grillwork that surrounds the
elevated bier that contains the remains, illuminated by a green glow,
chosen to create an aura of saintliness. In Tabriz, the Persian poets
have their own monument—call it a shrine—because poetry nearly
exceeds the status of religion among Iranians, and many will claim that
religion comes in a distant second. This is the Maqbarat-o-shoara, or
the Mausoleum of Poets, where poets representing a thousand years
of literary history are buried. In Qazvin the Peighambarieh Shrine is
the burial place of four Jewish saints believed to have predicted the
birth of Christ. Symbols of past Persian greatness were evident even
in a regional city like Qazvin. In the middle of a leafy, manicured park
stands the Chehal Sotoun, a handsome pavilion dating to the sixteenth-
century Safavid period, when Qazvin was the capital of the empire
before Shah Abbas moved it to Esfahan. Locals refer to it as Emarate
Kolah Faranagi, or "European Hat Mansion," because that is what it
resembles—a European visitor wearing a broad-brimmed hat. Today
the pavilion doubles as a calligraphy museum that contains one of the
most select collections in Iran. It displays the many styles in which
the art is practiced—Nastaliq, Shekasteh-Nastaliq, Sols, and Naskh.
Across brilliantly painted sheets of paper, lines of verse are not written
but drawn in dashes and curls that flow and bend and swirl. Qazvin
has been a center of calligraphy production for centuries, and many
of its past masters—Abdorrashid Deilami, Goharshad Khatun, Mir
Sadreddin, and Abdolmajid Taleqani—were born and learned their
craft in the city, where it is still taught.

A few days later, Aydin and I stopped at Takht-e Soleyman, or the
Throne of Solomon, now the remains of a Zoroastrian temple complex and sixth-century Sassanid-era fortress well off the beaten track
west of Zanjan. To get to it, we drove for more than an hour along a
two-lane road through a rugged, arid mountain landscape that rivaled

western Colorado in barren austerity and the eerie sense of loneliness that only desert mountain landscapes can evoke. The *takht*, or throne, sits in the middle of a high plain, and on that late December day a cold breeze was blowing from the north. Despite the bright sunlight, wisps of snow lingered in the shadows of the ruined walls.

Takht-e Soleyman began as a Zoroastrian fire temple during the fifth century, dedicated to Anahita, the goddess of water. It achieved greater importance when the Adur Wishnasp, one of the three Great Holy Fires, was moved to the temple during the third-century Sassanid dynasty. Zoroastrianism was then the state religion of the empire. Zoroastrian kings had to pay homage to the Adur Wishnasp before they could assume the throne. Historians speculate that the site was chosen because of the deep spring-fed lake that lies at the center of the complex and stands out like a smooth, liquid crystal on the windswept plain. Sassanid rulers later turned the site into a fortress, constructing formidable stone walls around the perimeter to protect it from invaders, but they were unable to stop Byzantine armies from nearly destroying it in 627.

After wandering around the stumps of the crumbling walls and columns, Aydin and I drove a short two miles to Zendan-e Soleyman, the top of a dormant volcanic crater where legends claim King Solomon kept monsters prisoner. Among Zoroastrians of the time, the Zendan-e Soleyman outranked Takht-e Soleyman in spiritual significance, and it stayed that way until the Adur Wishnasp was moved to the latter site, turning Zendan-e Soleyman into an also-ran.

After a scramble to the top of the crater we looked over the rim into an enormous, yawning cavern. Aydin told me that in more modern times prisoners were executed by being hurled into the abyss. In the distance we could still see Takht-e Soleyman very clearly, now even more pronounced on the bright winter day, spread out on the tableland beneath the sharp mountain backdrop. It was a setting, with all its austere beauty, scripted for an ancient religious site.

Surrounded by such cultural riches, with more to be found throughout Iran, it is no wonder that this stagnant generation would feel smitten, impotent, insignificant. It is also no wonder that America would emerge as the answer to all their ills. One could even say that if America didn't exist, young Iranians would have to create it.

"It's become a craze, almost an obsession, to dream of a new life in America," my guide Aydin told me, but almost disparagingly, suggesting that he recognized the facileness of the fantasy, or that he was not as impressed with America as the rest of his generation. Aydin was hard to read. At times he seemed to defend the status quo in Iran, or at least dismiss the most scathing voices. But he would also nod in agreement, however reluctantly, when I told him of the criticisms I had heard. "Students don't even think of applying to universities in Europe, Canada, or Australia, even if their chances of getting in are much better. They just want to get to America. It's America, America, America. Nothing else will do."

I was a little surprised by Aydin's cynicism, because he himself was an example of career stagnation. He had graduated from elite Tehran University with a master's degree in mechanical engineering but opted to lead foreigners around Iran because the pay was much better and job opportunities in his chosen path were extremely limited.

"I worked in Tehran for a while but the city was expensive and the salary I was getting wasn't high enough," he told me. "I had pretty good English ability and liked to travel, so I started to ask myself, 'What else can I do?'"

Aydin moved back to his parents' house in Tabriz, obtained a tourist guide's license, and began offering his services to the travel agents and tour companies authorized to handle Western visitors.

I asked him what it took to be assigned to Western tourists. Was it English ability? No, enough tour guides had that, though they might spend most of their time guiding groups of South Koreans or Russians. One of Aydin's colleagues was learning Chinese. The key factor, he said, was not to care about politics. I guessed that the qualification for tour guides was not to *appear* to care about politics, or at least to discuss it. This was not hard to understand, for politics was a constant theme when meeting young Iranians, and considerable political discussion took place at the late-night Zanjan café. The other popular topic among Iranian youth was religion, or the rejection of it.

"No one here believes in God," Javad boldly stated, followed by a quick translation for the rest of the group. Affirmative nods followed. "No one goes to the mosque. There's nothing for us to do, so we come here to watch football, or we go to Hadi's."

Who was Hadi? At that moment, on cue, Hadi entered, a wiry man with short-cropped black hair and a neatly trimmed black beard. Hadi was the owner of the café, and like many café owners, he had had numerous run-ins with the authorities. They had tried to close him down several times, and, as usual in such cases, the inspectors were more interested in stacking up bribes than enforcing the laws of the Islamic regime. That he ran a Western-style café that seemingly promoted Western-style debauchery—women were invited—placed him under suspicion. To please the authorities, he posted a list of house rules on the walls that accorded with strict Islamic values: no smoking was allowed, women could not congregate with men, no one under fifteen years of age could be admitted, no politics could be discussed, and so on. But enforcement was discretionary to nonexistent. Cigarette smoke floated in the air, and loaded ashtrays needed emptying, men and women gathered together freely, and for the last hour we had been talking about nothing but politics.

Then there was the matter of the pillows. The covers of the small backrest pillows that lined the sofa along the wall were printed with archival front pages of newspapers from the English-speaking world—the *New York Times*, *Washington Post*, London's *Guardian*. For the authorities, that was too much. Hadi was threatened with closure. What could he do?

Problems with the authorities usually have only one solution. "I went to the police station and paid them," Hadi explained. They never came back. The pillow covers remained.

When Parviz, Javad, and Hamid weren't watching football on the biggest of the wall-mounted TV screens, they were sometimes at Hadi's house, drinking his homemade wine.

"There's no way to have fun in Iran," Javad continued, "not for young people. We say it's illegal to laugh in Iran."

In conversations with Iranians, subtext is far more important than anything that is stated openly, and often what is not said is more important than what is. The silence after the mention of the wine meant that no offer to sample some of Hadi's personal vintage was forthcoming. As someone who had already fallen under the eyes of the authorities, he could take no risks, but he still wanted to play the gracious host in other ways. He asked where I was going after the café closed. Back to my hotel, I told him. Did I need a ride? I thanked him for the offer but assured him that my hotel was only a five-minute walk away. He still offered to drive me. I assured him that I wasn't trying to refuse his offer, but my hotel was, I assured him again, just five minutes away. I convinced him, and he was finally satisfied enough to let me strut the five minutes on my own. After he left, the young men returned to the TV set to catch the last minutes of Real Madrid action. I asked Javad for my bill.

"Oh, no—Hadi said you are our guest tonight," he replied, and he gave me a bag of peanuts in case I was hankering for a midnight snack.

Rural hamlets are sprinkled throughout the Iran countryside, and a few days later Aydin and I visited another, the village of Kandovan, about an hour along another twisting two-lane road that slowly rises up another mountain valley in the middle of the Sahand Protected Area. On both sides of the road the view is broad and sweeping both to the east and west, and the valley opens its arms to an arc of sky stretching overhead.

Kandovan is built vertically, on a steep hillside that ascends the southern side of the valley. But Kandovan's history, shaped by ever-changing geology, sets it apart from most of rural Iran. The landscape that now contains the village was formed approximately eleven thousand years ago, when the now dormant volcano Mount Sahand erupted, spewing lava and ash that over time hardened into volcanic rock. Water erosion did the rest—shaping the rock into cave-like formations that make the entire face of the mountain resemble an insect colony, or a collection of beehives. The rock was ideal for cave dwelling, shielding the interior from outside heat in summer and bitter cold in winter. The result was the energy-efficient houses the cave dwellers of Kandovan carved out of the hardened molten lava.

We parked at the edge of town and walked along the cobbled main street into the center, a crossroads where a turn to the right led to a bridge that crossed the stream that cut through the town and valley, and to the left to a lane that climbed into the village. It was the middle of winter but also Friday, the end of the Iranian weekend. Lingering day-trippers were wandering the streets and popping into the gift shops, open to catch whatever off-season rials might pass their way. The streets ascended the mountainside, ending where the balconies of the highest houses offered views of the mountain face on the other side of the valley.

Most of the residents of Kandovan are owners of seasonal gift shops and eateries, which open for business at the beginning of spring and close up at the end of summer, or when autumn crowds dwindle to a trickle, the fate of off-the-beaten-path, picturesque villages around the world that extend their life span by serving as rural getaways for city dwellers. But Kandovan has some year-round mainstays—the farmers and goatherds who market their wool products and locally made honey and handicrafts and cobble together the rest of their livelihoods by running a gift shop or homestay, a bed for the night for budget-conscious travelers. They have made the caves their homes, fitting them out with windows and balconies and exterior staircases to climb to their many levels—rock penthouses rebranded as ecofriendly lodgings for the back-to-nature tourist market.

Though eco-consciousness may be a prime motivation for lifestyle habits today, cave life in Kandovan was initially driven by the most basic need—survival. Most historians believe that it was the Mongol invasion in the thirteenth century that drove the people of the Kandovan region into the lava-formed caves. About ten minutes before we reached the town, Aydin and I pulled to the side of the road to take a look at a cluster of burrows dug into the slowly sloping hillside. Archaeological evidence dates these to the thirteenth century. Word of

Mongol savagery and its take-no-prisoners approach to conquest had reached this part of Iran, and the inhabitants soon saw that a life below ground was at least marginally safer than above it. The caves were dug, and their residents emerged during the day to tend to their fields and herds, and then hunkered in their subterranean hovels to avoid certain slaughter at night.

With the afternoon light fading and the temperature dropping, Aydin dropped me at the Laleh Kandovan International Hotel, where the rooms are caves cut into the rock hillside. He headed back to Tabriz to spend the night in the comfort of his own bed; I was left to spend the night as a cave dweller—twenty-first-century style. My room was outfitted in what could only be described as rural chic—hand-woven carpets on the stone floor and a matching hand-woven cover on the bed, track lighting in the stone ceiling, a flat-screen TV mounted on a stone countertop, and a working Jacuzzi in the bathroom, also hollowed out of rock.

All of this would have been utterly absurd had it not been so tastefully designed. What could have been a Flintstones theme park buried in the wilds of Iran was instead a subdued preserve of rural traditional life. The small terrace outside my door overlooked the valley, which was, after dark, not garishly lit, but swallowed in darkness. Only the dim lights outside the other rooms and the lights that lit the wooden walkways up and down the stone staircases shone in the winter night. The hotel restaurant was also dug into the rock, and that was where I had my dinner—*gormeh sabzi*, an herb-based stew loaded with lamb and vegetables and accompanied, as almost all Iranian dishes are, by a mountain of rice.

After dinner I took a stroll through the village, which was dark and quiet now that the day-trippers had left. Faint overhead lights illuminated the twisting lanes that wound up the side of the mountain, and fainter lights inside the rock-hewn houses showed that Kandovan was more than just a tourist showpiece that emptied with the departure of the last visitor, like a traveling circus folding its tents after its last performance. The few sounds that stirred the night—the barking of a dog, the babbling of the stream tumbling over the rocks as it passed under the wooden bridge—tugged at the silence for brief moments, but, when they receded, a hollowed quiet like that which can only be heard on a dark night deep in a mountain valley returned.

I was heading back to the hotel along the deserted main road when a near full moon rose above the ridgeline on the western side of the valley. Soon the cool light spread over the mountainside, drawing out the brightness in the wispy remnants of the snowfields near the crest of the ridge and throwing the barren trees into dark silhouette. Now I could imagine what it would have been like to have been hunkered in one of those cave homes of Kandovan back in the thirteenth century, waiting for a horde of Mongol tribesman to attack, looking for the glow of a light that could spell annihilation.

The nighttime walk and experience of the last few days had taught me an old lesson anew: the Persian identity didn't begin with Hafez and the great poets, and it didn't begin with the Arab-Islamic invasion. Those are certainly integral parts of an identity that today we call Persian, but they are still mere strands, however substantial, interlaced into a fiber that contains many others. If the story of a people is like the weaving of a carpet, it is not a pattern that simply repeats itself with never-ending monotony. It acquires more colors and designs as it develops, and over time the initial weave can barely be detected. These were the kind of thoughts better saved for the comfort of the Jacuzzi back in my room, which I plunged into before dropping off into a sound and listless sleep.

The next morning Aydin was ready and waiting for me at the entrance gate before I had finished breakfast. Punctuality was his forte. After we had been traveling for a week he had learned that if we agreed to meet at ten o'clock, I wouldn't appear until at least ten after, but every morning he was ready and waiting at the appointed time. We repacked his Saipa, shifting luggage here and there, and in less than an hour we were back in Tabriz. This time we bypassed the city to head north along the Jolfa Road, which ended at the Aras River, the border between Iran and Azerbaijan. As we neared the junction where the road ended, another ridge of mountains appeared directly in front of us. Beyond the ridge were more mountains, and tucked between the valleys were snowfields shimmering in the afternoon sun.

"That's Armenia," Aydin said, pointing to the distant snowcapped peaks. The other side of the river, close enough to reach by throwing a stone, was Azerbaijan.

The landscape of northern Iran offers a history lesson in the many invasions that the country has endured. After the Mongols poured across the northeastern border, razing cities and slaughtering thousands, the forces of the waning Ottoman Empire invaded, in 1914. It was a battle of weaklings. The Turkish Ottomans and the Persian Qajar dynasty were both on their last legs, though the two had fought numerous wars in their tussle for control of the Caucuses and the eastern end of the Anatolian Plateau. Long periods of Turkish occupation of northern Iran had left their imprint—much of the region, including the major city of Tabriz, was largely Turkish speaking. It was Aydin's first language, though he was also fluent in Farsi and English, and his German was competent enough to guide tourists from Munich and Berlin. But he had a cultural affinity for Turkish, which the Turkish pop music and traditional classics he had downloaded on an MP3 to play on the car stereo clearly showed.

The battles with the Ottomans were only a prelude to the next invasion—by British and Russian forces in 1941, to seize control of the country's oil fields, which the Allies feared would aid the Axis powers despite Iran's declared neutrality in World War II. During the interwar years Iran cultivated its ties to Germany, partly due to a distant and historical connection. The word *Iran* is derived from *Aryan*, and the Farsi language originated in central Europe before migrating across the Balkan peninsula, Anatolia, and finally down into Iran. But the main reason for Iran's favorable take on Germany was that, unlike the Russians and the British, Germany had no history of colonial domination. Still, the racial philosophies and antisemitism of the Nazis caused Iran to hold Germany at arm's length. More than 1,500 European Jews were clandestinely given Iranian citizenship by local embassies throughout Nazi-controlled Europe and then safe haven in Iran.

The tipping point came in midsummer 1941, when the Allied forces invaded Iran, the Red Army entering from the north and the British attacking from the Persian Gulf. Rasht, Tabriz, and Ardabil were pummeled by Soviet bombers. The British scattered leaflets over Tehran and Qazvin, urging the Iranian government to surrender. Victory for the Allies was quick.

The rationale for the invasion was twofold: Iran had refused to expel its approximately one thousand German expatriates, and the Allies needed Iranian territory to serve as a corridor for the transfer of military supplies to the Soviet Union. When it was all over northern Iran was divided, with the British controlling the territory south of Hamedan and the Soviets ruling the far north. Food was rationed to feed the occupying troops, which resulted in widespread shortages, hunger, and starvation. On September 16, 1941, Reza Shah was forced to give up power.

All this was now in the past. Aydin and I headed west on the two-lane road that hugged the Aras River until we reached a restored caravansary, now a restaurant in the tourist season. It was closed, but while we strolled the grounds Aydin told me about his ventures to the border as a boy in Soviet times, when the river was not the watery ribbon dividing Iran from culturally friendly Azerbaijan but from an atheist, monolithic, communist state.

"In the spring and summer, when the weather was good, our family would drive here for an afternoon on the weekends, but we didn't even look at the mountains. The Russians were not to be trusted. We thought that if they saw us they might attack us, take us prisoner. We actually believed that. We didn't know what might happen."

I asked him what kind of relationship Iran had with the Soviet Union during the dark days of the Cold War.

"It wasn't very good. There was constant tension. It was the same before the revolution and after. The revolution didn't change anything, and it was worse than the relationship between the U.S. and the Russians, and even the Russians and the Europeans, because we were right on the border. We don't have a good history with Russia, and we didn't have anything to protect us."

A journalist friend of mine from Tehran also recalled going to the border as a young boy, but without the fear and trepidation that filled young Aydin.

"We liked to drive up to the border," he told me. "It was exciting. "We knew the history wasn't good, but this was a chance to stand right at the border and look across it—there was the Soviet Union."

Both were right. The historical relationship of Iran and the Russians—Soviet or otherwise—has been miserable. In the nineteenth century the Persian Empire extended beyond the Aras River, placing present-day Georgia, Armenia, and Azerbaijan under its control. But in the early part of the century a series of wars between an ascendant imperial Russia and the hapless Qajar rulers resulted in Iran having to cede territories, piece by piece, in subsequent treaties, to the czars. This was quite a comedown, for at the end of the eighteenth century Mohammad Khan Qajar had expanded Iran and consolidated its territory by taking control of Mashhad to the east, and the region comprising modern-day Georgia, Armenia, and Azerbaijan to the north. But much further north, the czarina Catherine the Great also had her sights set on Georgia due to its strategic location bordering both Iran and the Ottoman Empire. After successive losses, Iran was forced to sign two treaties in 1804 and 1820, which resulted in a new Persian border being drawn at the Aras River and put the entire Caucuses region under Russian sovereignty. The Russian Revolution of 1917 drew the three tiny Caucuses republics into the arms of the newly formed Soviet Union, further frosting relations with Iran. Only an implosion of the communist state seventy years later allowed generally friendly ties to be established, but on the Iranian side of the border distrust still lingers.

What this history demonstrates, more than the constant battles for territory and geopolitical power so common in the eighteenth and nineteenth centuries, is the uncomfortable relationship Iran has had with Russia reaching back two hundred years. Even today, rather than allies, the two would be better described as "partners of mutual interest." In describing Iran-Russia relations, trust, candor, and confidence are not qualities that come quickly to mind.

We had a little further to go. Our destination was another fifteen minutes up the road, so we got back in the car and headed further up the valley, its steep walls narrowing into jagged plunges on both sides of the river, until we arrived at a sign that pointed the way up a narrower, windier side road that ended at the parking lot of the St. Stepanos Monastery, or Maghardavank in Armenian.

I had long thought that the Armenian presence in Iran dated back a hundred years, to the genocide that occurred during the collapse of the Ottoman Empire. But no. Armenians, and Christianity, have been present in Iran for more than a thousand years, since the beginning of Christianity itself. The apostle St. Bartholomew established a church on the present site of St. Stepanos in 62 CE. Six centuries later it was expanded into a monastery. Over the succeeding centuries it was damaged in wars between Seljuk Turks and the forces of the Byzantine Empire in Constantinople, then restored and rebuilt. In time it became an important center for the spread of Christianity in southwest Asia, disseminating liturgical artwork and sacred texts on Christian philosophy.

A turning point came in 1604, when Shah Abbas drove the Christian population out of northern Iran, reputedly to protect them from threats from the Ottomans. To ease the transition, he established an enclave in Esfahan and named it New Julfa, after the northern Armenian city of Julfa. After Iran lost the Caucuses region to the Russian Empire in the nineteenth century, what remained of the Armenian population migrated to Russia-controlled Armenia. By moving to Esfahan the Armenians may have lost their cultural and ancestral foothold, but rather than being ghettoized in the north they were integrated more fully into Iranian life. Their aptitude for business made them movers and shakers in the development of Iran for centuries beyond the reign of Shah Abbas and through the modernizing period of Reza Shah.

One of the Armenians with economic prowess was Yeprem Khan, born in present-day Azerbaijan, who had joined various groups that promoted Armenian nationalism against the overwhelming power of the Ottoman Empire. Under Russian rule these contacts earned him exile to Siberia, where he escaped and then fled to the Armenian-friendly city of Tabriz. There he rallied other Armenians to join the Constitutional Revolution to protest the rule of then shah Mohammad Ali.

The Constitutional Revolution, which took place between 1905 and 1909, was Iran's ill-fated attempt to usher in political rejuvenation by rebelling against Russian and British colonial power and the growing corruption and usurpation of wealth by the ruling class. During this time Iranian society entered a period of widespread political education and civic awareness, driven by the expansion of a free press and lively debate that drew in all levels of society.

At the beginning of the revolution Iran was ruled by Mozaffar ad-Din. Aging and sickly, the shah had run up massive foreign debts by selling off Iran's assets to Russian and British interests, including its oil profits, and negotiating uneven tariffs that crippled Iran's production of textiles and other goods. The country received little investment, and the bazaar merchants, the backbone of the economy, were suffering.

The revolutionary forces, centered in Tabriz, had had enough. A new constitution was drawn up that would create a parliament to have final say over all financial concerns, including foreign concessions and the national budget. The appointment of all ministers would be delegated to a special committee, which would also oversee the implementation of all new laws. Mozaffar ad-Din agreed to the revolutionaries' demands. Iran was on the verge of becoming a constitutional monarchy, with the shah remaining solely as titular figurehead holding little real power.

Before the ink was dry, Mozaffar ad-Din died and was replaced by his son, Mohammad Ali, who promptly abolished the constitution. In 1908 Yeprem Khan was a leader of a force from Tabriz that marched to Tehran to demand the ousting of Mohammad Ali and the seating of his eleven-year-old son Ahmed as shah. Mohammad Ali fled to Odessa, where he plotted a return to power, but he was ultimately beaten back by forces allied with Yeprem Khan. Meanwhile, Russian and British powers divided Iran into spheres of control, with the Russians taking the north and the British the south. Parliament ultimately dissolved, and Russian forces seized Tehran. Khan's victory was short-lived. In

1925 he died in battle in Shurchah at the hands of allies of Mohammad Ali, who sought revenge for the ousting of their favored leader.

Aydin and I wandered the grounds under a steely grey sky that occasionally brightened to allow the conical steeples—signatures of an Armenian church—to cast lengthy shadows across the stone floor of the inner courtyards. An adjoining museum displayed chalices, processional crosses, and illuminated Bibles written in Armenian. A large sign at the entrance, with text in Farsi, Armenian, and English, stated that the entire complex, a UNESCO World Heritage Site, was also registered as a symbol of the religious cultural heritage of Iran. Despite the significance of St. Stepanos in both Iranian and Armenian history, it is not the oldest church in Iran. That honor goes to the Monastery of St. Thaddeus near the town of Chaldiran, near the border with modern-day Azerbaijan. In Armenian it is known as the Qara Kelisa, or "Black Church."

Thaddeus may have beaten St. Stephen in bringing Christianity to northwest Iran, but not by much. The church that bears his name was built in 68 CE, but time has proven to be a great equalizer. Both churches, along with the Chapel of Dzordzor, perched on a promontory west of St. Stepanos, form a trio that make up the Armenian Monastic Assemblies of Iran.

By the time Aydin and I arrived back in Tabriz it was late afternoon, too late for any of the local museums, but time enough to take a long walk around El Goli Park, the city's postcard-perfect artificial lake and surrounding greenery. In the middle of the lake stands a former summer palace from the Qajar era that is now a restaurant. Picturesque balconies look out over the water. The sun had already dropped behind the spindly, barren trees on the western side of the lake, and the winter air had turned chillingly crisp. The broad walkway around the lake was crowded with Tabrizis strolling and mingling on the benches. Young families had toddlers in tow, and the health conscious worked their muscles on the exercise machines along the par course that began at the entrance. Yet the scene was not all straining and sweating in the cold winter air. Lining the walkway and running track were more Tabrizis gathered at cheap eateries behind thick sheets of plastic that formed a protective cover to shield them from the nighttime chill. There they sipped glasses of sweet tea, puffed on *galyoons*, the traditional water pipes, and finished off plates of grilled meat and *cholo kebab* in relative seasonal comfort.

It was Wednesday evening, beginning of the Iranian weekend, but still I was surprised by the number of people out enjoying the frosty air. In a few months, as soon as the mountain paths were clear of snow and the longer days of spring would begin to melt the icy buildup in the high valleys, the hiking trails would be filled with adventure-starved pleasure seekers.

I liked Tabriz at first sight—the clean, well-kept streets, the air of liberalism, Iranian-style, that pervaded the clean, well-kept streets, the prim storefronts and neatly tended parks sprinkled across the city. Even the traffic, though clogged at rush hour, flowed in an orderly way that put to shame the manic chaos of Tehran. Every morning, in the breakfast room of the towering five-star El Goli Hotel where I slept each night, I watched a girls' sports team mingle over the extensive buffet, headscarves barely covering their tumbling locks, baggy sweatshirts reaching only a few inches below their waistlines—"Islamic attire" that in many parts of Iran would have challenged the definition.

In the evenings I trotted from the hotel down to pedestrian-filled El Goli Park to jog four circuits of the pathway that circled the lake, passing the giant snowman statue at the entrance. Darkness had settled in along with the nighttime chill. Children licked plumes of cotton candy as they rammed their tricycles and scooters into the guardrail that surrounded the lake. There was no "purpose" to any of it, not the strolling, nor the muscle pumping, not even the sharing of dinner plates among the diners hunkered in thick jackets around the cafés' cranking space heaters. The only purpose, if it could be called that, was to be out among human company on a chilly winter night, and that was what made it so delightful.

On my last night in Tabriz I had dinner at a combination pizzeria and café, just a short walk from the park. With its bright, inoffensive décor and midrange prices it was the place to go for middle-class families from the neighborhood as well as dating couples out for an evening—in other words, everyone and just about anyone in liberal Tabrizi society. The menu was solely in Farsi—no English translation to aid the odd traveler—but the hostess recruited the help of one of the prep cooks to coach me through it. This aroused the interest of the group at the table next to me, a couple and two children—a little girl with a pink headband in her hair and a boy of about eleven sporting crystal-clear horn-rimmed glasses. They paid their check and were donning their jackets to leave when the boy came over and stood ramrod straight at the end of my table. He adopted the pose of a head waiter announcing the presentation of the next course.

"Thank you for coming to our country," he said with all formality. "We are very honored to have you."

3 | The Caspian Shore

RICE AND SPICE AND OTHER THINGS NICE

A newlywed bride wanted to make fluffy steamed rice but did not know how, so she turned to her mother-in-law for help. "First you wash the rice," the mother-in-law instructed. The bride nodded and said, "Yes, I know." "Then you soak the rice in lightly salted water for a couple of hours." "I knew that too," said the bride. "Then you cook the rice until the grains are tender." "Yes, I knew that as well." The mother-in-law decides to teach the bride a lesson: "Last, put an adobe brick on top of the rice, cover it, and cook for an hour." The bride prepares the rice as instructed and the disintegrated brick ruins the rice.

—Persian fable

It was closing time, and most of the diners had left, but the rain was still pounding on the canopy that covered the café patio adjacent to the pizzeria next door. The rain was welcome and long overdue. The fields and hills around Ramsar, and all of northwest Iran, had endured years of drought, so a good, heavy dousing couldn't have been more welcome.

For the past hour or so I had been talking to Alireza, an Iranian American chiropractor living in southern California who was back in Iran for a few months to deal with "family business," a catchall term for the limitless list of reasons that compel Iranians from the diaspora to return, often to resolve legal matters stemming from the 1979 Islamic Revolution. We had been paired together by one of the restaurant staff, who, noticing me sitting alone at one of the tables lining the wall, thought I should have some company, and so he introduced me to fellow countryman and English-fluent Alireza, who had also been sitting alone, munching on a pizza.

"Would you like some?" he asked several times after he plopped what was left of the pie between us, and each time I told him I had already had dinner and my stomach couldn't absorb another bite. As the last of the guests paid their checks and left he told me his story.

He was born in Tehran and had gone to the U.S. to study physical therapy in the late 1970s, a few years before the beginning of the Islamic Revolution. When the country exploded in open rebellion against the oppressive rule of Shah Mohammad Reza, he concluded it was not the best time to return to Iran. Already he had shifted his career path and enrolled in the Life School of Chiropractic in Atlanta. He graduated, moved to Southern California, and still did not return to Iran, not for another fourteen years. The reason was simple. The devastating Iran-Iraq War had erupted, and he refused to be drafted into the Iranian army to serve as cannon fodder for what had become an ideologically driven regime that was using the nationalistic sentiments of the war to stoke its own special brand of Islamic fervor. So he remained in Southern California, where he has lived ever since.

All of this came out in very no-nonsense fashion, and the longer Alireza and I talked, the more I found him emblematic of so many diaspora Iranians who had lived for decades in the West but had been born and come of age in prerevolutionary Iran. They found greater comfort in Western values than those of the Islamic Republic, yet they remained attached to a very different Iran, one that had been almost a hybrid of Asian-Persian culture and Western ways, that still floated in their imaginations. Family members who had remained behind were the unbreakable tie to both these expats' homeland and the lives they had lost. For many a return occurred every year, usually in the summer. For others, the gap between trips could be years, even decades, but they did occur, if only to assure themselves that the Iran that they had known still existed, if only in the equally sentimental imaginations of friends and relatives.

"You sure you don't want a slice?" Alireza asked again, and again a few minutes later—the impulses of Persian hospitality returning—and again I declined, and again I assured him that I had just eaten. I was not put off by his persistent politeness. I knew where he was coming from. It was not pushiness. Old habits had resurfaced, and quickly. He was "home," and therefore my host, and I was therefore his "guest," and in Iran it was the sacred duty of a host to ensure that his guest wanted for nothing.

I asked him what changes he had seen in the country since he was last back, fourteen years ago.

"Back then, there was so much change. First the revolution, which completely transformed the society, and then came the war, which went on for eight years. The biggest problem was that even after it was over there was no opportunity for reflection, for the people to realize what had happened and how it had affected them. Everything was all about suppression, and it came from the government. This government is all about suppression, suppression of even the normal instincts of human beings. It doesn't encourage exploration of any kind. It's afraid that anything will lead the people away from the path of Islam. All through the war everything was all about slogans, how the country and the revolution had to be defended—simple statements, simple beliefs, anything to whip up support for the war. That was why I could never come back, not then. When it was over, there was no opportunity for the people to come to terms with what they had experienced, inside."

There have been reams of prose written about the effects of the Iran-Iraq War and war in general, but I had never heard them expressed with such depth and razor-edged simplicity. I asked Alireza if there were any difficulties he faced in adjusting to this new Iran. He threw his head back, paused.

"It took me a while to learn what the new rules were, of how people are supposed to act in society. Everything was turned upside down. All of a sudden an entirely new set of principles were forced on us. We were supposed to become an 'Islamic society,' but what did this mean? We were never that religious, never in our entire history. After the revolution and the war people were told they were supposed to look at themselves in a different way. They were supposed to relate to others in society differently. Yet something had been driven deep down inside them that they didn't know how to express."

Around the café there were a few tables of diners left, groups of young men and women chatting and laughing with as much ease as any group of young men and women anywhere in the world. On the surface, nothing seemed amiss. But this was, perhaps, a lesson in the illusions presented by surface impressions. I knew Alireza was on to something. The Islamic Revolution and the ensuing war had distorted Iranian society beyond all recognition. His years in a land that celebrated free expression almost to a fault had sensitized him to this "new normal" that had shifted the foundation of Iranian society away from one that for centuries had celebrated personal expression and indulgence in sensual experience to one that denied any experience that was not in line with "Islamic values"—as government officials interpreted them.

Alireza continued along this theme, clearly one of his pet peeves with the "new Iran." "People need to be free to express what they experience, and that is what is missing here. There is no opportunity for growth. That's why I find it hard to stay here for any length of time. A few weeks, even a few months, is fine, but after that. . . ." He paused to search for the right words. "I can feel that. . . ." Another pause. "I'm not . . . 'moving.' My life isn't moving. There isn't any opportunity to grow."

Alireza was licensed to practice in Iran, and he took out his wallet and showed me his membership card in the Iranian Chiropractic Association, but he never saw patients, not on this trip, not on any of his previous returns. These were personal pilgrimages severed from the life that he had established in Southern California, not opportunities to develop professional contacts. That kind of effort would force him to combine phases of his life he still hadn't reconciled. His trips back to Iran were akin to religious retreats—a rare chance to turn his back on his life in the U.S. and return to his roots, to reassemble the pieces of what had become a fragmented identity. If he were ever to accomplish that, his American life would have to be left behind.

I asked him if he could speculate on the direction Iran might be headed?

He leaned back, again threw his head back. "Every time I'm back it isn't the same. There are more restaurants, more boutiques, more of a Western way of life."

He was buoyed by this. He was smiling. It seemed to assure him that the path on which Iran was headed in the days of the shah hadn't been completely lost after all.

As for his view on this "new Iran," I had to agree. There had been a proliferation of stores selling high-end fashions, restaurants that would be classed as "upscale" in the West, and, most noticeably, a coffee shop explosion. In cities all over the country, social oases for mingling while sipping cappuccinos and espressos and munching on cakes and pastries had sprouted, and the background music that floated from their sound systems would have been banned just a few years ago as "Western cultural hegemony"—flamenco and bossa nova, jazz classics, American pop staples, and even what had come to be known as Farsi pop, pumped out by Iranian American bands centered in "Tehrangeles," the capital of diaspora Iranian youth culture in Southern California. All of this had finally found its way to Iran, primarily through the e-waves that manage to pierce the most formidable e-walls erected by government censors. It was a losing battle, and hardline government figures seem to have realized it was simply no longer worth the effort, which could be better directed to the suppression of overt political challenges.

"This has really helped," Alireza went on, pointing to the laptop I had been carrying to catch up on emails and check out news websites. "The internet didn't exist during the first twenty years of the revolution. Now people know what the rest of the world is like. There is exposure to other ideas and what is happening in other parts of the world. The government isn't able to lie like it used to."

There was a problem here. A little way into our conversation, Alireza had lamented how the government had wedged religion into every aspect of Iranian life: "We have forgotten what it means to be Iranian," he had said. At the time I knew it was a bit of exaggeration but let it pass. After all, I had been introduced to Alireza because one of the café employees thought I shouldn't be sitting alone—a gesture of social decorum consummately Iranian. But Alireza had a point. Almost forty years of oppressive Islamic rule had sowed a degree of confusion about the Iranian identity.

"We are still looking for our religion," Alireza had said, and this had a resounding ring of truth. Islam had arrived in Iran 1,400 years ago, and it was still trying to find a foothold in the Persian identity. Then he added, with a ray of hope, "We have had such great philosophers. I hope we will find ourselves by rediscovering the thinking of another time."

It was no secret who and what he was referring to—the works of the great Persian poets who had both shaped and defined Persian culture and created a distinctively Persian literature—Hafez and Saadi, Rumi and Omar Khayyam, Ferdowsi.

But now everything was muddied. "Looking for our religion . . . we will find ourselves . . ." Alireza was talking about the Iranian identity, but it involved a lot more than Islam and Hafez.

All this was a little too much to pick apart over cold pizza near closing time, so I presented Alireza with a more immediate question: If the Persian identity were as confused as he claimed, wouldn't the infusion of Western values, channeled through the e-stream of the internet, muddy the mix even further?

"There is nothing foreign or strange about American culture," he said, the ceiling lights reflecting off his glasses and brightening his eyes more than they already shone. "We need to have a good relationship with America."

He could have been referring to the heady days of Shah Moham-mad Reza Pahlavi at the height of the Cold War, when Iran, with its anticommunist stance, was viewed as a convenient bulwark against Soviet expansion. The high-water mark was arguably the champagne toast shared between the shah and U.S. president Richard Nixon. But for devout Muslims, the image of the shah raising a glass of champagne still stands as a shameful betrayal of Islamic values. For more secular

Iranians it is a wistful reminder of the more modern image that the shah sought to project.

"We all used to watch American movies as children," Alireza went on, with obvious nostalgia. His face beamed. "I grew up on American cartoons. We connected with America."

Word that there was an American guest in the house had circulated among the staff, and now that the kitchen had closed the two cooks and one of the waiters sidled over to our table. They stood at a slight distance, polite, respectful, but curious. One of the cooks said something to Alireza, who translated.

"He wants to know why you came to Iran."

"I always thought it was a nice country, and I wanted to see it."

Alireza translated, and the faces of the group nodded approvingly. The waiter asked what I had seen in Iran, and as I rattled off the names of the cities I had visited wide grins spread across the faces, and then there was a spark of laughter.

"You've seen more of Iran than any of us," said the cook.

Another man joined the group. He was short but stocky with close-cropped black hair and a neatly trimmed beard. This was Hossein, the owner of the restaurant and café, and a friend of Alireza's.

"I love America," he blurted out, in halting English. "That is my dream, to one day go to America."

"Everyone wants to go to America," I replied, lamely. I had learned that this was the only approach to take with America seekers, not only in Iran but anywhere in the world. Always there was the whiff of a faint, delusional belief that I might, just might, be a conduit to the land of their dreams, and the only effective response was to express understanding and empathy.

"Do you think I can get a visa?" Hossein continued.

"It's hard," I said, lying. It wasn't hard. For someone like Hossein, who had never been to the United States and had no ties in the country, it was next to impossible. But I wouldn't tell him that. I didn't want to spoil the party. Another employee appeared with a box of saffron cookies. The waiter produced a smartphone and began snapping photos—me with Alireza, the two of us with Hossein, me surrounded by the rest of the group. The restaurant may have closed, but the party was just getting started.

"You're really from America?" asked the other cook, and I knew what was coming. It was part of the ritual when meeting Iranians and as formalized as a mating dance in the natural world. "What state?"

I told him, and there were more nods. After more than a month of touring Iran I had noticed that the more remote one's city or state of origin the more pleased the questioners appeared, as though they were collecting pieces of America like some people collect stamps, coins, or bottle caps. This made Pocatello, Idaho, and Tuscaloosa, Alabama, blue-chip properties, and it made these Iranians feel connected to America, not just New York, California, Miami, and other well-known spots but also the remote hinterlands, the "real America" they had seen only in pirated American movies and TV series.

The last of the diners had paid their checks and left. One of the kitchen staff was sorting silverware at one of the empty tables. Hossein glanced around the room to make sure it had cleared out and then leaned toward me. "Would you like something?" he almost whispered, and then, after a loaded pause: "I like Americans. Would you like something? Wine? Whiskey?"

"You have some?" I replied, but cautiously.

He consulted with the cook.

"Whiskey. No wine. Or some cognac? Would you like some cognac? It's good. Homemade. But it will take a little while. It's not here."

Alireza cut in, assuring me that Hossein did make some very good cognac, but if I was ready to sample it I better watch out—it was *strong*. "Iranians like strong alcohol," he said. With that, the waiter disappeared out the front door, and I heard his motorbike start up and tear off into the night. There was some debate over whether the lights in the café should be dimmed in case the police passed by, but Hossein said there was no need and then explained.

"After I opened this place the police came around and looked into every bottle in the kitchen. They even checked the bottles of the flavored syrups for the coffee drinks. They had heard that I might be serving alcohol, but I knew they weren't really looking for anything. They just wanted money, so I paid them and then they stopped coming. If they came by now I'd give them a bottle and they'd go away."

The lights stayed on.

After about ten minutes the waiter returned with a liter bottle of Absolut vodka spray-painted black, except for the Absolut logo that leaked through. Hossein produced two glasses. Alireza uncapped the bottle and poured. The cognac, clear as crystal, rained into my glass with the soft, tinkling sound of clinking ice cubes. I twirled the glass, swirling the contents, and it ran down the inner walls of the glass in evenly tapered lines—the sign of a first-rate cognac. I placed my nostrils over the lip. The aroma was heavy, woody, pleasantly smooth. Then came the test.

"Let's drink to the future of Iran!" Alireza said, hoisting his glass. We clinked glasses, and I took a sip. I expected to be hit with a blast of liquid lightning, but the cognac went down clean and smooth with only a gentle suggestion of its strength. But Alireza was not kidding. It was *strong*. *Very* strong, but in the pleasant way the sun shines on a bright, clear fall afternoon. I could feel its warmth seeping through me, producing a sensation of cozy contentment. I was ready to curl up in front of a roaring fire.

Alireza refilled our glasses. Again I twirled mine, watched the clear, even stream run down the inside of the glass, inhaled the soft, woody aroma.

Alireza took a sip, deeper than mine. "Iranians are very emotional people," he went on—the cognac was working its magic—"We can think and analyze, but sometimes we can think and analyze too much. In the end we are led by our emotions. The problem these days is that we don't know how to love. We can read about it in the works of our poets, but we only know it in the abstract, as something to write about, or read about, but what about the experience?"

He refilled our glasses. If any of the Ramsar police had dropped by I have no doubt Hossein would have placed more glasses on the table, sent the waiter out for another bottle, and the party and the discussion that it generated would have continued.

It continued anyway, as conversations have no trouble doing when they are aided by fine cognac, but once the last drops had been drained from the bottle, Hossein told us it was time to lock up. Alireza extended an invitation to keep the evening going.

"Why don't you come up to my house? I have some good home-made wine that's been waiting to be opened."

I asked him if he wasn't concerned about the authorities, the same who had tried to shut down Hossein's café and pizzeria.

Alireza waved a hand. "Here no one bothers us. My house is far back up in the hills. No one from the police ever goes up there. And no one up there wants anything to do with them. If we have any problems, we work it out ourselves. No one would think of calling the police. That only brings trouble. Everything in this country is all about relationships. If you have good relationships, you don't need the police."

I wanted to accept Alireza's invitation, but my senses weren't drowned in enough cognac to not realize it was impossible. "No one bothers us . . . everything in this country is all about relationships," he had said, which was true—for Iranians who know the right people. But the prospect of being nabbed drinking illegally made wine in an Iranian home by a rogue police officer who didn't put much stock in personal relationships wasn't something I wanted to chance, not as a foreign visitor, and an American to boot. So I politely declined Alireza's offer, taking a rain check till the day when alcohol could be drunk freely throughout Iran—whenever that may come.

It was time to go. Hossein was about to turn out the lights. I didn't have to call for a taxi because Alireza had his car out front and insisted on giving me a ride to my hotel, also tucked away in the Ramsar hills. The rain was still coming down as he steered his white Peugeot up the zigzagging streets to the driveway of the hotel. We pulled up to the door, and he seemed reluctant to shut off the engine, or drive away. He took a business card out of his wallet and scribbled his mobile number on the back.

"Now you have another friend in Iran," he said as we bid our farewells.

The next morning I expected to wake up with a head the size of a kettledrum, but the crystal-clear homemade hooch had passed through without leaving a footprint. The rain had passed, and occasional shafts of sunlight were breaking through the cloud cover. Conditions were ripe for a climb to the ruins of a thirteenth-century fort set high atop a promontory overlooking the city.

After breakfast, Aydin and I hopped in the Saipa, headed south, and then angled through a neighborhood of one-story houses to the beginning of a trail that led up to the fort. The steep rock trail was slick with cold morning dew that also reflected the sunlight as it danced off the dripping leaves. In fifteen minutes we had reached the base of the walls of the fort. From the ruins of the ramparts it was easy to see why Alireza would choose Ramsar as his home-away-from-home, or home-back-home, depending, of course, on whether he felt he had a home anywhere at all. Ramsar was Southern California reimagined on the shores of the Caspian. The city, with its apron of white stucco houses topped with red-tiled roofs, spread out along the silvery blue coastline. Along the seafront boulevard palm trees gently nodded in the morning breeze.

"I'm Iranian and I love Iran, but I could not live here," I recall Alireza saying. "It's 'the system,'" he added, using the catchall term for the Islamic government and its suffocating laws, but for Alireza it also meant a backward mindset that represented all that ailed Iran. "It doesn't encourage growth, the growth of the individual. Every time I come back I know that I can only stay for a few months. After that I feel that I have to leave. I feel like my life is standing still."

Alireza's life could almost be summed up by the tired phrase, "You can't go home again," but he had proven it wrong. He could go home again—as long as "home" was defined as a little fortress of his own, deep up in the Ramsar hills to keep the realities of present-day Iran at a distance.

After the trek up to the fort, Aydin and I drove to Ramsar Palace, the prime reason for Ramsar's inclusion on the tourist trail. The palace was built in 1937 by Reza Shah Pahlavi to serve as a summer getaway whenever he wanted to escape the congestion of Tehran. The relatively small building, with its white marble façade, almost swallowed up by an extensive, manicured garden, reminded me of the kind of bunga- low Russia's Catherine the Great would have given to one of her many lovers once she was ready to toss him aside. The summer residences of the Russian nobility scattered around St. Petersburg tried to mimic the grand opulence of the French royalty, but Ramsar is a slightly dif- ferent case.

To call Ramsar a palace is something of a misnomer, for the chunky, compact house lacks the sprawling layout, glitter, and grandeur of Ver- sailles or Peterhof. Ramsar could be better seen as representing the period from the late nineteenth century and into the twentieth, when significant European influence, from France in particular, spread east- ward. The palace could also be seen as symbolizing the bifurcation of the Iranian identity—devotedly and defiantly Persian but also reaching to embrace Western ways.

Today, Ramsar Palace also stands for something else, which ties it, ironically, to the Islamic regime—the alienation of rulers from the Ira- nian people. The majority of Iranians are nowhere near as consumed by religion and Islamic principles as the ruling mullahs would like them to be and believe they should be. Likewise, during the reign of the Pahlavis a wide swath of Iranian society was not as enamored of Western ways as the secular ruling class wanted them to be and believed they should be. Many will claim that this disconnect, as much as his megalomania and repressive policies, led to the downfall of Mohammad Reza.

"The shah did do a lot to modernize Iran," one friend, born just before the Islamic Revolution, told me, "but he moved too fast for some of the people. The more liberal elements were opposed to his authoritar- ianism, but the conservatives and many people in the countryside saw him as betraying Persian values."

Today it may be rimmed with seasonal homes owned by the urban, monied class in Tehran and the rest of northern Iran, but the Caspian shore was slow to develop. The western slopes of the Alborz Mountains shielded it from settlers moving north from central Iran, for centuries an intimidating Russian Empire glowered to the north, and to the east lay the open sea. The Caspian shore remained a backwater. Yet it became the source for one of Iran's most well-known exports—caviar, *khaviyar* in Persian—specifically beluga caviar, the "Iranian diamond," so named because of its high quality. Beluga sturgeon, the fish that produce the tiny dark eggs, have been known to live up to one hundred years.

Oddly, caviar has never played a significant role in Persian cuisine. Iranians don't "do caviar." Most of the caviar for consumption is found in five-star hotels for foreign visitors, in other words, business travelers and tourists seeking a taste of Iran that in everyday terms is not very Iranian. The majority of the tiny black fish eggs, tightly packed in small, round tin containers, are exported to distant parts of the world and identified, for marketing purposes, as "Iranian caviar." What these glossy ads do not say is that overfishing of the Caspian, combined with increasing pollution and economic sanctions, has meant that Iran's caviar industry has been hit hard, reducing it to a fraction of its former size.

The port of Bandar-e Anzali, near Rasht, is another fading star. At the beginning of the last century, the city thrived off trade with imperial Russia, but the Bolshevik revolution of 1917 slammed the door. After seventy years of hibernation, trade with Russia picked up again following the dissolution of the Soviet Union, but once again it dwindled when economic sanctions hampered all economic activity with Iran. Nevertheless, the one-hundred-year-old "Russia connection" managed to leave a mark on Iranian politics through the export of communism and socialist thought, which would take shape as the Persian Communist Party and become an influential force in Iranian politics up to the reign of Shah Reza Mohammad Pahlavi. The shah's fierce anticommunist stance earned him American backing until his Western leanings were cast into doubt, a key factor that cost him Western support during the 1979 Islamic Revolution.

Before plunging into more questions of politics, Aydin and I decided to seek the peace of the countryside. We drove about twenty miles outside the city to the Gilan Rural Heritage Museum, where cottages and farmhouses and fishmongers' hovels, and even a rural mosque, had been uprooted from their foundations and reconstructed in a sylvan preserve that was part living history, part woodland retreat.

For a couple of hours, as dusk fell, Aydin and I wandered the paths that weaved through the forest, stopping at building after wood-framed building to get a glimpse into nineteenth-century Persian life. It had been an overcast day at the beginning of winter. All day the sky was somber grey and the trees barren of leaves, but the starkness of the surroundings never translated into a sullen mood. Even when the late-afternoon sky darkened and the chill in the air grew heavy I found peace in the silence and serenity, and most of all the simplicity of a time that had faded into the past in countries far from the borders of Iran.

This artificially created preserve, as isolated from the current strife as it could be, wasn't the only opportunity for retreat in Iran's north. There was also the village of Masouleh, a hamlet of several hundred houses squeezed onto the top of a mountain valley about thirty miles from Rasht. Masouleh has nothing to recommend it except that it is a quiet, timeless, rural hamlet surrounded by a landscape of extraordinary beauty. And then there are the houses.

The entire village of Masouleh was built on a steep hillside that is a waning link of the Alborz Mountains. So steep is the slope and so crowded the construction that the front terrace of one house becomes the roof of the one below it, tier by tier, from the top of the ridge to the valley floor below. Because of the configuration of the town and the tightness of the streets, cars can go no further than a parking lot spread out where the road ends and the village begins. In Masouleh, foot traffic is the only traffic.

Aydin and I had stopped by on a brilliantly bright winter day with low-angled sunlight seeping through the naked branches of the trees that filled the valley. We spent a couple of hours climbing streets that at their narrowest and steepest become staircases cutting through tiers of mud-brick hovels. Rarely was anyone home. After decades of little use, most of the houses had become the seasonal getaways of families that had long ago moved to the urban centers of Tabriz and Tehran, or closer by—to Rasht, Qazvin, or Zanjan. With the arrival of spring the town would reawaken. The Noruz holiday, or Persian New Year, would draw visitors by the thousands: day-trippers, weekenders, and the owners of the homesteads, who would sweep them out to get them ready for weekend visits that would last into the fall.

There was a reason to follow the narrow, twisting road up to Masouleh besides the radiant winter light and remote beauty of the setting. The reason was the *girich* patterns that decorate many of the doors. Masouleh is estimated to be a thousand years old, and the practice of girich in Islamic art and architecture covers most of that time. A girich pattern consists of interlocking and overlapping geometric designs, usually emanating from a polygon star. The eye of the viewer can organize them an almost infinite number of ways. A girich pattern may be a flat surface, but one that suggests depth and even the mystery of infinity. They are prominent on the wooden window grills of some of the larger houses, and on the balconies overlooking the tiny, postage-stamp squares that dot the town.

Aydin and I sat in the sunlight on the terrace of a restaurant overlooking the valley, sipping tea and slurping on bowls of *aash*, a thick noodle soup, as the sun sank slowly beyond the ridgeline and the earth-colored façades of the village gradually deepened. A group of Korean backpackers left the ecofriendly hostel on the other side of the street, and other day-trippers gathered at the tables to also drink tea and nurse steaming bowls of aash.

I was glad to be here in the middle of the week in the middle of the winter, because on any summer afternoon or the beginning of Noruz the near-empty lanes would be crammed with curiosity seekers, the terrace tables packed, and the souvenir shops rimming the parking lot and lining the streets leading into the village full to bursting. The lot itself would be chockablock, and cars would be lined up bumper-to-bumper one, even two miles, down the winding road, and the footpaths that began where the town's lanes ended would be lined with hikers. But all of that was months away. Today was reserved for an Iran of a more quiet, innocent past, and the joy of winter sunlight cutting through barren trees.

"Iranians are like city people anywhere these days," Aydin said as we basked in the sun. "They spend all week at their desks, and when the weekend comes they want to get out of the city and get some exercise, enjoy the outdoors. Towns like this get a new life."

I didn't have any trouble believing this. At the edge of North Tehran, at the Velenjack trailhead, I had walked one of the mountain paths to a viewpoint where a small café was selling drinks and snacks to dozens of other mountain strollers. The ruggedly adventurous continued further, far up into the remote wilderness in the direction of Mount Damavand, at 15,300 feet the highest peak in the Middle East. Iranians have always had an affinity for natural environments, and Persian poetry is packed with natural imagery. In these lines from Rumi, the great Sufi master, nature offers lessons for human life:

> Be like the sun for grace and mercy.
> Be like the night to cover other's faults.
> Be like running water for generosity.
> Be like death for rage and anger.
> Be like the Earth for modesty.

Saib Tabrizi, a seventeenth-century poet from Tabriz, also saw the natural world as instructive:

> If like the very dew you do not leave the fragrance
> Inside the sun's gaze you will not find a place.

The fourteenth-century writer Hafez could never escape the beauty of the imagery found in nature:

> When the wine sun fills the bowls of the East,
> It brings to her cheeks a thousand anemones.
> The wind breaks ringlets of hyacinth
> Over the heads of the roses
> As among the meadows I inhale
> The fragrance of her rich hair.

Given the political turbulence and economic hardship that is part of day-to-day life, it is easy to understand why many Iranians escape to rural retreats for quick holidays or a simple walk in the woods. There was no escape from the recent political unrest once we were back in the Rasht. As we zipped through streets, a neon sign in the window of a café-restaurant caught my eye: Escape Room.

Aydin dropped me at my hotel, near a large, leafy park, ideal for an end-of-the-day run, and so I donned my Nikes and "Islamically appropriate" workout clothes—long pants for men—and strutted over to the park.

Rumors that there would be demonstrations that night had apparently reached the security services, for all the paths into the park were guarded by black-clad, truncheon-wielding members of the basij, donned in riot helmets and black balaclavas and spaced every forty or fifty feet around the park perimeter. A tough-looking basij commander made the rounds of his forces while communicating with higher-ups via smartphone and radio. It was clear that all of this was to ensure that the park did not become a congregation point for any group seeking to hijack the protests for political ends, particularly any green movement forces emerging from hibernation.

This time, unlike the 2009 postelection riots, the protests caught the government off-guard. What was unusual about these was that they had begun in Mashhad, Iran's second-largest city, and not exactly a hotbed of antiregime fervor. They quickly spread to Kermanshah, where a recent earthquake had killed more than six hundred residents, and to Qom, Hamedan, and other cities not known for green movement activism. On the contrary, these protestors represented the Iranian heartland, upholders of the status quo who were generally allergic to political upheaval.

Nothing is static or predictable in Iran, surely not protests. Within days the message had changed from protests against corruption to attacks on the character, competence, and even the legitimacy of the Islamic regime. In Rasht and Ramsar, and far north in Ardebil, near the border with Azerbaijan, I watched reports on state-sponsored English-language Press TV in the cozy comfort of my hotel rooms, and the state-funded message, channeled through English-fluent anchors, was true to form: "outside forces" were sowing seeds of dissent, antigovernment agitators wanted to destabilize Iran. Ayatollah Khamenei stated, "In recent days, enemies of Iran used different tools, including cash, weapons, politics, and intelligence services to create troubles for the Islamic Republic."

This time the problem with the government's rebuttals was that they were refuting the legitimate gripes of their traditional supporters. One odd twist was that the protests had been stoked not by the remnants of the green movement but hardliners seeking to attack the reformist impulses of President Hassan Rouhani. The second odd twist was that latent liberal forces quickly saw an opportunity to voice their own grievances and were able to steer the protests in another direction.

Surprisingly, the activity in the park continued as "normal," but in Iran "normal" spans a wide spectrum of definitions. Parents amused their children on the playground slides and swing sets. Couples discreetly nuzzled on the benches in the more shadowy recesses of the park where the basij had not ventured, not that they would have bothered with such minor breaches of "Islamic values" anyway. They may even have been glad to see it—more nuzzlers meant fewer protestors. Other runners, out for their evening jaunt, pounded the footpaths with me. I sprinted along the park perimeter, passing basijis cloaked in their antiriot gear. That I was a foreigner, and a Westerner, generated no interest. Far more important was heeding the orders of their commander and eyeballing the residents of Rasht for any spark of rebellion.

As an American in Iran it was refreshing to be dismissed for a change. I finished my laps around the park and then angled through the streets back to the hotel. Again there was a sense of déjà vu, drawing on memories of the 2009 postelection riots. Just a few blocks from the besieged park, life carried on as "normal." Afterwork shoppers popped into the brightly lit spice shops and grocery stores and other storefronts before making their way home, where news of the demonstrations would receive scant coverage on the state-run broadcasting outlets.

About an hour later Aydin met me in the lobby to head out for dinner at a reputedly good and authentic—he claimed—Italian restaurant. Thursday-night nightlife in Rasht was in full swing. By the time we arrived at the restaurant it was eight o'clock—early for dining in Iran—but a stream of customers was beginning to fill the ground-floor tables. All of the popular social media sites—Snapchat, Twitter, and, most important, Telegram, the message-sharing pathway of choice for Iranian youth—had been blocked. Aydin had downloaded a VPN onto his phone to circumvent the government censors, but still none of the sites would open, and he subscribed to all of them.

Watching all this was enlightening. During the 2009 demonstrations the government had simply cut off internet access as well as the cell phone network, and that was enough to stymie e-communication and any political activity that depended on it. But since then the world of social media, with all of its sprawling paths for communication, had exploded, and the government had taken up the challenge and raced ahead of the e-subversives, keeping Facebook and Instagram and Telegram and Twitter out of the hands of not only the refuseniks but appointed tour guides like Aydin, collateral damage in the battle against political dissent. Our food arrived—a vegetarian pizza for me and a lasagna for Aydin—and we split a bottle of the sparkling, slightly sweet grape juice that now passes for red wine in once wine-saturated Iran.

It was awful, but as bad as it was I enjoyed it, purely for the illusion of having a real bottle of mellow smooth Shiraz on the table. Still, it was hard to reconcile this with the fact that the world's oldest sample of wine was discovered in Shiraz, dated to 5,000 BCE. Imaginary though it was, the ruby bubbly washed down the dinner, and then it was time to walk it off.

We headed toward the city hall, the buzzing pedestrian shopping streets, and the spacious plaza where they all intersected. It was the center of Rasht nightlife. Children darted around on bicycles, and the latest of late-night shoppers scooped up last-minute purchases. Like many pedestrian zones in urban spaces, Rasht's was peopled with bronze figures engaged in everyday activities—a reader sitting on a bench, a woman huddling under an umbrella, an old man about to mount a bicycle, strollers carrying imaginary shopping bags.

The air of normalcy would soon be punctured. We had turned down a side street off the main square and were heading back to the hotel when we met a phalanx of several hundred regime supporters, or counterprotestors, who had been called in to support the regime. They were marching down the middle of the pedestrian lane, waving posters of Khamenei and Khomeini while a sound truck followed along, blasting proregime slogans. Chants of "Long live the revolution!" rose from the crowd. Oddly, there were no signs proclaiming, "Death to America!" and "Death to Israel!" The insurrection may have erupted so quickly the Revolutionary Guard hadn't had time to print them up. Following further behind was an army of basijis, gunning the engines on their souped-up motorbikes as they careened onto the sidewalk, challenging pedestrians in a show of thuggish intimidation, to erase any doubt among the people of Rasht who controlled not only the streets but the country itself.

Aydin tugged me out of the path of the basijis as though I were a toddler who needed to be shielded from playground bullies. This was understandable. As a foreign visitor who had been granted a tourist visa to enter Iran, I was, in keeping with the protocols of Persian hospitality, a guest of its government, and therefore my safety was the responsibility of the tour agency that had arranged my visit. Aydin, the guide assigned to serve as my host, was also, in effect, my babysitter. But it was not all gracious Persian hospitality at work here. There was also more than a little self-interest at play: God forbid that news reports carry a story of an American tourist being injured in an antigovernment demonstration in Iran.

The tour agency had been so worried that for the past two days Aydin had been fielding calls from the Tehran office, morning and afternoon— "How was everything going? Had we run into any problems with the demonstrations? Had we seen any of the protests?"—the voice on the other end of the line asked.

Earlier that day his phone rang again, as we were approaching Rasht after leaving Ardabil. I asked Aydin if it was the office again, knowing the answer was yes. I recognized the other voice as the young woman who had come to my hotel in Tehran to collect the payment for the tour the day before I left.

"What did they want this time?"

"They heard there might be some demonstrations in Rasht and told me that if you go out tonight I should come with you, keep you away from anywhere that might be a trouble spot." And that was why he had joined me for dinner and the stroll to the plaza and through the shopping streets. But the futility of this was obvious. Riots, protests, demonstrations—they could erupt anywhere. The cat-and-mouse game between protestors and the security forces had long ago reached the point where it defied predictability. The green movement forces had learned to play catch-me-if-you-can on the streets, on the internet via social media websites, even via text messages through downloaded VPNs. Antigovernment protests were largely conducted in the e-sphere—the new guerrilla warfare of the twenty-first century. A former journalist for several reformist publications told me their offices were constantly being closed down by government authorities, but the impact on alternative voices was minimal: "We just moved somewhere else and reopened," she told me.

"I'm flattered that I'm so well looked after," I told Aydin.

"As long as you're in Iran they are responsible for you," he replied, opting for a neutral, professional response, but with forced formality.

Of course, it wasn't that simple. In Iran no political issue is. I suspected that the tour agency had suspected (correctly) that I had written essays about my previous travels in Iran, and so they wanted to keep me away from any events that might provide grist for newsprint. Not that they cared what I might write. But if the foreign ministry learned that the agency had issued a tourist visa to a visiting American who then scribbled stories about political dissent, and the agency supervising his movements did nothing about it—that would never do.

Tonight, what was most noticeable were the reactions of those going about their usual business on a Thursday evening. While the demonstrators shouted their proregime slogans, and the basijis gunned the engines of their supercharged motorbikes, the strollers and shoppers ignored them, as though inattention had become a form of counter-protest. Up and down the pedestrian street, small crowds gathered to watch the spectacle, but along the sidewalks where the basijis buzzed the strollers and behind the storefronts, the mood was one of helpless, strained tolerance.

Once the protestors had moved on, Aydin and I headed back to the central square, passing the music stores and DVD outlets, budget cloth-ing stores and high-end boutiques. At the end of the square the historic city hall and its iconic clock tower were brightly lit. We popped into a sweet shop for a quick dessert and cup of tea, and Aydin chatted with the pastry chef in Turkish about the events. The chef had little to say. He just wanted it all to go away so business would get back to normal.

The impact of the proregime sideshow may not have been as lacklus-ter as it first appeared. Beneath the veneer of calm, passions had been stirred. After we returned to the hotel I went out and sat for a while in a café down the street. Small groups of young Iranians traipsed in to spend the rest of the evening sipping cappuccinos. Couples with children in tow gathered around the tiny tables to munch on slices of cheesecake from the pastry case. The menu was printed only in Farsi, but a woman at the next table had heard me struggling to communi-cate with the barista and came to the rescue. She got me a black tea with a small side of milk, but also saw an opportunity to air her views on the events in Rasht.

Her name was Tahereh, or Tina, as she called herself in Canada, where she had lived for the past twenty years. She was back in Iran for a few months to spend time with family members and take care of "other business," which she referred to in typically opaque terms. Tahereh was another long-term expatriate who, out of desire and necessity, had long kept her feet planted in two lands. She had listened to President Rou-hani speak to the nation earlier that evening in a half-hearted attempt to calm the political waters, but she came away unmoved.

"All this is talk, talk, talk," she said. "The people on TV, they say the protests are all about prices and inflation, and all the corruption in the government, but none of that is the real problem."

"And what is that?" I asked.

"Nothing is going to change until they get to the heart of things."

"And what is *that*?" I asked.

She paused a moment and then replied, almost cautiously: "Freedom. That's what no one wants to talk about. The people simply want more freedom. Instead of giving it, these people in the government, they say all the social problems are left over from the time of the shah, or the fault of the West. What they're really saying is that the people should just forget about that time and the more liberal values, the more open lifestyle. They say that if we would just forget about those things we would have an Islamic paradise."

She leaned a little closer. "Yes," she said, "no doubt there are problems. People are going through very hard times, and some of it is because of the sanctions, but the real need is simply greater freedom in every form—expression, behavior, dress, thought, beliefs."

I knew that some of these freedoms were novel concepts in Iranian society. During the reign of Mohammad Shah Pahlavi true freedom of expression was nonexistent. Prisons were busting with political activists, as the visit to the Qajar-era prison museum in Tehran showed. This lack of candor, even call it fear, had deep roots in Persian culture, in which open criticism of anything or anyone is something of a no-no. Iranians, as Iranians say, constantly live "behind the mask."

Tahereh was standing close to my table and the café was not crowded, yet she spoke quietly, measuring her words, careful not to say too much or to be overheard—by whom? As in former communist countries, there is always the fear of the watchful eye, the open ear. Public encounters must be accompanied by strict social protocols—politeness, obligatory graciousness, little intimacy or candor—all while maintaining a protective shield around the personal self. There is nothing particularly new about this separation of the private and the personal, nothing that can be blamed on current political life. It is as old as Persian culture itself, but the presence of a paranoid and repressive government has a way of reinforcing tradition.

After a few days in Rasht and Ramsar, and the side trip to Masouleh, Aydin and I were ready to make a break for Tehran. There was a lot of coast yet to see, and we breezed through it along a narrow, two-lane highway that could pass, with a little imaginative assistance, for California Highway 1. The sea was to our left, the coastal fields and waning dribbles of the Alborz Mountains to our right. The road split the two—sea on one side, mountains on the other—and between the road and the mountains was a broad plain with just enough room, and just enough rainfall, in welcome wet years, to produce two of the crops most closely associated with Iran's agricultural output, not to mention Iranian culture.

The Caspian shore has been the tea-growing center of Iran since the late 1800s, after several attempts over the centuries to cultivate the plants had failed. Prince Mohammad Mirza, a native of Lahijan, near Rasht, came to the rescue. The prince had been the Iranian ambassador to British India and, being a fluent French speaker, succeeded in passing himself off as a French laborer to learn the secrets of tea cultivation while working in tea plantations. The scheme worked. He managed to smuggle tea plants and seeds back to Iran to cultivate around Lahijan, and the result is what we could see from the roadside as we drove along the seaside highway—field after field of ripe green tea plants, their leaves fluttering and flapping, row after row, in the coastal breeze.

After tea, came rice. The region around Ramsar has long been the rice-growing center of Iran, the origin of the heaps of fluffy grain served with every meal, topped with butter or seasoned with fresh saffron. As we passed, the waterlogged rice fields shimmered steely grey under semi-cloudy skies, with the mountain backdrop casting long shadows across pools now dormant in the winter but waiting for the first sign of spring to burst back to life.

After rice came the mountains, the ragged, rugged peaks of the Alborz range. A few miles past Chalous, the road to Tehran turned sharp right and began its climb into the mountains, running parallel to a stream that cut through the Alborz on its way to the Caspian. The road to Tehran followed the path of the stream in reverse, gradually rising as the stream descended, offering dramatic views into the valley, which gradually became a deep gorge plunging from the side of the roadway. The road continued to rise, and rise, high into the mountains. The receding snowfields became snowdrifts, the snowdrifts knitted themselves together, and soon the slopes were shrouded in an even cover of shimmering, glittering snow, iridescent under the glare of the sharp winter sun.

We were nearing the top of the pass. The air was frosty cold. Just before the highest point on the road we stopped at a rest area where many other drivers had pulled over to pick up snacks and steaming cups of coffee before beginning the descent. Rest stop though it was, it was also the last chance to view the high alpine scenery before it would recede into rearview mirrors, and memory. Other drivers pulled into the parking lot to snap selfies against the background of the Alborz. Others stamped their feet, wiggled their shoulders to shrug off the cold, and exhaled clouds of steam as the gas station attendants filled their fuel tanks.

Then it was all downhill—almost. There were still a few kilometers to the top of the pass, but after we crossed it, Aydin was able to shift into higher gear and take some of the load off his straining Saipa. As the kilometers rolled by, the snowfields that covered the mountains in sweeping white blankets gradually thinned. The air was still crisply cool, but the deep freeze had lifted. Bare ground appeared. We passed side roads that led to the ski runs that drew Tehranis away from the city for weekend escapes—from its congestion, its chronic smog, and of course even the stern oversight of the regime and the daily stresses— economic, social, and political. As the road became level I was a little disappointed to see the last remains of the snow disappear. Apartment blocks and industrial parks crowded the roadside, sparse at first but then thicker, until mega-urban sprawl obliterated any sign of the alpine glory we had left behind.

Then we were back. The traffic stumbled and lurched through the city streets as it always does in Tehran. We passed Azadi Square and the landmark Azadi Tower, which strikingly resembles the logo on Aydin's Saipa. And then down Enqelab Avenue to Enqelab Square, where the hard realities of life in Iran returned. The threat of protests, in the government's eyes, had not receded, like the snowfields of an hour ago. An army of basij forces decked out in full riot gear encircled the square. The gates of Tehran University were similarly "protected" from any social and political unrest. There soldiers stood guard and army jeeps were parked to the left and right of the gates. Meanwhile, students passed in and out with visible nonchalance. And that was what was most striking about the dramatic and at the same time demure scene. Along the streets around the university, shoppers, sidewalk strollers, and office workers who had ducked out early went about their business with the same casual disregard. Unrest, intimidation, warning, crackdown—this was all part of life in Iran, as natural as the falling of snow and seasonal melting in the nearby mountains.

4 | Mashhad

SHRINES OF ALL KINDS

Listen: this story's one you should know,
You'll reap the consequence of what you sow.
This fleeting world is not the world where we
Are destined to abide eternally:
And for the sake of an unworthy throne
You let the devil claim you for his own.
—Ferdowsi

I felt a tap on the side of my arm. It was gentle at first. I thought it was an inadvertent bump from the passing crowd. Then I felt it again, more deliberately, and then a voice spoke softly, almost in a whisper: "Please, please . . ."

It came from a man of about thirty-five, wearing sunglasses, a black jacket, and sporting a goatee. We were standing at the entrance to the Imam Reza Shrine in the center of Mashhad. A throng of pilgrims was going in and out, and we were planted in the middle of the passing current. I had been snapping photos of the goings-on, as any tourist might at the gate of one of the holiest shrines in the world of Shiite Islam. Mustafa, my guide, had told me that this was fine before he wandered off in the direction of the market stalls selling souvenirs all around the shrine.

There was another tap, and now the bearded man with the tinted lenses was tugging on my arm.

"Thank you, thank you," he almost whispered, now tugging the sleeve of my jacket. Then he pointed at my camera and mumbled something in Farsi he should have known I wouldn't understand. The repeated thank yous were a blind stab at politeness. He kept tugging at my sleeve, trying to pull me in the direction of the security booth near the entrance gate. I didn't move. Again he tugged and again mumbled in Farsi. Then another man appeared, who confronted Mr. Tinted Lenses. An argument ensued, but Persian style, with neither man raising his voice, pounding a fist, or in any other way exhibiting the heat of open confrontation.

Both men, I realized, were plainclothes members of the security services, stationed at the gate to keep an eye out for suspicious activity and, when boredom took over, perhaps to grab a photo-taking foreign tourist.

What was surprising, but also characteristic of Persian culture, is that no matter how contentious an argument becomes, voices are never raised, and this was the case of the sparring security men. They discussed, argued, or debated—it was hard to tell which—and then Mustafa appeared. The three then parried, but quietly, back and forth. Mustafa was asked to produce some sort of document, which he did. Mr. Tinted Lenses squinted at it, and the debate continued.

It was decided that the photo-taking foreigner would be delivered to a higher authority. As a simple tour guide, Mustafa had no vote. He and I were led to the security booth, where the debate continued. Mustafa showed the men his paperwork, the security men squabbled, but civilly and quietly. Tinted Lenses tried to press his case, but from what I could tell he was having a hard time of it. A decision was reached. Mustafa folded up his paperwork, and we left.

Then Mustafa told me what it was all about. Tinted Lenses had spotted me outside the entrance to the shrine wielding a camera and taking photos, which was allowed in normal times, as Mustafa had told me. But these were not normal times. A little more than a week before, an unexpected spate of protests, driven largely by the frustrated working class, had erupted, first in Mashhad, but then quickly spread to other cities. It had been eight years since the Iranian streets had seen anything approaching open dissent. This time the security services were careful not to overreact, as they had been accused of in the postelection demonstrations in 2009. Still, itchiness was in the air. The regime couldn't allow the protests to spiral out of control. It was an unenviable balancing act and a test for paramilitary forces that hadn't had much practice in the intervening years.

In the closed quarters of the security office it was decided that it was Tinted Lenses who overreacted. "He didn't know why you were taking photos," Mustafa told me. "He kept saying we should look at your camera, see where you've been, maybe you're a spy."

"If I was a spy would I be taking pictures in front of the entrance?"

Mustafa shook his head in a way that said, I know, I know . . .

"These security people, some of them want to prove themselves. They think they will win points with their superiors, that they might catch a spy someday."

"Standing in front of the entrance in the middle of the afternoon?"

More head shaking. "The other guys, they were more sensible. I showed them the papers stating that you were a tourist and that I was your guide. The second guy who appeared, he kept saying, 'What are you bothering him for, he's a tourist?' The guy with the beard, he kept saying they should look at your camera, see where you've been. Maybe you *were* a spy. . . ."

I reminded Mustafa what he had told me, that it was fine to take pictures outside the entrance. It was a way of digging a little deeper, seeing if there was anything I wasn't being told.

"I know, I know. . . . It is. This guy just got all crazy about it. The boss in the office, he thought the whole thing was silly."

The experience carried an odd sense of déjà vu. On my first trip to Iran in 2009 I was taking pictures of signs mounted on a fence that circled a large villa in Esfahan. One of them read, "And you should treat all women with respect." I had taken two or three shots when a hand tugged at my arm. This time it was a solider, who took me by the wrist and led me down the street toward the entrance. I loped alongside, like a dog on a leash, wondering, What is *this* all about?

At the entrance gate another soldier was stationed at a guard booth. Sohrab, my guide, who had wandered a little ahead, came running down the street. He chatted with the soldier at the gate but didn't bother to produce any documents, and when it was all over the soldier at the booth spoke to me in Farsi, adding a deferential nod. The jumpy soldier also nodded my way and smiled, but grimly.

As we walked away I asked Sohrab what it was all about.

It turned out that the villa was the home of the governor of the Esfahan Province. Then, too, times were tense. The postelection riots were rocking city after city, and the jumpy soldier was hell bent on "maintaining security."

I asked Sohrab what the soldiers had said to me when we left.

"They wanted to apologize."

I asked him what he had said to produce such a turnaround.

"I just told them you were a guest in our country, and what the hell did that guy think he was doing, grabbing you like you were a criminal. I said you're not a murderer, there's no reason for him to behave like that."

I heard an echo of Sohrab from a previous run-in with regime flunkies: "They push, you push back. Don't take their shit."

It might have been a simple exchange, and a surprising one, to walk away with an apology from a member of a security service, but there was also a lesson to be learned in the dynamics of a security state: The eyes of anyone pressed into the service of the state are directed upward, never outward. The aim of the lower-level functionary is to please the slightly less-lower-level functionary above him. Social and legal principles are abstractions not to be bothered with, for one quickly realizes that *service* means achieving the aims of the system, and one acts accordingly.

There was another lesson to be learned here, in Persian conflict resolution. The first rule is: The more direct the confrontation, the more restrained the debate. This allows each party some breathing room, a chance to maneuver, to adjust, to allow reflection to supersede emotion, and most important, to save face by not being driven into a position from which there is no retreat, where compromise and ultimately resolution become impossible.

In Esfahan we walked away with apologies. No apology was forthcoming from Mr. Tinted Lenses. As Mustafa and I left the security office he was still arguing with his boss, probably that I was likely a spy, that my camera should be confiscated, and who knows what else. But his boss wasn't listening, and Mr. Tinted Lenses' attempt to keep the Imam Reza Shrine free of wandering spies probably cost him more brownie points than he thought he had earned.

Even before this episode, I had not looked forward to Mashhad. I had heard that Mashhad was deeply conservative, due to the presence of the Imam Reza Shrine, and so I imagined it to be another Qom, where arrogant, self-assured mullahs strutted the streets with pompous certainty, holding their turbans high as an emblem of political and clerical authority. And that it would appear derelict and decrepit, an outward manifestation of the moral rot that almost forty years of Islamic rule had brought.

But I was all wrong about Mashhad. Around the shrine, pilgrims from all over the Shiite world passed in and out of the entrance gates, with the women displaying a kaleidoscope of colors and styles of dress. And there were more secular Shiites in contemporary, if conservative, clothing, from Iraq or Lebanon, Bahrain or Syria, paying respects to the imam without promoting any particular spiritual allegiance. A few blocks from the shrine Mashhad was a clean, orderly city laid out in a patchwork of geometric grids. Away from the shrine, and the pilgrims, the residents of the city went about their business, making ends meet in the nearby bazaar by catering to the everyday needs of the residents— selling spices, housewares, and coffee and tea—as well as the casual needs of the pilgrims and souvenirs for them to bring home.

I quickly learned that despite the presence of the Imam Reza Shrine, Mashhad is paradoxically one of the more liberal and socially tolerant cities in Iran. It is also the only major city facing Afghanistan and points east, and Iran's second largest. Geography made Mashhad a crossroads

throughout its history, and crossroads have always been just that—
places where various races, religions, and belief systems cross, mingle,
and mix, in the process gaining acceptance through familiarity, chipping
away at the forces of tribalism and exclusion that would otherwise arise.

My arrival was equally smooth and trouble-free. Mustafa was waiting
for me at Mashhad airport, holding up a printed paper with my name
miserably misspelled. The sign helped me spot him, but he had little
difficulty picking me out of the crowd of Iranians passing through the
arrivals hall. As soon as I caught his eye, his hand went up, he folded
up the sign with the jumble of letters, greeted me with typical Persian
graciousness, and led me to his car, waiting in the parking lot.

The Mahan flight from Tehran to Mashhad was something of a mile-
stone for me because it was the first internal flight I had ever taken in
Iran. More important, for the one hour that the plane was aloft, I was
free for the first time from the enforced guardianship of a tour guide.
The guides I'd had on past trips had never felt like a burden, more like
knowledgeable traveling companions, but for this single hour I was
traveling solo, and began to feel something like all the other Iranians.

In Tehran, Mohammad, a driver hired by the tour agency, dropped
me at Mehrabad Airport, the takeoff point for Iran's domestic flights.
At the moment the car door closed and he pulled away I was free to
wander. I could have skipped the flight and disappeared into the subversive underground to plan the resurrection of the green movement,
steal nuclear secrets, or start an underground newspaper. A million
scenarios spun in my head as the taillights of Mohammad's Khodro
disappeared. But I had other plans. Mashhad was ahead. I grabbed my
bag, entered the concourse, and moved to the check-in desk.

After we had buckled up and the plane was about to begin its sprint
down the runway, an Islamic prayer sounded over the loudspeakers, customary on all flights on Iranian airlines. But where Iranian airlines are
concerned, an Islamic prayer is not a spurious gesture. Iran Air, Mahan
Airlines, and Aseman all have appalling safety records, largely due to the
unavailability of spare parts for their aging fleets, almost solely resulting
from the international sanctions slapped on Iran for decades due to sus-

picions about its nuclear program and—many Western governments contend—support for terrorist groups. In February 2018 an Aseman flight went down near Semirom, Iran, killing all 68 aboard. In January 2011 a Boeing 727 operated by Iran Air crashed in Orumieh, in northern Iran, killing 81 of the 105 passengers and crew. In February 2003 an aircraft operated by the Iranian Revolutionary Guard crashed in the desert near Kerman, killing all 275 onboard. In 2014 a Sepahan flight departing from Tehran crashed after takeoff, resulting in 38 deaths and 10 injuries. There have been many more accidents, crashes, and "incidents" over the years, making the skies over Iran among the most treacherous in the world. It should be no surprise that after the 2015 nuclear agreement was signed, Iran bought new planes from Boeing worth $166 billion.

My hour flight from Tehran to Mashhad was not added to the long list of Iranian air disasters. After we landed, all of the passengers trudged through the jetway safe and sound. I found my bag rotating on the baggage carousel and then Mustafa, holding up the misspelled name card. The anticipation of traveling unchaperoned over such a long distance became a nonevent.

Later, inside the entrance to the Imam Reza shrine, Mustafa and I were greeted by one of the official guides designated to lead non-Muslims around the site. For the next two hours Mustafa shared my role—the guide leading the guide assigned to me. Either way, Reza took the helm, leading us into the first courtyard and launching into his often-delivered account of the shrine's history, sprinkled with autobiographical bits about the man who gives the complex its reason for being—Imam Reza.

To understand the significance of the shrine, and the man who received such a grand resting place, we have to backtrack, to 632 CE, when Islam divided into its Sunni and Shiite branches.

Theologically speaking, the gap between Sunnis and Shiites is no wider than that between Roman Catholics and the many strains of Protestantism and the Eastern Orthodox Church, or, we might say, as wide. Both Sunnis and Shiites agree on the fundamental principles of Islam but quibble over the fine points. In particular, Shiites believe in the Twelve Imams, inheritors of the spiritual message of Prophet Mohammad who have been assigned by God to guide the rest of the Islamic world. This line of succession began with Ali, both cousin and son-in-law to Prophet Mohammad, who married the Prophet's daughter, Fatima. According to the Twelver doctrine, the last imam has already been born, in Samarra, Iraq, sometime around 868, is alive and well and roaming the world as we speak, and will announce himself when Jesus Christ returns to restore eternal peace and justice to the world.

In 765, Musa Ibn Jafar Al Kazim, the seventh of the Twelve Imams, had a son, Ali Ibn Musa Ar-Reza, or Ali Reza, who inherited the title of Eighth Imam. He was in his early twenties and not popular among the local religious powers, though in his religious studies he proved himself to be so ahead of his years that he was allowed to issue fatwas from mosques and interpret passages from the Quran.

Despite his lineage, it was not a good time for Ali Reza to be named Imam Reza. The death of Prophet Mohammad one hundred years earlier still sent battles raging between Persia and the Sunni Abbasid caliphate, seated in Baghdad. Conflicts erupted in other parts of the Islamic world, pitting faction against faction, powerful feuding tribes against one another. The situation had become so chaotic that Al-Massum, the Abbasid leader, offered to make Imam Reza his prime minister, all to project an aura of unity that would, hopefully, put the conflicts to rest. But Al-Massum had other aims: to give his corrupt leadership an air of legitimacy and use the union as a window into the goings-on in the Shiite world. Or, as Godfather Michael Corleone advised, "Keep your friends close but your enemies closer."

Imam Reza accepted the offer, but Al-Massum's plan backfired. The ascension of Imam Reza lifted Shiism's popularity. Al-Massum's bosses in Baghdad sought to depose him, prompting Al-Massum to head to Baghdad to argue his case. Imam Reza accompanied him. En route, the vizier, or primary minister, of Al-Massum was assassinated. Al-Massum believed it was time to unload Imam Reza, considering the political baggage he had become, and poisoned him in the town of Tous. Al-Massum had Reza buried in nearby Mashhad, which means "place of the martyr."

This early in Islamic history, political power and religious influence were two strands of the same cord. Imam Reza was on track to become the most important leader in the Muslim world. And yet, in spite of the prestige and clout he was about to inherit, he had become well known for his humility and simplicity. He decorated his house to resemble that of a common villager. His food was equally simple, and he had the habit of eating with the household help, waiting until everyone was present before signaling that it was time to begin. A suggestion that the servants and members of the household eat separately was soundly rebuffed: "All are created by God. . . . Why should there be any discrimination in the world?"

Aside from his personal character, what I find admirable about Imam Reza is not his religious or political status, which was foist upon him, but his skill in maneuvering political minefields. What speaks for his character far more than the circumstances of his life are the values he adhered to, and these were often expressed in brief sayings, a measure of true wisdom:

> Ignorance reveals itself in the following:
> Being angry without cause,
> Speaking without need,
> Rewarding the undeserving,
> Not distinguishing between friend and foe,
> Revealing a secret,
> Trusting everyone.
> The ignorant never realizes his mistake
> nor accepts advice.

And there is this:

> A man's folly is demonstrated in three ways:
> Talking about matters that don't concern him
> Offering comments when not asked
> Interfering in other people's affairs without understanding.

And:

> He who thinks he is the wisest is the most foolish.
> A foolish man speaks without thinking;
> A wise man thinks before he speaks.

Though Reza died at the age of fifty, he was able to step back and view life from an enlightened distance that only maturity can bring:

> In the rise and fall of fortunes there are lessons to be learned.

And:

> Stay with the truthful, no matter how few.
> Stay away from the false, no matter how many.

As a reflection of his personal humility, Imam Reza also recognized the value of self-reflection:

> The greatest defect is to point out a defect in others
> Which you possess but fail to see in yourself.

As both thinker and wordsmith, he could also master metaphor and the aphorism:

> Envy is to man what rust is to iron.

Some of my favorite quotes are the shortest, for to say the most in the fewest words is a true sign of a perceptive mind:

> A favor is a trust that you must return.

And:

> The best revenge is forgiveness.

The shrine of Imam Reza is a matrix of interlocking courtyards. The day we visited it was early afternoon and the day was bright and sunny, so the first courtyard, and the one we visited next, and the one we crossed into after that, were crowded with pilgrims mingling and gawking like any tourists would do, but some were actually praying. The afternoon sun sparkled off the tilework and brightened the turquoise domes in the clear, crisp air, but the strongest impression by far was of the absolute massiveness of the place. The eleven courtyards, some larger than a football field, had been knitted together beginning in the tenth century, when ground was first broken on the site of a former Zoroastrian fire temple. Over the centuries new courtyards were added and existing ones expanded, until the entire complex had grown, amoeba-like, to become the largest mosque in the world and the second largest in the number of supplicants it can hold, rivaling the Grand Mosque in Mecca, Saudi Arabia.

The Imam Reza Shrine survived the thirteenth-century Mongol invasion that devastated much of the Khorasan Province, as well as the incursion of Miran Shah, son of the Uzbek warrior Tamerlane, in the fourteenth century. The shrine's fate was helped by the fact that local Mongol warlord Sultan Mohammad Ilgiatu converted to Shiite Islam, and that Miran Shah was too busy destroying the Persian capital of nearby Tous to be bothered with Mashhad.

Near the end of the sixteenth century the legendary Safavid ruler Shah Abbas managed to evict the Uzbek occupiers from all of the Khorasan Province surrounding Mashhad and set out to repair the damage that centuries of invaders had wrought. Throughout the 1800s the Qajar kings continued to tweak and tinker with the shrine, adding more courtyards, domes, and porches, a minaret or two, and splashing the interiors with mirrors, a Qajar decorative favorite. Considering all of the hands that have meddled with the shrine it's a wonder that it hasn't grown into an utterly grotesque monstrosity. Instead, the place has become a sprawling architectural labyrinth where no part bears any relationship to any other. The saving grace is that it covers such a vast area that each courtyard is self-contained, adjacent to another yet resolutely distinct, like mountain peaks of a single chain.

The room where Imam Reza lies buried was off-limits to me, an infidel (in the harshest terms) or an unbeliever (in gentler ones), since only Muslims are allowed to enter the innermost sanctums of the shrine. No matter, I thought. I had seen enough, and I had seen enough shrines to have a pretty good idea of what lay beyond the public courtyards—a bier draped with a silk cloth, lit in harsh, lime-green light that rained down from spotlights above. It would have been shielded by metal grillwork, which pilgrims occasionally touched and kissed between recitations of prayers offered on the surrounding carpets.

When we were finished, Mustafa and I took a stroll through the Mashhad bazaar, which was unremarkable as Iranian bazaars go. But there was an exception—the spices for sale came from a single multi-colored bin, each seasoning in its own unicolor tier, like ice cream flavors too distinct to mingle without spoiling the unique quality of each.

Like many places in the world that hold religious significance, Mashhad has had its brush with sectarian-inspired violence. In June 1994, on the Shiite holy day of Ashura, a bomb exploded in the threshold of the shrine, killing twenty-five. The perpetrator was Ramzi Yousef, who was also convicted of the bombing of the World Trade Center in New York City the year before. There was an odd parallel here. In New York the target was the "infidel" neocolonial West; in Mashhad it was renegade Shiites. Who would ever guess that the U.S. and Iran would be linked, both being targets of radical Islamic terror?

Ironically, Mashhad's growth to become the second-largest city in Iran was largely due to violence, this time originating from outside the country's borders. When the Mongol invasion destroyed the nearby capital of Tous in 1219, the survivors fled to Mashhad. Historians estimate that the invading force numbered anywhere from 100,000 to 700,000. Whatever the number, it was too much for the measly army assigned to protect the city from nearby Merv, in present-day Afghanistan. Seeing the writing on the wall, the governor of the Khorasan Province offered to surrender under the condition that none of the city's inhabitants or its defenders would be harmed. Genghis Khan's youngest son, Tabu, who was leading the attack, accepted—but then slaughtered almost the entire Persian force. His thirst for blood was still not quenched. Tabu marched further into Iran, attacking Nishapour, seventy-eight miles from Mashhad. In one of the battles, Genghis Khan's son-in-law was killed. This so enraged Tabu that no living thing in Nishapour survived. He even killed the cats and dogs.

Invaders from the east weren't finished with Khorasan. A century later Uzbek forces swept through Mashhad and Tous and ravaged Nishapour once again. At the time, the population of the city was estimated at 1.7 million, making it one of the largest in the world. The Uzbeks showed even less mercy than the Mongols. By the time they were finished, thousands of the residents' heads were piled into pyramids.

Seven centuries later, in 1941, British and Russian armies would invade northwestern Iran and seize the nation's oil fields to prevent the precious crude from being shipped to the German forces, which Iran tacitly backed. This prompted many of the rural villagers in the west to move to the city, swelling Mashhad further. Four decades later, the Iran-Iraq War drove many residents of Khuzestan and other battlegrounds near the Iraqi border eastward, and the city most removed from the fighting was Mashhad.

My religious observances done for the day, it was time to hit the town, and Mashhad can boast an abundance of nightlife for both the faithful and the secular. For the devout, early evening is one of the best times to visit the Imam Reza Shrine, for the low rays of the setting sun glance off the tile work of the towering iwans and spread across the courtyards like a rolling carpet of saturated light. Instead of emptying out, the shrine prepares itself for the next wave of visitors, those who stayed away to avoid the heat of the day, preferring to bask in the cool of the evening. And so the courtyards fill up once again.

Throughout the Middle East, night carries none of the associations of fear and foreboding that it does in Western cultures. In Iran, as in most of the Arab world, night represents relief from the punishing heat of day. It is a time of retreat and relaxation, a moment to dismiss one's cares, to connect with family members and neighbors, to swap news and tell stories, to fill the darkness with the joy of human interaction. At the Imam Reza Shrine this means that the courtyards become venues for family gatherings, as the illuminated minarets throw light into the darkened sky and floodlights bathe the interiors.

In the diagonal streets that radiate from the shrine, the secular life of Mashhad also spins into life. It is shopping time, and the stores up and down the main boulevards displaying smartphones and TV sets and men's suits see a stream of buyers. The lanes of the nearby bazaar are more crowded than in the afternoon, as when Mustafa and I had strolled through. The shopkeepers are busy weighing sacks of walnuts, pistachios, and, of course, crystal saffron candy, *sohaan*, traditional toffee brittle, and other Persian sweets.

I had dinner down the street from the hotel at the Almas Restaurant, which Mustafa had recommended. It was a no-frills place that prided itself on quality food rather than extravagance of décor. I didn't expect the best Persian cooking. To hope for that would only invite disappointment. It isn't that Persian cuisine is uninspiring. On the contrary, it mixes nuts, fruits, and spices with rice, and wraps roasted chicken, lamb, meat, and fish in a cocoon of mystical flavors. It has inspired many of the great Persian poets.

> To him who is stinted of food,
> A boiled turnip will relish like roast fowl.

So wrote the twelfth-century poet Saadi.
It was Omar Khayyam who added the memorable lines:

> A book of verses underneath the bough,
> A loaf of bread, a jug of wine, and thou.
> Beside me singing in the wilderness,
> And wilderness is Paradise now.

One Persian saying goes:

> The origin of the body's destruction
> Is the removal of dinner.

Naturally food has found its way into the expression of Persian wisdom. A popular proverb says:

> Before eating always take time to thank the food.

And another:

> It is better to return a pot you borrowed
> With a little something you cooked in it.

In Persian culture food is always inseparable from social life:

> The man who eats alone eats with the devil.

Striding along Imam Reza Boulevard in the direction of the Almas, I had plenty of time to whip up images of my own Persian banquet. To start, there would be *aash-e jo* (barley soup), *gazane* (soup from nettle), or *aash-e anar* (a thick soup made from pomegranate). This would be accompanied by thick loaves of *barbari* bread, *sangak*, a leavened flat-bread, or the extra-thin *lavash*, maybe also a side dish of *must-o khiyar*, thin yogurt mixed with mint, garlic, and cucumber. For a main course I'd choose between *khoresh-e fesenjan* (pomegranate-walnut stew), *baghala ghatogh* (a vegetable stew made from beans and dill), maybe with a side of *dampokhtak* (turmeric-seasoned rice spiced with lima beans), *khoresh-e bademjan* (a tomato-based eggplant stew seasoned with saffron), or, if my sweet tooth needed soothing, a plate of *shirin polow* (a rice dish mixed with raisins, almonds, and sweet carrots). Before the Islamic Revolution all of this would have been washed down with a hefty glass of golden-ruby Shiraz wine, but without a waiter to sneak me some, or a friend like Ali Reza in Ramsar to provide some of his homemade, I would have to settle for a glass of pomegranate juice. If my belly had any room left, I'd squeeze in an order of *fereni* (rice pudding flavored with rosewater), a concoction of the Achaemenids that had been a summertime favorite among the royal families.

Sadly, in today's Iran I could enjoy this dinner only in my imagination, for the best Persian cooking is now found in family kitchens, where recipes several hundred years old have been tweaked with an alchemist's precision. In today's Iran the enjoyment of fine food and the social rapport that must accompany it is experienced in the private home, where alcohol may be consumed, Western music played, and mixed-gender dancing going on, all out of view (and interest) of the authorities. The problem is not food. Good food does not violate Islamic principles, but much of what goes on while fine food is being sampled, shared, and enjoyed does. The problem was that I was a visitor in Iran, and to make things worse, a Western visitor, and an American, so I could never be invited to an Iranian home because of the intrusive, ubiquitous eyes of the security services that would follow my host long after I had walked out the door.

"I'm sorry I can't invite you to our home," a friend in Tehran wrote to me during my second trip to Iran. "I'm ashamed for my country."

For my friend the great shame, I knew, was being unable to extend the cardinal Persian virtue, which has almost defined the Persian identity for millennia—hospitality. But I did not take offense, because I knew that the current "Iran" was not really Iran. This was a postrevolution, twenty-first century, theocratic "Iran," not the Iran of the Achaemenids, the Safavids, or the Sassanids, or the Qajars, or even of the days of Mohammad Reza Shah. This was a corrupted, distorted Iran that bore no relation to its 2,500 years of history. Seen that way, this was not Iran at all. This was another "Iran" in which a foreign visitor could not be invited into a Persian home, which in truth was no Iran at all.

Tonight the Almas would have to suffice. It was too bad that it wasn't the beginning of Noruz, the Persian New Year, for then the Almas, and every restaurant worthy of the name, would have added special dishes to their menus. *Reshteh polo* (rice, noodles, and lamb chunks) might be one, accompanied by *dolma borg* (grape leaves stuffed with rice and meat), or *sabzi polo ba mahi* (fresh fish with herb-flavored rice). The centerpiece, likely spread out on a table near the door where guests entered, would be the *haftsin*, samples of seven foods that all begin with the letter *s*. Lentil sprouts (*sabzeh*) and wheat pudding (*somanu*) would represent grains. Druj berries (*senjed*), cropped apple bits (*sib*), and sumac leaves (*somaq*) would stand for fruit, and the entire presentation would be topped off with chopped garlic (*sir*) and vinegar (*serekh*).

A taste of these would have brought me good luck for the new year, because of the number seven, and in ways that would set my life in a direction I could have never dreamed. The apple would make me irresistibly attractive. The garlic would assure good health and teach me patience. Hyacinth, along with the garlic, would refresh my spirit of purpose, and the rice pudding might even bring me children, while a sprinkle of the golden sumac would make me rich. A mirror added to the *haftsin*, and the glow of lit candles, would set my gaze on the future; a few painted eggs could bring me even more children. A swarm of goldfish circulating in a perfectly round fishbowl would remind me of the continuing fluidity of life.

There was no more time to imagine a Persian feast-of-all-feasts because I had arrived at the Almas, which didn't offer a feast of any kind. But I didn't expect one. Despite Mustafa's recommendation, my chances to have a dinner as fine as the finest Iranian cook could offer were low. I also knew that Mustafa could never have invited me to his house, as he would have liked, so the best he could do was steer me to the most suitable Persian cooking to be found anywhere near my hotel. In this respect he succeeded. The *gormeh sabzi* I ordered (herb stew with lamb and lima beans) was as good as any *gormeh sabzi* I'd had anywhere. The lentil soup that preceded it was thick and exhaled the aroma of cumin and coriander. Two times the waiter passed by my table to plop down flats of steaming, freshly baked *lavash*, just pulled from the *taftoon*, or oven, by the hands of the resident baker.

I knew the food would be good, but the food was never intended to be the Almas' selling point, for me. I was more interested in the reception a foreigner, and a non-Muslim foreigner, would get here in Mashhad, a few blocks from the Imam Reza Shrine. I placed my order with the combination receptionist and headwaiter, who coached me through the Farsi-only menu by referring to the pictures of the dishes on the plastic laminated card and an illuminated signboard behind the counter. When I had it down he gave me a number to take to my table. The soup and bread came fast, delivered by a smiling waitress who seemed to take extra care to smile a little brighter than she would for a casual diner. Beyond her I could see, through a window that ran almost the width of the dining room, the prep area of the kitchen, where the finishing touches of the dishes were added. The view into the inner workings of the kitchen, the endearing smiles of the waitress, the hand-scribbled check in indecipherable Farsi, and even the leftover stains on the tablecloth made me imagine—with some stretching— that I wasn't in a restaurant at all but the coziness of a Persian home.

There wasn't the inevitable "Where are you from?" possibly because those few words were beyond the linguistic ability of the staff, or perhaps because the perpetual flow of pilgrims from all over the Islamic world had worn them out. As I finished each dish it was removed with formal ease, and when I was ready to go the waitress brought the Farsi-scribbled check with the total added in painstakingly clear international numerals. As I paid the receptionist-headwaiter, the waitress, the bread boy, and the kitchen staff on the other side of the window smiled and nodded in farewell, the bread boy placing his hand across his chest and extending a slight bow. I was reluctant to leave, but leave I did, and hopped into a taxi to head to the next destination on my whirlwind night in Mashhad.

Shrines like that of Imam Reza, and those housing the remains of dozens of other Shiite notables, are not the only kinds of shrines in Iran. The coffee shop explosion has produced shrines that are less architecturally grand but far more important to the liberal class that honors the icons of American movies and music and all things that emanate from the pop culture of "the Great Satan." The Café Zhork, where I headed next, was one, and here I noted one advantage that the secular shrines have over the religious. After visiting three or four, the Shiite shrines appear one and the same. There is the mosque-like interior, the silk-draped bier illuminated in garish green light, the surrounding protective grillwork that receives the kisses and tender touches of the devout. The secular shrines vary in design and décor, with idiosyncrasies that can never be found in their religious counterparts. The Café Zhork had echoes of the Café Cinema in Zanjan, yet it added a bit more funk. The walls were covered with black-and-white photos of Hollywood icons—Leonardo DiCaprio and Marlon Brando, Robert De Niro, Al Pacino, and Russell Crowe. In the corner, a bearded man with shaggy brown hair strummed a blues guitar.

I downed a hot chocolate and soaked up a little of the blues before moving on—to the Café Eden. It was easy to find. I zigzagged through the backstreets of Mashhad, which reminded me, vaguely, of residential Manhattan—quiet, tree-lined blocks, neatly kept and swept, fronted with apartment buildings that catered to the upper-middle and upper-upper-middle class. At the intersection of two of those streets was the Café Eden, offering a comfortable space and an island of retreat for the night owls of Mashhad, like any café in Greenwich Village or SoHo. But nothing in the interior aspired to shrine status, secular style. No American movie stars or pop icons decorated the walls, only a few photos of Mashhad in earlier times. The Eden was meant for Mashhad's culturally restless and stifled. The soft, wood-paneled interior and polished wooden tables oozed comfort, but the room was tight and compact. Beyond the countertop the espresso machine hissed whenever a new order was placed, and the steaming cups were placed on a tray to be delivered to one of the seven tables. But what filled the room with even greater sensual soothing than the glow of wood and the aroma of the coffee were the sprightly, tinkling notes of the *dutar*, a traditional string instrument, played by a bald young man with a scraggly beard seated at a corner table.

The Eden was an escape zone that allowed Iranians to forget, as much as they could, that beyond its doors still lay the Islamic Republic. No deities of Western pop culture were given their due here, rather an Iranian identity that predated the Islamic Revolution and the cultural and social repression that followed. A group of four or five, men and women, gathered at a large table in the front window. The women may not have removed their headscarves, but they did allow them to slide far beyond the crowns of their heads. The conversation, however, was free of any covering. At the table across from me a young couple spoke softly, looking into each other's eyes. The woman propped her chin in her hands while gazing across the table with flirty nonchalance. All the while the soft, tender strains of the dutar swept up the muffled voices and the intermittent hiss of the coffee machine, mixing with the smoothly polished wooden walls and soft yellow light that made them glow.

One of the group, a man with oddly reddish hair and a beard to match, came over to my table and asked in smooth English, "Do you mind if I smoke?"

Almost anywhere else, smoking in such a small room would have been terribly forward, and is prohibited by law in most of the Western world, but this was Iran, where indoor smoking is commonplace, and therefore the grace with which he made the request made me reply, "No, that's fine."

The Eden reminded me of the café in the Saad Abad arts complex in Tehran, with its softly lit interior and wood-themed décor. But the Saad Abad café was more of a shrine, this time to the jazz and crooner era of the 1940s and 1950s. Nat King Cole, Louis Armstrong, Marilyn Monroe, and Bing Crosby were given their due in a lineup of black-and-white photos, while the mellow, oozy voice of Sarah Vaughn circulated among the tables with the same silky nonchalance as the waitstaff.

I propped my laptop on the table and hooked up to the café's Wi-Fi to catch up on the news, both far away and close to home, but in Iran news generated far away always has the tendency to reverberate close to home. The protests over inflation and economic mismanagement were still shaking the cities in the provinces, where the country's working class had suffered the brunt of international sanctions. And there was the continuing chatter about missile strikes on Iran's nuclear sites and the "failure" of the 2015 nuclear agreement by the persistent, redoubtable anti-Iran voices.

No doubt neither the chatty group in the window nor the schmoozing couple across from me would have wasted much attention on any of this. Over the decades Iranians have learned to live with their country in the international spotlight, never for the best of reasons, but geopolitical dynamics can change as quickly as the weather, and Iranians have learned that they have little influence over either. Better to chat and schmooze and extract some enjoyment from an ephemeral life than get worked up over daily headlines.

Closing time arrived, but there was no slapping down of checks or rush to the door. The dutar player finished a few chords while the chatting and schmoozing went on. The evening was left to trail off like the final notes of the dutar. The Eden's lone waiter brought me my check, the amount again calculated in clear Western numerals.

I went to the counter to pay. The waiter accepted the note I handed over, returned some change, and then added, "Thank you for coming. We're honored to have you."

Here we go again, I thought. It had all gotten a little annoying—the constant deference to Western visitors, the expressions of appreciation for coming to Iran and not being deterred by negative media images, the feeling of being elevated to celebrity status for simply stepping into a country where few go. All of this prevents one from slipping into the role of invisible traveler, who is there to observe, to listen, to learn, in order to experience life as it is lived. But that is not always possible in Iran, and there is nothing one can do about it. So it becomes one of those inconveniences of travel, like bad food or foul weather in other places, that one learns to tolerate. And it has to be tolerated for the simple reason that these expressions of appreciation are, in the end, heartfelt and well-intentioned, not the fawning of souvenir sellers or tour promoters only eager to mooch a dollar. For the waiter, the museum ticket-taker, the hotel desk clerk, or a man or woman on the street, the presence of a foreigner restores a speck of national pride: See, everyone isn't afraid of us. But in situations like the one at the Eden I didn't want to acknowledge any of this, or answer with a simple "Thank you." It would make me feel that I was accepting a level of status that was unearned and undeserved.

"Why is that?" I asked, dumbly.

"Because you're a foreigner." "Foreigner," in this instance, meant a Westerner, or one from far away, which might mean Asian, but definitely not anyone from within a stone's throw from the region.

"I'm just a customer," I replied.

He drew a blank, which gave the conversation an opportunity to move on. I was grateful. The dutar player joined in. So did the barista behind the counter. Here was a live foreigner ready to pluck for opinions, views from outside, points of view that weren't Iranian. Again I was in the spotlight, but little did they know that from my perspective they were too. Here was my chance to pump a few café-going Iranians for their views. I decided to fend off the usual litany—Where are you from? Why did you come to Iran?—by launching questions of my own: What caused the recent protests? Who was behind them? What were they all about?

No one had an answer, and no one could have offered one anyway because when it comes to questions of politics in Iran there is never a clear answer, only guesses and speculation, and usually more guesses. There are many reasons for this—social, political, economic, domestic, international—that play on every issue. Add to this the fact that the Persian culture is by nature, choice, and definition obtuse. The result is an aversion to the appallingly simple sound bite, which to the Western mind can crystalize complexity but to the Persian says nothing. So the barista, the dutar player, and the waiter clammed up. But to let such a pointed question go unanswered would never do either. There was a crystal clear fact on which they all agreed.

"You know," the waiter started, "there isn't enough freedom in Iran."

The dutar player translated for the barista. The barista nodded. Then the conversation shifted gears. They asked how I had voted in the 2016 U.S. presidential election. Was the U.S. serious about attacking Iran? Why was the U.S. so hostile to Iranians?

I offered what I could, in typically American, overly simplistic talking points: The U.S. needs an enemy, the hostage crisis still loomed large in the American mind, Americans really know very little about Iran.

I was able to escape before getting in too far over my head. The waiter had called a taxi for me, and it had arrived. Before I could get to the door the dutar player had to get in one more question: "How much is a flight from the U.S.?"

That, at least, had a simple answer.

That next morning Mustafa was waiting for me in the hotel lobby before I straggled in from the breakfast room. He was typically on time for our ten o'clock rendezvous, and after only two days together had grown accustomed to the typical ten to fifteen minutes I was always running behind. He didn't seem to mind. He killed the time texting and checking emails in the cushy comfort of the hotel's oversized armchairs.

Once we were on the road the topic turned to cars. I'd noticed that Mustafa had a heavy foot on the accelerator, as he tried to get more power out of his Iran-built Saipa than it could muster.

"I like Cadillacs," he said proudly as we coursed through the Mashhad traffic, which was actually in motion, a condition not to be taken for granted on Iran's car-clogged streets. They had become much worse since my first visit here in 2009. Getting around Tehran in any efficient manner was almost impossible most of the day. When the traffic backed up, which was frequently, a twenty-minute trip could stretch to two hours. In Zanjan, in northern Iran, we had to circle the block just to reach the front of the hotel so I could drop off my bag, and the circuit took almost half an hour. But now, oddly, the road was smooth sailing, fit for the Cadillac Mustafa pined for. I asked him if he had ever driven one.

"No," he said, in a sagging tone, and I had a good idea why the American classic was his wheels of choice. It couldn't have been the roar of the engine, which he had never heard, nor the pull of its power as it accelerated, which he had never felt, nor the ease with which the lengthy mass of metal rounded corners. Never mind that. It was Cadillac's image as an icon of American indulgence and self-assertion, enshrined in its oversize grill and capacious back seat, sweeping tailfins and coal-black tires, which clawed the road and pulled the two-ton rig forward like a charging leopard. Like the U.S., Iran had miles upon miles of larger-than-life landscapes that ranged from deserts to alpine mountain valleys, but no homegrown motoring machine that could make any driver the master of them.

We were "on the road again," in classic American (or Iranian) style, this time on the way to the town of Tous, the capital of the Khorasan Province before the Mongols razed it and the surviving population fled to Mashhad. Tous would have dwindled into insignificance, like any of the one-gas-pump pit stops that dot the American landscape, if it weren't for its claim to the birthplace, and burial place, of the first of Iran's great poets—Abu Al-Qasim Ferdowsi Tusi, or simply, Ferdowsi.

Ferdowsi's literary reputation rests on one work—the *Shahnameh*, or "Book of Kings"—an epic poem three times longer than Homer's *Iliad* and the longest epic poem ever written by a single author. It took thirty-three years to complete, and when it was finished Ferdowsi had spun a fantastic tale of myth and fantasy. It begins with the Sassanid creation story and then pulls the reader through a series of interwoven tales in which characters, both real and fictitious, appear, disappear, and resurface again. Some live for centuries; others are typically mortal. Normal concepts of time are suspended.

In the beginning, Keyumars, the first man, also becomes the first king of Persia, tying the history of the empire with that of humanity itself. His grandson, Huolong, discovers fire, and succeeding tales chronicle the lives of sons and grandsons. Similar to Greek drama, there is more than a drop of modernism in Ferdowsi's characterizations, for the upright and admirable exhibit deep flaws, and the most lowly show redeeming qualities. In true Shakespearean fashion, family members are done in, generating revenge murders and blood feuds.

The swashbuckling hero of the tale is Rustam, a warrior who unknowingly kills his own son in battle and is ultimately killed by his half-brother. But let us backtrack. Rustam was the son of Rudaba, a princess from Kabul, and Zal, a renowned general. The birth of most mythological heroes is either shrouded in mystery or bestowed with unusual circumstances, and Rustam's was the latter. He had grown so large inside his mother's womb that he had to be delivered through the Persian equivalent of a Caesarian section. He showed his extraordinary abilities quite young, killing an elephant that had gone mad with a single blow from a mace when just a child. He then inflated his reputation by conquering and pillaging a fortress that sat at the top of Mount Sipand, one that his great-grandfather, dying in the attempt, had failed to take years earlier. Then Rustam proceeds on the *Haft Khan-e Rustam*, or "Rustam's Seven Quests," to save the king, who has been captured by evil forces.

Along the way Rustam loses his horse, and his search takes him into the kingdom of Samangan. There the king of the realm puts him up, and

Rustam meets the lovely princess Tahmina, who makes him an offer: she will return his horse if he fathers her child. Rustam agrees, and his horse is returned, but before he leaves Samangan he gives Tahmina a jewel and a seal. If the child is a girl, Tahmina is to weave the jewel into the girl's hair. If the child is a boy, she should attach the seal to the boy's arm. Tahmina gives birth to a boy and names him Sohrab.

Years pass. The drums of war begin to beat, pitting the Persians against the kingdom of Turan, where Sohrab has grown to become Turan's most accomplished warrior. No one on the Turan side will fight the legendary Rustam, so Sohrab steps forward. The two face off in a struggle to the death, which Rustam eventually wins, breaking Sohrab's back before thrusting him with his sword. As he expires, Sohrab tells Rustam that his father will avenge his death and produces the seal that Rustam had given to Tahmina. True to tragedy, Sohrab cannot be saved, and Rustam is finally done in by his own jealous half-brother Shaghad.

Even if Ferdowsi's tale hadn't been as colorful, sweeping, and epic in scope, he still would have been credited with arguably an even greater achievement—saving the Persian language.

Incursions into Iran throughout the first millennium threatened more than its territory and the lives of the people who inhabited it. The Arab invasion of 651 brought the Islamic religion, which gradually replaced Zoroastrianism as the approved faith. Equally important, Arabic was imposed as the new lingua franca. The cuneiform Pahlavi script in which Farsi had been written for almost eight hundred years was replaced with the Arabic alphabet. Arabic words and phrases were introduced, particularly those that concerned matters of religion. Pushback occurred, and Farsi's grammar, syntax, and vocabulary were not substantially altered. Later, in the ninth century, New Persian was developed, which essentially recast the Persian language in the still recently adopted Arabic alphabet.

When Ferdowsi began work on the *Shahnameh* he intended it to not only document early Persian history but serve as a counterpunch to Arabization and preserve the Persian language. He took care to use terms and phrases that had special meaning in Persian culture, chose vocabulary that would represent the language's idiosyncrasies and shades of meaning, and consciously wrote in a style that reflected Persian thought and manner of expression. In the end, the long-winded tale doubled as a lexicon and linguistic handbook that was able to serve as a reference for future generations. Farsi, as the language of the Persian people, was saved.

Ferdowsi, being a Shiite, was deemed an infidel by a local Sunni cleric and denied burial in an Islamic cemetery, so his final resting place became the garden of his house on the outskirts of Tous. It is all for the better, for the setting has passed the test of time. It is quiet and peaceful, and surrounded by a quadrangular garden with reflecting pool that serves as a reminder of the one that sat at the center of his house. The house is long gone, and on the site stands a massive stone cube that contains his bier and a small museum that honors the author and his work.

Ferdowsi was born in 940 to wealthy landowning parents. His early years are a mystery, and if he wrote any poems in his youth, no trace of them exists. But he must have achieved a literary reputation of note, and early, for in 977 the king chose to give him the task of writing the entire history of Persia in verse. For his efforts Ferdowsi would receive 60,000 pieces of gold, one for each couplet that would be written, to be paid when the work was completed. The king gave Ferdowsi a room in the palace decorated with paintings to provide inspiration.

Ferdowsi went to work, and thirty-three years later his literary behemoth was finished. But along the way Ferdowsi and the king had their spats, with Ferdowsi believing the king didn't hold his work in high enough regard, and the king believing Ferdowsi was, to put it simply, a little too full of himself. When the time came to collect his payment Ferdowsi was given not 60,000 pieces of gold but silver. As to the reason, accounts differ. One source claims that the court functionary sent to deliver the money replaced the gold with silver because he regarded Shiite Ferdowsi as an infidel. Other sources contend that Ferdowsi was simply being stiffed.

Whichever is true, or neither, Ferdowsi was outraged, and in a fit of pique gave the money away. Now it was the king's turn to voice his rage. He gave Ferdowsi a death sentence—he was to be stomped on by elephants. Rather than face the music, Ferdowsi fled to his native Tous, hiding along the way with friends and royal protectors, but eventually he realized he had overplayed his hand. He sent the king an apology, and the king had a change of heart. He sent Ferdowsi 60,000 pieces of gold to make good on his original offer, along with a caravan of camels loaded with spices, fabrics, and other gifts to help patch things up. As luck would have it, Ferdowsi died of a heart attack just before the caravan arrived. His own funeral procession was exiting through one of the gates of Tous just as the king's gift train was entering the city. Reflecting classic Persian ambiguity, the date of Ferdowsi's death is uncertain. One account has him living to the age of eighty, dying in 1020; another adds five years to his life, ending it in 1025.

We arrived at Tous in the early afternoon. Outside the tomb, in the clear winter light, couples strolled in the garden and children cavorted on the stone plinth that supported the epic block of stone. Along the edge of the garden souvenir stands sold laminated bookmarks bearing quotes from the *Shahnameh*, pen sets honoring Ferdowsi, and greeting cards with miniature paintings depicting *Shahnameh* episodes. Business was good, and I added to it, buying a coffee mug imprinted with *Shahnameh* excerpts, and a *Shahnameh* battle scene. Also imprinted on the mug, curiously, was a quote from the Sufi poet Rumi, which represented something of an escape from the chains of history, myth, and tradition, and anything else that constrains the human spirit. It would seem to debunk everything I had just seen, but not really. Ferdowsi is Ferdowsi and Rumi is Rumi. The two can coexist in the same universe, just like black and white, up and down, right and left, and every other dichotomy, which aren't dichotomies at all unless we choose to see them as such. In his *Shahnameh*, a jaded, cynical Ferdowsi had written:

> I turn to right and left, in all the earth
> I see no signs of justice, sense or worth:
> A man does evil deeds, and all his days
> Are filled with luck and universal praise;
> Another's good in all he does—he dies
> A wretched, broken man whom all despise.

But I would rather end this chapter with the ever-joyous spirit of Rumi:

> Dance, when you're broken open.
> Dance, if you've torn the bandage off.
> Dance in the middle of the fighting.
> Dance in your blood.
> Dance when you're perfectly free.

5 | Kermanshah

KURDISH LANDS AND WARRIOR KINGS

The kingdom that had been wrested from our line I brought back and reestablished it on its foundation. The temples that Gaumata had destroyed, I restored to the people, and the pasture lands, and the herds and the dwelling places, and the houses that Gaumata had taken away. I settled the people in their place, the people of Persia, and Media, and the other provinces. I restored that which had been taken away, as it was in the days of old.

—Darius I, inscription at Bisotun

On November 12, 2017, an earthquake rattled Kermanshah. It registered 7.3 on the Richter scale according to readings by the U.S. Geological Survey. In the hours that followed there were fifty aftershocks. It was the most dramatic rumbling of the Earth in Kermanshah since 1967, when another earthquake measured 6.1. This time the quake killed 630, injured approximately 8,100, destroyed 12,000 homes, and left approximately 70,000 to sleep on the streets. By Iranian standards this was small potatoes. In 2003 a temblor near Bam, in southeastern Iran, registered 6.6 and killed 30,000, though some estimates are much higher.

The moral of this story is that Iran lives on shaky ground. In the case of the Kermanshah quake, the cause was the Arabian plate rubbing against the Eurasian, a fold under the Earth that produced the Zagros Mountains, which begin just north of Kermanshah and angle southeast toward Shiraz. In Kermanshah, once friends and relatives had been buried and the rubble cleared away, the people made a simple observation: that many of the buildings that withstood the quake were built before the Islamic Revolution, while newer buildings collapsed. It was further evidence in an ever-lengthening catalog of instances of government corruption. This time the result was shoddy construction, which produced the death toll.

For a couple of months Kermanshah simmered, but when antigovernment protests erupted in Mashhad in January 2018 they quickly spread to Kermanshah. Political fault lines are no different than the geologic. A rumbling in one part of the landscape inevitably stirs another. In this case, what Mashhad and Kermanshah have in common is that neither are known as hotbeds of Green Movement activity, adding more fuel to the claim that the protests were fomented by hardliners with the aim of besmirching the administration of President Hassan Rouhani.

Earthquakes, both the geologic and political, are forever unpredictable, impossible to foresee and to prepare for, but the Kermanshah protests did produce a new, unforeseen weapon for antigovernment protestors to wield—humiliation. One night, in the midst of one of the melees, one of the basijis was grabbed by the crowd just as he was about to swing his baton. Did the crowd kick him to the ground, stomp him to death? No, they pulled his pants off and sent him fleeing back to his comrades, trouserless.

The major seismic issue that has created off-and-on political instability in northwestern Iran is, euphemistically, the "Kurdish question." Together with neighboring Turkey and Iraq, and along with Syria, Iran has a significant Kurdish minority. In Iran they number approximately five million, spread across several provinces in the northwest, and the "capital" of an imaginary Iranian Kurdistan is Kermanshah. To make matters worse—and in Iran's neighborhood anything that can provoke instability is by default "worse"—some Kurds are Shiite and some are Sunni. Thus they straddle the Middle East's major sectarian fault line.

First, a little background on the Kurds and the designation *Kurdish*. In the third-century Sassanid era, the nomads who roamed northwestern Iran were informally called *kurds*. The term never designated a specific ethnic group, not for a thousand years, when the term *Kurdish* came to define the nomadic, *"kurdish"* tribes of the northwest. Whatever they were called, the Kurds, as an ethnic group or a band of roaming nomads, were long a significant presence in the region of Kermanshah, even after they were defeated in a lengthy war between the Kurdish king Madig and the Persian emperor Ardeshir I at the beginning of the third century. As part of the resolution of the war, and in an act of magnanimity, a *"kurdish"* prince was put in place to rule over Kermanshah.

Much later, in Safavid times, the Kurds became significant power brokers in the constant battles for control of the region, and the valuable trade routes, between the Persians and the Ottoman Turks. But in the middle of the thirteenth century the Mongol warlord Hulāgu tore through Kermanshah in Mongol fashion, razing the city and slaughtering most of its inhabitants.

When the Sykes-Picot Agreement of 1916, drawn up by the foreign ministers of Great Britain and France, delineated the modern boundaries of Syria and Iraq, the "Kurdish question" was not in question, or was not one that Sir Mark Sykes and François Georges-Picot wanted to raise. The Kurdish people existed as a people with a distinct language and cultural identity across today's Iran, Iraq, Turkey, and Syria long before the modern states of Iran, Iraq, Turkey, and Syria appeared on the global map. But as far back as Sassanid times, Persian-Kurdish conflicts had a bad habit of erupting. A thousand years later Kurdish dynasties would bubble up in the region around Kermanshah and eastern Iraq, and a certain Sultan Sanjar managed to establish a Kurdish-ruled region near the present-day city of Hamedan.

These efforts at homeland building, heartfelt though they may have been, were feeble and short-lived. Once the Safavids came to power in the sixteenth century, things went south for the Kurds. The Safavids weren't too pleased by the limited self-rule the Kurds had established for themselves in areas of western Iran and tried to rein them in. The Kurds pushed back but lost big. Historic Kurdish towns were razed and the people dispersed. The seventeenth century saw the Kurds' circumstances spiral further downhill. Their defeat in the yearlong battle of Dimdim in 1610, along with their subsequent dispersal, wasn't good enough for the Persian rulers. The remaining vanquished were slaughtered, and Shah Abbas gave the order for additional massacres in the towns of Mukriyan and Beradost.

For about two hundred years tensions cooled, but at the end of the nineteenth century they rose again. This time the instigator was Sheikh Ubaedullah, who led several revolts against the Qajar rulers. These were successfully squashed, but they paved the way for Simko Shikak, a Kurdish nationalist leader who led another series of revolts against Persian rule after World War I. Questions remain over whether Simko's rebellion was an honest attempt to create a Kurdish homeland or whether he was simply riding piggyback on the Kurdish nationalist wave for personal gain, namely, the pillaging of regional wealth owned by Iranians and even fellow Kurds.

The Kurds were not alone in navigating the turbulent ethnic waters that have long characterized Iran. Since the medieval era Kermanshah has also had a significant Jewish minority. In the nineteenth century the city had three synagogues and an estimated Jewish population of a few thousand. Most were small tradesmen and local merchants, but some rose to positions of prominence, like Hakim Aqajan, a Talmudic scholar and man of science, and Elyahou Pirnazar, one of Iran's first Jewish lawyers. Shemuel Yehezkel Haim became the editor of Iran's first Persian-language Jewish newspaper, *Ha-Haim*, and he was named the Jewish representative in the Iranian parliament.

But for Jews, like the Kurds, Kermanshah was not always a place of tolerance. In 1919, at the time of the Kurdish uprisings, rumors spread that Jews were using the blood of Muslims in the baking of Passover matzo—the well-known accusation of "blood libel" that also occurred in Christian Europe. The result was that dozens of Jewish homes were razed and many more ransacked. But to their credit, many Kermanshah Muslims took in those who had been rendered homeless and provided food and other aid.

Simko may have not put the best face on the cause of Kurdish nationalism, but still the cause did not die, even after Simko was killed in an ambush organized by Reza Shah in 1930. Reza Shah had tried the tough approach, exiling many prominent Kurds. The Kurdish leader Mohammad Rashid saw another opportunity to restoke the nationalist cause when the British-Soviet invasion during World War II threw northern Iran into chaos, but he, too, was ultimately repelled. Thirty-five years later another uprising of Kurds was pushed back by forces under the control of Mohammad Reza, who also had little sympathy for the cause of Kurdish nationalism.

Then came the Islamic Revolution, which the Kurds backed, believing they could fare no worse under Ayatollah Khomeini. They were wrong. The new Islamic government viewed the Kurds, with their separate language, culture, and allegiances with fellow Kurds in Syria, Iraq, and Turkey as unreliable backers of the new ruling order. In short order, Iranian forces were sent out to the Kurdish regions to take control of cities the Kurdish nationalists had seized during the chaos of the revolution. In the process, thousands of Kurdish nationalists were executed, entire villages were flattened, and thousands of civilians killed. Ayatollah Khomeini even declared the fight against Kurdish separatism a holy war.

In the past ten to twenty years, Kurdish protests against brutality on the part of the security forces have been met with increasing brutality. Kurdish newspapers have been closed and journalists jailed. Two Kurdish political prisoners—Ettam Fattabrian and Fasish Yasemani—were executed on the charge of "enmity against God." Serious efforts at rapprochement were made during the administration of Mohammad Khatami in the 1990s, with Khatami offering public praise of Kurdish history and culture, but once he left office any notion of Kurdish independence, or even greater autonomy, was roundly denounced.

Such has been the Kurdish experience in Iran, and it remains, to greater or lesser degrees, similar to that of other Kurds in the areas of the countries that form historic Kurdistan. The obvious question is how any minority could pose not so small a threat to such a large nation like Iran. The answer is the "brushfire" effect. Iran, like neighboring Iraq and Syria, is not a homogenous society. It is composed of many ethnic groups. Granting autonomy to one could spark similar movements among the Turkmen, Baluchis, Arabs, Turks, and others, resulting in an unraveling of the national fabric and the definition of national identity. Brushfires must therefore be stomped out before they have half a chance of spreading.

Then there is the "chink-in-the-wall" effect: The concept of the nation-state, and the kind of supranationalism that might embrace all its members, is quite new in Iran's neighborhood. In the case of Iran and many of its neighbors, the wall is not only fragile but still in the process of being built. Iran may have never been colonized like the other countries that surround it, but it has long had to contend with ever-feuding, never-complacent minority groups. Ethnic and cultural identities still trump identity by passport not only in Iran but in many parts of the world, so a chink in the fragile wall of national identity runs the risk of not just fracturing the wall but bringing down the entire edifice.

And then there is the "fear-of-our-own-more-than-the-other" effect. It can be easier for Iranian powers to extend tolerant policies toward religious minorities who will forever be minorities, and therefore never a threat. Muslims who represent the other branches of Islam are another matter. Shiism itself is a minority within the entire Muslim family, and minorities themselves are aware of the threat that they could pose if given the opportunity. In Iran's neighborhood the various ethnicities and overlapping Muslim identities are many, and the Kurds could, might, and actually may present a threat to Persian inclusiveness, from one of many angles in which tribal allegiances may be spun.

There is the nationalist card—Kurds representing a "state" without a state; the ethnic card—Kurds seizing on ethnic identity to separate themselves from their Iranian citizenship; and, worst of the worst, the sectarian card—Kurds being mostly Sunnis within an almost exclusively Shiite Iran.

Even in the murky world of Middle Eastern political and sectarian conflicts there are moments when a flicker of clarity appears. In this case what is clear is that when the modern Middle East was carved up one hundred years ago, the Kurds were dealt out of the game. Efforts to kick the Kurdish can down the road hoping it will one day fall off the horizon have been flights of fancy. Conflicts in the Middle East cannot be diffused over time. On the contrary, they do not wane, they simmer, and the people of the Middle East have long memories. As American novelist William Faulkner said about the American South: "History isn't past; it isn't even history." But Faulkner never spent any time in the Middle East.

Politics aside, Kermanshah is one of those rare places in Iran that failed to leave me with any lasting impression. The hotel where I stayed was another throwback to the 1970s and the reign of Mohammad Reza Shah, and in typical shah style—a little gaudy and overdone. Driving through the city one passes grocery stores and bland retail outlets, in between local branches of Bank Melli, Etka supermarket, Bank Pasargad, and the discounter Ofogh Koorosh. In search of dinner the first night, I hopped into a taxi and headed toward a local eatery that promoted its "Persian-style buffet." It did have a "Persian-style buffet," within a cavernous dining hall where no table seated fewer than twelve, which suggested its primary clientele were wedding parties that numbered into the hundreds. Waiters in black slacks and crisp white shirts easily threaded their way through the maze of tables, serving soft drinks and fruit juices to the few diners who kept them minimally busy between bookings.

Back at the hotel was where the real action was happening. An actual wedding party was in full swing, in the ballroom just off the lobby. I was fiddling with the internet connection on the computer near the reception desk when the guests began filing in—women whose knee-length skirts and loose headscarves more than pushed the boundaries of regime correctness for dress. All of the men were wearing staid business suits, but many sported neckties, a feature of male dress not seen in public since the days of the shah.

After the Islamic Revolution, neckties were frowned upon in Iran because they were associated with Western culture, and Western culture was regarded by the new ruling order as the source of all that had ailed Iran for at least a century, through cultural domination and at times flagrant invasion, subterfuge, and internal meddling. And so, for more than thirty years, the open-collar shirt became the politically correct fashion statement for Iranian men up and down the social ladder. Some high-level officials like Foreign Minister Javad Zarif have taken to wearing starched white collarless shirts to inject male garb with a touch of posh. But here in the lobby of the Parsian Hotel were neckties—double-stranded, Western-style neckties—as if the years of Islamic rule were but a dream.

For an explanation I turned to Shaheen. Shaheen was the desk clerk who had directed me to the hangar-like mess hall for a "typical Persian buffet."

"When it comes to weddings and other occasions, things are a little more relaxed," he told me. In short, the permission of neckties was another example of playing fast and loose with Islamic rules, bending them when needed to keep domestic discontent at bay.

And did this policy of flexibility extend to women displaying bare calves and forearms, with hardly a nod to the mandatory headscarf?

Shaheen smirked and nodded. I had seen this many times, which left a question hanging: What *were* the rules? Were neckties "permitted"? The answer, I knew, could only be given from a true Persian perspective: yes—and no. Or, no—but yes—sometimes. Behavior was dictated by circumstances and had to bend with the ever-shifting, never-stable social landscape. It was a fact of life that the regime had learned over its nearly forty years in power: when, how, and under what circumstances to let air out of the balloon and diffuse the tensions of the masses.

Iran has no shortage of tensions—social, political, and even some that spill over into the realm of sport. And they have a way of traveling, of not knowing their place. In February 2017 Kermanshah became the host of the Freestyle Wrestling World Cup, with global contenders arriving from Russia, Malaysia, Turkey, Georgia, and the United States. The final came down to a series of matches between Iran and the U.S., which the Iranians handily won, wrestling being Iran's de facto national sport. The national team, always a powerhouse at the Summer Olympics, has won gold medals in the last six. But the matchup almost didn't come off. Initially the members of the American team were refused visas, in the customary tit for tat that occurs in diplomatic relations. The Trump administration had denied all visa applications from Iranian citizens, so the Iranians responded in kind, and if it meant nixing the American team from World Cup competition, so be it. But the prestige of the competition was at stake.

"A World Cup competition without the Americans would not have been a real World Cup," said Iran's Wrestling Federation chairman, Rasoul Khadem.

In the end the visas were granted, and the American team arrived, in the middle of the night, with Iranian wrestling fans at the airport to greet them with roses, and pizzas at the hotel when they checked in. The American loss was not one to be ashamed of, for on the wrestling mat almost no one beats the Iranians.

I found myself dragged into a wrestling match of sorts with one of the locals, and it happened in the unlikeliest of places—Kermanshah's Jummah Mosque, or "major mosque." The midday prayers had just finished, and word had circulated that a foreign visitor, an American, had stopped by the mosque. One of the men edged over. A few others followed. One asked, with help from an interpreter friend, what I thought of the new administration of Donald Trump. A quick thumbs down cast my vote, and earned a handshake from everyone in the group. But these were not limp-wristed pleasantries. This was Kermanshah, so no one, foreigner or Iranian, would go away with a fish-flopping handshake. These were vice-grip tight, manly exchanges of brotherhood.

When the last of the group stepped forward, he shook my hand but held on just as I was about to let go. There was a standoff. We both squeezed harder, and the handshake turned into an arm twist. He began forcing my fist to the right in a standup arm wrestle. I pushed back. He fought back. I could feel the muscles tighten from his fingers up through his forearm, upper arm, and on into his shoulder, strained and taut. He pressed. I held. He pressed harder. Our fists were locked. I pushed back. There was only one outcome. A draw. Like tired boxcars after a long journey, our hands uncoupled. There were smiles all around, and more handshakes, again vice-grip tight.

≈

Halfway between Hamedan and Kermanshah, Sohrab and I stopped in Kangavar to have a look at the Temple of Anahita—named for the Zoroastrian goddess Anahita, the goddess of water, one of the four sacred elements in the Zoroastrian faith. This is the common view about the origin of the site, but it is still speculation. Even among Iranian scholars, debate still bubbles. Ali Akbar Sarfaraz, in the Department of Archaeology at Tehran University, believes that, based on the appearance of the ruins, it was not a Zoroastrian temple at all. Masoud Azarnoush, who unearthed the site, agrees. On the other hand, ancient sources refer to the site as a temple of Artemis, and in Persian terms Artemis was intended to be an indirect reference to Anahita.

Forget the bickering over the origin of the site—Persian, Zoroastrian, or Hellenist. What I enjoyed most, wandering around the grounds, stepping over the toppled columns, and weaving around the still-standing stumps, was the ambiguity of it all. Here history and science part. Science is about evidence, objectivity, clarity, but what makes history fascinating, I realized, is the exploration of the unknown. Here the special treat was not knowing what the place was all about. It could have been a temple, a palace, maybe a grand reception hall and showpiece of the empire in its northern provinces. Any of these could have been possible, or none. It was a playground for the imagination, and that alone made it worth seeing.

I had almost free run of the entire site. Two or three other tourists were taking turns selfie-snapping as they assumed heroic poses on the tops of columns. Now and then a car or two passed on the highway, but aside from these fleeting breaks in the stillness there was only radiant sunshine, piles of broken stone, and the aura of the water goddess.

As ancient goddesses go, Anahita was quite an appealing goddess in the pagan pantheon. She represented all the cleansing and life-giving forces of water, her primary element, but in the Zoroastrian sphere she also stood for wisdom and purifying forces of all kinds. In the *Aban Yasht*, a Zoroastrian hymn, Anahita is described as

> The life increasing, the herd increasing, the fold increasing who makes prosperity for all countries. She is wide flowing and healing . . . associated with fertility and purifying the seed of men, encouraging the flow of milk for newborns. As a river divinity, she is responsible for the fertility of the soil and the growth of crops that nurture both man and beast.

The *Aban Yasht* refers to the Yazata, the life-giving river that was the source of all creation. Anahita's complete name was Aredevi Sura Anahita, which means "damp, powerful, and pure." Representing the holy element of water within the Zoroastrian cosmos, she was the source of all creation. Another Zoroastrian text, the *Bundahishn*, from the early Middle Ages, goes on to credit Anahita for being the source of all life:

> All the waters of the world created by Ahura Mazda originate from the source Aredvi Sura Anahita, the life increasing, herd increasing, fold increasing, who makes prosperity for all countries. This source is at the top of the world mountain Hara Berezaiti, "High Hara," around which the sky revolves and that is at the center of Airyanem Vaejah, the first of the lands created by Mazda.

The text continues much more colorfully, in 3-D Hollywood form:

> The water, warm and clear, flows through a hundred thousand golden channels towards Mount Hugar, "the Lofty," one of the daughter-peaks of Hara Berezaiti. On the summit of that mountain is Lake Urvis, "the Turmoil," into which the waters flow, becoming quite purified and exiting through another golden channel. Through that channel, which is at the height of a thousand men, one portion of the great spring Aredvi Sura Anahita drizzles in moisture upon the whole earth, where it dispels the dryness of the air and all the creatures of Mazda acquire health from it.

Later writers felt the need to give Anahita more physical representation. Water imagery was not enough, so she was dressed in golden robes, wearing a golden crown and jewelry, and, as an odd fashion statement, ankle boots with golden laces. To get around, she cruised the heavens in a chariot drawn by four horses whose names also evoked water in all its forms: Wind, Cloud, Rain, and Sleet.

For all her power in the Zoroastrian world, Anahita had relatives, other goddesses who shared many of her characteristics in other pagan pantheons. There was Mat Zemlya, the "Moist Mother Earth" in Slavic lands; the Egyptian goddess Isis; the Roman Venus; Ishtar, the Mesopotamian goddess of sex and war; and Nana, from Bactria.

In Babylonian times, the beginning of the New Year was seen as one of the best times for marriage plans, because it was celebrated as the union of Heaven and Earth. And if problems in the realm of the sensuous appeared, Zoroastrians believed that an invocation to Anahita could help:

> To increase passion or sexual confidence, take a warm bath before meeting your partner. Perhaps add some lusty aromatics to the water (cinnamon, vanilla, mint or violet) to put you in the right frame of mind. Let Anahita's waters stimulate your skin and your interest, then enjoy!

Considering Anahita's powers, it shouldn't be surprising that she was also designated the guardian of prostitutes who worked within the temple, whose task was to "purify the seed of men and the womb and the milk of women," wrote the Greek historian Strabo.

Whether or not sex appeal was the driving force, the image of Anahita so captivated the Achaemenid king Artaxerxes II that he advertised his fixation for the water goddess through a means previously unknown in the Persian Empire—statuary. While the Greeks and Romans were fond of representing their deities in marble, the Persians held back, not believing that gods bore the likenesses of men and women. Then along came Artaxerxes with his obsession for Anahita. According to the Greek historian Herodotus, stone likenesses of Anahita began to spread throughout the empire. In contemporary terms, Anahita had gone viral. Her image appeared in Armenia and the Caucuses, Turkey, Syria, and Palestine. Along the way she acquired avian symbols—the peacock and the dove. In Armenia, eligible young women performed their religious duties at a lavish temple dedicated to Anahita at Eriza before choosing their husbands. As late as Sassanid times, images of naked or minimally clad women on silverware are believed to depict a lustful Anahita.

Anahita's image on silverware reminds me of an odd habit of Iranian dining—that rarely is one given a knife as part of the silverware set. Usually a spoon and fork are meant to suffice. One might conclude that the voluptuous figure of Anahita can not be confined to the narrow diameter of a table knife. But no, the reason has more to do with Persian cuisine, a waiter in Tehran told me: "One only needs a knife to cut meat, and in traditional Persian cooking meats are usually in stews or made tender before they are grilled in kebabs, so there isn't any need for a knife to cut them. Most of the time they can be pulled apart with a fork and spoon."

After a walk around the ruins I headed back to the road where Sohrab had dropped me off, saying he would be back "in a little while," with, of course, that perfect Persian obtuseness that refused to even hint at what "a while" meant. I waited, and after a few minutes his white Volvo appeared, along with an explanation for his tardiness: he had gone in search of a quick lunch. My hunch was that demands other than the nutritional had kept him away, but in keeping with Persian ambiguity, I knew only that I would never know for sure.

This night I had a special dinner to look forward to, with or without a knife, with or without a sinewy image of Anahita to wedge its way between the fork and spoon. It was December 21, the shortest night of the year, otherwise known as Yalda in Iran and other countries where Zoroastrianism is practiced. Yalda night is—after Noruz—the most important date on the Persian and Zoroastrian calendars.

In the forty years since the Islamic Revolution the regime has tried to quash all reminders of Iran's Zoroastrian past, but with abysmal success. Like Hanukkah for Jews, Christmas for Christians, Diwali for Hindus, and numerous pagan festivals that commemorate the longest night of the year, Yalda continues to be a special occasion for Iranians.

The term *yalda* is not Persian, but Syriac, and it came with the arrival of persecuted Syrian Christians, who found sanctuary in Sassanid Persia from the first to the third centuries. In the Middle Aramaic dialect *yalda* means "birth," and so it became the name for Christmas before it spread beyond the early Christian communities. In third-century Persia a bit of Christian and pagan crossover took place, where the Prophet Jesus as the "Light of the World" became a force of brightness and light to ward off the evil spirits of Ahriman (or others of your choosing). Linguists speculate that the Old Norse *Yule* may have derived from the Arabic *yelda*, or "dark night."

Whatever one's language or religious heritage, on Yalda night it is important to stay up late, preferably in the company of friends and family members, telling stories and jokes, dancing, doing anything to vanquish the dark forces of Ahriman. Get through the night and the next day begins the lengthening of the days, and the birth of the Zoroastrian goddess Mithra, goddess of—what else?—light. She can also go by the name Mehr, which is also the seventh month of the Persian calendar. The fourteenth-century poet Saadi saw the festival as an opportunity for renewal and staring down the dark elements of life that suppress the brighter possibilities of human beings:

> With all my pains there is still the hope of recovery
> Like the eve of Yalda, there will finally be an end.

Saadi also tied Yalda to the favorite theme of all Persians—love:

> The sight of you each morning is a new year,
> And night of your departure is the eve of Yalda.

Almost everywhere in the world the celebration of festivals centers around food. Yalda is no exception. On Yalda night it is advisable to nibble on slices of watermelon and pomegranate, because their bright red color symbolizes the glow of the sunrise and the resurgent forces of light. If no watermelon or pomegranate is available, beets or apples will suffice. To guard against insect bites, eat some carrots, peas, or green olives. To ward off joint pain, garlic will help. But watermelon is also ideal, because it fights off any discomfort brought on by summer heat. A fistful of nuts—almonds, pistachios, or hazelnuts—along with dried figs, apricots, or any other fruit has to be part of the mix because no Persian feast is complete without them.

My own feast, at the Shayli in the center of Kermanshah, began with a greeting by the host. On display in the middle of the room was an arrangement of nuts and dried fruit, and sliced pomegranate and chunks of watermelon forecast the sunrise.

Ancient societies all over the world depended on seasonal celebrations to restore faith in stability and continuity, which the cycle of the seasons represented. Chaos and disorder, violence and war, these were the result of human conflict. The reliability of the seasonal cycle brought psychological comfort, especially in times of political upheaval. Yalda is therefore a celebration of the stronger forces of nature over those of fickle, unpredictable humans.

The host sat me at a table at the end of the room with the best view of the hall. I was early. Iranians are typically late diners. As the hour approached nine, the tables began to fill up, and when the room reached its breaking point, one of the waiters brought around a collection of sealed envelopes, each of which contained a verse by the fourteenth-century poet Hafez. This was the introduction to another important ritual of Yalda night. In the privacy of their homes—and here in the Shayli—Iranians typically make a wish and then flip through a dog-eared copy of Hafez and pinpoint a passage. The words of the master are supposed to deliver a reply to the wish. All gathered attempt to define the meaning.

I didn't have the luxury of choosing my own Hafez lines. The answer to any wish I might have made was left to fate, and the host who handed me an envelope as he circled the room. I breathed deeply and tore it open. It read:

If the gardener desires the company of flowers, for a day or two,
> for the bitter separation must bear the patience of a
> > nightingale,
Oh heart, snared in the curls of the lover, do not despair;
> a clever bird caught in the trap must show patience!
A rebel rend and expedience, why should he care?
> laying plans and caution relate to those with possessions!
In the way of tarighat reliance on piety and gnosis is heretical;
> the journeyer, even with a thousand talents, must yield to
> > God,
With such tresses and face, no roving eyes to catch
> the face of jasmine, her jet black curls smelling of hyacinth.
Love her wind and her coyness:
> this frenzied heart is mad for her black hair and tresses.

I was glad that I had forgotten to make a wish, so I had no hint as to whether it would be made true or dashed. I was able to listen without a worry to the Persian music that had started up, played by a band of musicians that had gathered at an empty table on the other side of the room.

More diners arrived to replace those who had left. Music played. Strands of the santour, tar, ney, dutar, and daf circled the room, aided by the soft curve of the walls.

> Oh Saghi, how long will you neglect circulating the vessel?
> The impossible, when with lovers, must turn infinite.

So wrote Hafez, and in the way only he could—not only the choice of words but their arrangement, and the context in which they are used, combine to create a baffling number of interpretations. Throw in the poetic tools of symbolism, nuance, and double and triple meanings, and the "meaning" of the poem can be as elusive as the seeds of a dandelion released to a summer breeze.

What the hell, I thought. If my fate was laid out somewhere within this tangle of imagery, it was worth taking a whack at. Hafez referred to a garden and distance, and the anguish of the heart ended with a plea for patience. Then he mentioned, or advised, "laying plans and caution," and took a swipe at knowledge. Then came the thousand talents of the journeyer. Hafez's choice of the term *gardener* made me wonder if he had me in mind at all, and the "god" he mentioned could easily be a stand-in for fate, or serendipity, or any other force outside our control. "Her jet black curls" threw the door of meaning open wide, for every reader of poetry knows that female imagery can stand for anything but the female in the flesh—perhaps a dream, a desire, maybe an ideal, or a flight of fancy.

It was easy to see how Iranians could delight in this. It was a verbal and mystical game of hide-and-go-seek—twisting and tweaking the choices of wording and shades of meaning like the combinations of a lock, but one that was destined never to open.

None of the other diners seemed bothered very much. The fun was in the parsing of possibilities, and to solve the puzzle would have spoiled the fun. The Shayli's other guests passed their envelopes around the group, while the waiters circulated serving trays piled with slices of watermelon, followed by red apples and figs. A cluster of musicians seized a santour, a dutar, and a *ney* and started putting out more traditional tunes. At the front entrance, all the Yalda foods were arranged on a *korsi*, or ceremonial display, and these slowly disappeared as the plates and bowls filled with dried fruits and nuts and other goodies made their way around the room.

There was a slight skirting of tradition, for if this had been a true Yalda, observed to-the-letter, the waiter and cooks and kitchen help would have taken their places at the tables, and the customers would have become servers. The children would tell their parents when it was time to leave, and the parents would obey. The Shayli's owner would wash the dishes and sweep the floor, for Yalda night is also a celebration of disorder and turning the world upside down, letting chaos reign in a confused world to rattle the evil intentions of Ahriman.

It was not yet midnight, meaning the partying still had a ways to go. I trusted that the revelry going on all over Kermanshah would be enough to protect me from Ahriman, so I caught a taxi to head back to my hotel. Also breaking with Yalda tradition, I let the driver take the wheel, and when we arrived back at the hotel, the night clerk was snoozing in a ratty armchair, as he should. He was still wearing his rumpled sport jacket, and the woman closing the office hadn't shed her scarf and manteau, which meant, in Yalda terms, that all was still well with the world.

The next morning all *was* still well with the world. The axis of the Earth had trembled but righted itself. It had weathered the night of Ahriman. Ahriman would be back next year, to try again, but no matter, today the sun rose, a bright, pink glow just like the slivers of watermelon and pomegranate that had long been cleared from the Shayli's serving trays, and a minute earlier than it had the day before. In the hotel's breakfast room the guests were munching on slices of feta cheese laid across thick warm slices of *barbari* bread, while the waitstaff dutifully tended the coffee machines and orange juice dispenser, as their duty sheet prescribed. Sohrab showed up in the hotel lobby to pick me up with his usual punctuality.

In Kermanshah the best was saved for last. In Kermanshah the most significant and heavily visited historic sight is Bisotun, not quite within the boundaries of Kermanshah but not far away, about twenty-five miles along a two-lane road that skirts a line of sloping, craggy rock formations. As we breezed along the road the sun rose higher and the morning chill burned away a cover of low-lying fog. A few millennia ago the road was a dirt track that connected the Persian Empire with the Babylonian kingdom of ancient Mesopotamia, and it was a later link in the caravan routes that served as the commercial corridor funneling goods between western and central Asia. Today, the sheep were nonplussed as the Volvo cruised past. They had seen so much traffic that the tire tracks of a single car were just another imprint on a groove dug centuries deep.

At Bisotun is where the Achaemenid emperor Darius I made his mark, in stone and in imagery. After the death of Cyrus the empire faced challenges of succession from nine opportunists claiming to be the rightful heir to the throne. Persian history refers to them as the nine imposters. Darius fought a series of nineteen battles against them, defeating them all to preserve the integrity of the empire. At Bisotun, in enormous relief sculptures carved out of the rock two hundred feet up the cliff face, Darius is shown squashing one of the defeated under his foot. Victories over the other upstarts, their necks looped with ropes and hands tied together, are also memorialized in the rock. The unfortunate figure lying under Darius's boot is believed to be Gaumata, the last of the nine pretenders Darius defeated, somewhere near Bisotun. The sculptural panorama is believed to date from 522 BCE.

It is reasonable to believe that this is where Darius would take his victory dance, memorializing the event in stone to serve as a warning to future moochers who might pass along the ancient road. To add a little divine weight to the warning, above Darius the winged image of Farvahar, the symbol of Zoroastrianism, hovers. Several inscriptions were carved into the stone to describe Darius's victory. One of the oldest states:

> The kingdom that had been wrested from our line I brought back and I reestablished it on its foundation. The temples which Gaumata, the Magian, had destroyed, I restored to the people, and the pasture lands, and the herds and the dwelling places, and the houses which Gaumata, the Magian, had taken away. I settled the people in their place, the people of Persia, and Media, and the other provinces. I restored that which had been taken away, as it was in the days of old. This did I by the grace of Ahuramazda, I labored until I had established our dynasty in its place, as in the days of old.

To ensure nothing would be lost in translation, Darius wrote his entire text in three languages: Babylonian, Elamite, and Persian. Elamite came first, as it was the lingua franca of the time. The others were added later. It is this feature that persuaded UNESCO to give Bisotun World Heritage status, for nowhere else had three versions of the same text been written in cuneiform script, and the Bisotun inscriptions became the

key for deciphering the ancient language, making Bisotun as important to cuneiform as the Rosetta Stone is to Egyptian hieroglyphics.

We pulled into a nearly empty parking lot with bright morning sun
streaming along the face of the rocky cliffs and the broad open valley
that swept by. Soon we were not alone. As the morning warmed up,
other cars pulled into the lot, and, high up the tall slab of broken limestone, their passengers could be seen making their way up the access
trails as bright blotches of color against the sun-splashed stone.

The cool, crisp air was ideal for a morning hike. I dug into the slope
and began the trudge. Every five or ten minutes I stopped to look back
over the fertile valley. Some historians believe that Bisotun was chosen
as the site for what would have been a victor's memorial because it was
here that Darius had vanquished Gaumata, the last of the impostors.
But why would he make his statement, in pictures and text, so distant
from the caravans that would plod by far below? In twenty-first-century
terms it was bad advertising strategy, placing a rock billboard out of
view of the passing traffic.

Apparently I knew nothing of promulgating a message in the ancient
world, because the reliefs and the text did draw attention, for about two
thousand years. Explorers, military men, and diplomats from France,
Italy, and England, with other Middle Eastern religions on their mind,
believed the reliefs represented either the twelve lost tribes of Israel or
Jesus Christ and the twelve apostles. Linguistic light began to appear
in the late eighteenth century, when Carsten Niebuhr, a surveyor from
Germany, reproduced the text in a published description of his travels in
Iran. This enabled Georg Friedrich Grotefend to begin work on cracking
the cuneiform code. In 1802 he concluded, correctly, that each of the
wedge symbols stood for a letter of the alphabet rather than a syllable,
and the arrangement of the wedges did not represent a pictorial sign,
as in the case of hieroglyphics or East Asian languages.

The most persistent pursuer of the mystery of Bisotun was Henry
Rawlinson, an officer in the British East India Company. Between 1835
and 1893, with the help of boys from the surrounding valley, Rawlinson used boards and ropes to get a closer look at the portions of the

text too difficult to view. The effort paid off. He and a team of Asian linguistic scholars were ultimately able to connect the wedge-shaped symbols into an entire rendering of Darius's message.

I have always found this to be one of the most humbling experiences in the ancient world—visiting temples, monuments, and memorials whose scale reflects the vision of their builders. To fully appreciate them we have to dismiss any views on the religious values they represent and even the megalomania that often drove their construction, and see them solely through the eyes of their own times. And considering the tools and technical knowledge available to build them, the accomplishments loom greater than the battles and other events they commemorate.

For all the weight that Bisotun carries in Persian history, the site has also been a source for legends, and like most legends, how much is truth and how much is fiction is encrypted within the stone of the mountain. According to Ferdowsi, the eleventh-century poet and crafter of legends, there was once a man named Farhad, who had fallen in love with Shirin, the wife of King Khosrow. Once this was found out, Farhad was punished by being ordered to find water within the mountain. But there was a caveat—if his labors bore fruit, the king's wife would be his. For years Farhad toiled away, and one day water sprung from a hole he had dug. But rather than being rewarded with a bride, Farhad was told that Shirin had passed away. He lost his mind and died on the spot. But it was all a ruse. Shirin was alive and well, and was devastated on hearing of Farhad's death.

Ferdowsi would never let a tale end on such a bleak note. When Farhad was told the grim news, fake though it was, he hurled his axe down the mountain. The axe was made from the wood of a pomegranate tree, and where it landed a pomegranate tree later sprouted, and fruit from the tree had the power to heal the sick.

We had another stop to make. A few miles out of Kermanshah we pulled into a parking area on the north side of the road. Sohrab told me nothing as we got out of the car and followed a paved path that led through what appeared to be a roadside rest area with a reflecting pool as its centerpiece. We strode on a little further, and the figurative curtain was pulled back.

We were at Taq-e Bostan. In simple terms, Taq-e Bostan is a series of gigantic relief sculptures carved onto a rock face and framed by archways topped with the images of women in various forms of dress—luxurious, thinly veiled, and in some cases no dress at all. In historical terms, Taq-e Bostan is another celebration of Persian glory in large-scale stone images. Call them stone billboards that once advertised the greatness of the empire for passing traders.

In Persian terms, the carvings at Taq-e Bostan are still "young"—less than two thousand years old, having been chiseled out of the rock between the fourth and seventh centuries. True to their times, they portray the Sassanid kings Ardashir II, Shapur II, Shapur III, and Khosrow II in suitably regal fashion. In one of the reliefs, Ardashir II is becoming ruler of the empire as he and another figure, believed to be his predecessor, Shapur II, trample Julianus Apostata, a vanquished Roman emperor, with their feet. In another, Khosrow II demonstrates his kingly qualities by shooting a boar while saddled on his favorite horse. Both horse and rider are decked out in full warrior gear. Smaller reliefs portray the kings enjoying their favorite pastime—hunting. The god Mithra also appears, standing on a lotus flower and bearing a *barsum*—a handful of branches that was the symbol of divine power. For anyone wondering what the whole display is about, inscriptions—captions, in contemporary terms—are cut into the rock. The inscription for Shapur III reads:

> This is the figure of Mazda-worshipping Lord Shapur, the king of kings of Iran and Aniran, whose race is from the Gods. Son of Mazda-worshipping Lord Shapur, the king of kings of Iran and Aniran, whose race is from the Gods, grandson of Lord Hormizd, the king of kings.

Little of this would have been eye opening in Greece or Rome, or other parts of the world where ancient cultures once flourished, but in today's Iran, reliefs like those at Taq-e Bostan have added meaning. They are ever-present reminders that much of Persian culture, and therefore the Persian identity, predates the arrival of Islam. In today's Iran, the Islamic message attempts to sweep away over five thousand years of history, but Persia's past continues to bleed through, a litany of indelible facts that cannot be washed away. For many Iranians, reliefs like those at Taq-e Bostan also stand as a symbol of lost greatness, with the kings of former dynasties replaced by a government of hardline mullahs and two Supreme Leaders whose ruling principle has been adherence to a religious doctrine that has no deep roots in Persia's cultural history.

Leaving Kermanshah we headed south and then east on the way to Esfahan, skirting the Zagros Mountains and snow-capped Mount Sefidkhani, its graceful ridge rising above the winter-brown valleys. Cross-country driving is often like this in Iran, using the broad, sweeping valleys to zigzag around the mountain ranges that cut north and south, east and west, dividing the landscape into distinct regions that, interwoven, form the identity of the country.

Halfway between Kermanshah and Esfahan we passed through Arak, an industrial city that straddles the fault lines of ancient and modern Iran. The name itself carries the weight of history. *Arak* derives from the Arabic *Al-Iraq*, which linguists speculate may have descended from the Hebrew *erech*, meaning "long." Erech was also mentioned in the book of Genesis as a city in the kingdom of Nimrod. Etymology aside, in the eighth century BCE, the region stretched from Arak to the border of today's Iraq and beyond, under the rule of the massive and sprawling Median Empire. The ruins of ancient cities stand, or lie, as remnants of the Arab spillover from the Babylonian kingdom.

Arak, today, is one of Iran's industrial centers, a product of Mohammad Reza Shah's modernization campaign to thrust the country into the twentieth century before it passed into the twenty-first. In 1974 Wagon Pars began making railroad cars and engines, and the bright blue-and-white trains have managed to reach speeds of one hundred miles per hour. Arak also generates steel, aluminum, and petrochemicals, but its highest-profile and most controversial industry has been the heavy water reactor at Khondab, about twenty miles northwest of the city.

Whether the reactor has been producing so-called heavy water to aid in the production of weapons-grade plutonium has sent jitters through countries worried about Iran's nuclear program, rumbles at least as tremulous as the 2018 quake that shook Kermanshah. Inspections by the International Atomic Energy Agency (IAEA) and studies by nuclear experts have been—fittingly, in Iranian terms—inconclusive. Concrete was poured into the reactor core in January 2016, and the IAEA has stated that there is no evidence that the heavy water from the reactor has been used to produce weapons-grade fuel. Yet Iran is still Iran, one of the few countries in the world capable of combining the facts of hard science with political ambiguity.

6 | Hamedan

CITY OF THE JEWISH QUEEN

The great god is Ahuramazda, greatest of all the gods, who created the earth and the sky and the people, who made Xerxes king, and outstanding king as outstanding ruler among innumerable rulers. I am the great king Xerxes, king of kings, king of lands with numerous inhabitants, king of this vast kingdom with far-away territories, son of the Achaemenid monarch Darius.
                    —Cuneiform inscription at Ganjnameh

The layout of Hamedan is emblematic of today's Iran. The center is dominated by a traffic roundabout where six radial roads converge. In the center stands a circular relief sculpture of Ayatollah Khomeini, and the first Supreme Leader appears, as he does everywhere, severe and grim-faced, his bushy eyebrows hovering over darkly piercing eyes. The majority of Hamedan's residents pay him little notice as they circle through the roundabout, while small bundles of flowers left beneath Khomeini's stern gaze wither in the midday sun. It is a grim metaphor: Shiite Islam lies at the core of Iranian society, around which most Iranians navigate while trying to ignore it as much as possible.

Still, there is a normalcy to Hamedan, an "anywhere" feel, as there is an "anywhere" feel to Des Moines, Iowa, and other cities in Middle America. With half a million residents, Hamedan is neither a traffic-choked megalopolis like Tehran nor a regional backwater. It lacks the spellbinding architecture of Esfahan and the cultural legacy of Shiraz, but it has a university with two thousand students and other landmarks that give it a place on the Persian map. And some historians believe it to be one of the oldest cities in the world, dating to at least 1100 BCE.

We rolled into Hamedan after a two-hour drive from Kermanshah, zigzagging through the smooth rolling hills and open fields that form the apron of the Zagros Mountains. I had been to Hamedan once before, in June 2009, during the postelection riots that followed the reelection of Mahmoud Ahmadinejad. Being a university town, it was inevitable that the turmoil in Tehran would find its way there. On the day I arrived, there had been clashes between protestors and the security forces, but by late afternoon the dustups had settled into a tense standoff. The Revolutionary Guard had parked their troop carriers around Azadi Square and other strategic points in the city, from where they eyed the troublemakers with the same severe gaze as Khomeini at the roundabout.

Now something else was brewing, but this time more personal than political, or historic, or cultural. An hour out of town Sohrab had made a couple of calls from the car and spoke in the coy, mellifluous tone men use when they are conversing with women they are not married to. He had a wife and three children, but over our many hours of road talk he freely admitted that he "played around a bit," so I sensed he had inserted a late-day dalliance into the day's itinerary.

Since we had left Tehran, Sohrab was allowing me much freer rein. In the capital, the discovery of an American wandering loose without his guide could have left him with many questions to answer to the authorities. But here in the hinterlands, the risks were reduced, so he agreed to drop me at Hamedan's famous stone lion and pick me up a few hours later at the mausoleum of the Avicenna, the eleventh-century physician and, many claim, the founder of modern medicine. In between—he said with a straight face—he had to have the car serviced.

Hamedan's stone lion is just that—a lion carved from a block of stone hauled out of the nearby mountains.

The lion is one of a pair that guarded the gates of the city for almost a thousand years, well after the Arab invasion of 633 CE. The Iranian Organization of Cultural Affairs claims it was left by Alexander the

Great when he tore through the Persian Empire in 331 BCE. The Macedonian conqueror made it in honor of one of his soldiers, Hephaestus, who passed away in Ecbatana (Hamedan's former Persian name). But another narrative claims that the lion was carved during the Arsacid dynasty, which ruled the Kingdom of Armenia from 54 to 428 CE. This is proven—as much as any archaeological claim can be—by the style of stone, later also found on sarcophagi in the area.

Whatever the origin of the lions, in 931 the Zoroastrian warrior Mardavij tried to move the lions to the city of Rey while attempting to wrest control of Hamedan from Muslim invaders, but one was destroyed. The lone lion remains, though badly weather-beaten and with a broken paw, a reminder of the many invasions Iran has borne.

It was a beautiful spring afternoon. The rays of the late-afternoon sun streamed through the thick boughs of the oak trees. Young mothers pushed baby strollers along the pathways as they ran errands to the neighborhood markets. Old men gathered on wooden benches, leaning on canes and playing endless rounds of backgammon and chess.

I was strolling along one of the footpaths when I was approached by a young man dressed in neat slacks and a button-down shirt, carrying the clean-cut look of a medical student. His name was Javad, and he worked as a journalist for one of Hamedan's media outlets. Or so he said. Naturally, he asked where I was from, and naturally, when I told him, his eyes brightened. Then he was not about to let me go. One after the other, the questions tumbled out: How long had I been in Iran? Had my ideas about Iran changed? What would I tell friends back home? But something did not feel right. I was used to being bombarded with questions by curious Iranians, but Javad rattled his off as though he was reading from a prepared script, like a junior interviewer who needed to polish his skills. Government informants are known to linger around tourist areas, eyeing foreign visitors to latch on to, and then pepper them with questions as a way of feeling them out. With luck, they might uncover a Western journalist, or better yet—the gold medal—a foreign intelligence agent.

I answered with the appropriate evasiveness: Yes, Iran was impressive. No, it was not what I thought. And then I told him that I had to meet my guide. He asked where. At the mausoleum of Avicenna, a good ten-minute walk away, I told him, thinking that would shake him off, but no. With Persian politeness, he offered to escort me there. So as long as I had to bear him I decided to get the most of it—to grill him as he had grilled me. I asked him if, as a working journalist, it was possible to write anything he wanted.

"Oh, yes," he said, a little too quickly.

"Really, *anything?*"

"Of course—as long as it is *factual.*"

"And opinions?"

"Oh, that's no problem. We can express *any* views."

"Any at all?"

" Yes—as long as they have *validity.*"

And so it went. Maybe Javad wasn't a government informant. But if he wasn't, it was clear that he was only capable of scripted answers, talking points issued in journalism school to prospective regime toadies. What he believed, if he believed anything at all, was never going to be revealed to an American visitor he had corralled in a park.

Then Javad became curious. He asked about restrictions on American journalism: Was it true that newspapers in the U.S. could publish *anything* they wanted?

"Well, almost, but certain standards have to be maintained."

"What if lies are spread, about people's reputations?"

"There are laws against slander and libel."

He had heard that European countries had laws against such things like hate speech—didn't Americans believe in any limits?

Javad's questions were horribly reductive, but the fact that he had posed them at all held promise. He could have been of two minds: he may have absorbed just enough regime propaganda to get him a job as a journalist, or as a working journalist he may have harbored genuine curiosity about the principles of international media. Both could have been true. Or neither. Maybe he simply wanted to feel me out. There was no way to tell. He was a cipher, and therefore the perfect public face of an authoritarian government.

We were passing through Azadi Square, which had been chockablock with military personnel transport trucks the last time I was there. But now students were gathered at a colorful juice bar that opened onto the street, and others were lounging on the grass, flipping through textbooks as they absorbed the receding rays of the early summer sun. I fumbled through a few more answers to Javad's inane questions, and then we arrived at the mausoleum of Avicenna. With customary Persian politeness he wished me a pleasant time in Iran and thanked me for showing interest in the country. For the first time I actually believed something he said. But before he could get away I thought I'd get mischievous. I asked him where I could find the home of Shirin Ebadi. The 2003 Nobel Peace Prize winner and international human rights advocate had been born in Hamedan.

Javad's grin vanished into a look of confusion. "Oh, she doesn't live here anymore," he said.

I knew that. Shortly after the 2009 postelection riots Ebadi had to flee Iran, driven out by crackdowns and intimidation, and since then she had divided her time between London and Toronto. Her office in Tehran had been closed, her sister briefly detained. This was long-common regime practice—to harass the relatives of dissidents living safely outside the country as a way of intimidating and muzzling them.

"I mean the house where she grew up."

"Why are you interested?" Javad queried.

"There might be a plaque outside it. After all, she is Iran's first Nobel laureate."

This was sheer folly, and I knew it. Anything to do with Iran's premier human rights advocate would not have been advertised, least of all in Hamedan. If anything, the information would have been buried, lest her childhood home turn into a pilgrimage site for Green Movement types—flowers left at the front door in the middle of the night, graffiti sprayed on the exterior walls.

"I'm sorry, I don't have any idea," Javad said, wagging his head. And with that he shook my hand and again wished me a very pleasant stay in Iran. And again he sounded like he meant it.

I had lied to Javad about meeting Sohrab. He wasn't due for at least an hour. I just wanted to shake him off, since there was nothing to be gained by talking to him further. Any question on any "sensitive" subject—and there are many in Iran—would be met with predictable regime blather, all the more nauseating because of its pretended sincerity, as if any sincere thought went into the answers at all. And so, with time to kill, I went looking for the tomb of Esther and Mordecai and the synagogue complex where both are buried, long a pilgrimage site for Sephardic Jews.

Whether or not the biblical figures actually lie in the tomb has long been a subject of debate. Some historians claim that they were moved to present-day Israel and laid to rest in Baram, near Haifa. The twentieth-century German archaeologist Ernst Herzfeld believed that they were buried in nearby Susa, today's Shush, the Persian Empire's capital in Esther's time. But no historical bickering obscures the fact that Jewish history has been entwined with the history of Iran, and the history of Iran has been entwined with Jewish history, and so a visit to the tomb, whether Esther and Mordecai lie there or not, was anything but a waste of time.

The first Jews arrived in ancient Persia in 722 BCE, when the Northern Kingdom of Israel was conquered by Shalmaneser V, king of the Assyrian Empire, driving the Israelite tribes into exile. Those who fled to Persia arrived in Khorasan, the region that today straddles Turkmenistan and western Afghanistan. In 586 BCE more Jews sought exile in Persia, this time when the Babylonians expelled the Jews from the Kingdom of Judah, and for two hundred years the Persian Empire became the repository for many of the Middle East's Jewish exiles.

Cyrus's policy of religious tolerance played a role. As the empire expanded, freedom of religious expression was enshrined as the rule of law, and in 529 BCE this was codified in the Cyrus Cylinder, often regarded as the world's first declaration of human rights. In 537 BCE Cyrus allowed the Jews to return to Jerusalem to rebuild the Temple. The second volume of the Book of Chronicles states:

Thus saith Cyrus, king of Persia: All the kingdoms of the earth hath the lord, the God of heaven given me; and He hath charged me to build Him a house in Jerusalem, which is in Judah. Whosoever there is among you of all His people—the lord, his God, be with him—let him go there.

In recognition, Cyrus is the only non-Jew to have been given the title "Lord's Messiah," or divinely appointed leader. Cyrus died before the Temple was completed, so it was left to his son-in-law and successor Darius to see the project through. More than forty thousand Jews are believed to have accepted Cyrus's offer to return to the ancient land of Israel, but among those who chose to remain behind were Esther, an orphan, and her guardian and uncle, Mordecai. And so begins a tale of intrigue with all the convolutions of a Greek drama.

One night in the middle of a six-month feast—wining and dining were something of a marathon sport in the Persian Empire—Ahasuerus (believed by some to be Xerxes, the son of Darius), summoned his queen Vashti to appear before his guests so they could admire her beauty. But Vashti refused, igniting a storm of controversy. Ahasuerus's advisers warned him that if word of Vashti's rebellion got out the news would rock the kingdom, so she was ousted from the court, and a yearlong contest to find a replacement was won by Esther, who became the wife of Ahasuerus and queen of the Persian Empire.

Esther fell easily into her role, and the scandal that Vashti may have caused soon faded. Then things changed. One day, Esther's uncle Mordecai overheard two soldiers manning the city gates planning an assassination of the king. Mordecai relayed the news to Esther, who conveyed it to Ahasuerus, and the king had the plotters executed. Mordecai rose in the king's favor but was otherwise unrewarded—for the time being.

Enter Haman the Agagite. Haman was a well-known prince, and Ahasuerus, believing that a person of such esteem should receive his due, ordered that anyone encountering Haman in the street should bow to him. The commoners accepted Ahasuerus's dictate, but there was one holdout: Mordecai, who claimed that one should only bow to God.

One day the two passed in the street, and Mordecai refused to bow. Haman was so offended he plotted to rid the empire of all the Jews, and he began to work on Ahasuerus, eventually convincing him that they were planning to rise against him. Driven by haste and fear, Ahasuerus signed an order stating that all the Persian Jews were to be executed.

Seeking to protect not only her uncle but the rest of the Persian Jews, Esther took it upon herself to figure a way out of the mess. She soon cooked up a plan. The first step was asking both Ahasuerus and Haman to be her guests at a private banquet. Both agreed, and walking home from the banquet that night Haman again encountered Mordecai in the street. Again Mordecai refused to bow. Haman, doubly affronted, sought the permission from Ahasuerus to hang Mordecai.

That night, while mulling Mordecai's fate, Ahasuerus recalled the time when Mordecai had saved his life by revealing the assassination plot. The tables then turned. The next day he asked Haman what would be a fitting reward for someone the king wanted to honor. Thinking that the king was referring to him, Haman said that such a man should be escorted through the streets on horseback, clad in royal garments. Ahasuerus agreed and commanded Haman to deliver that treatment to Mordecai, and told him that Mordecai had once saved his life.

Mordecai was now back in the king's favor, but the fate of the rest of the Jews still hung in the balance. At another banquet a few nights later, Esther took the opportunity to ask the king a favor. Ahasuerus said he would be glad to grant her anything she wished, so she begged him to withdraw the order mandating the Jews' destruction. She acknowledged that she herself was Jewish, and that it was Haman who had plotted to rid the empire of its Jews, and all because of his tiff with Mordecai.

Furious, Ahasuerus sought revenge on Haman. Fearing the worst, Haman fled to Esther and begged her to save his life. But the loop was closing. A raging Ahasuerus tracked him down in the queen's bedchamber, and now Ahasuerus imagined the worst—that Haman was trying to seduce his wife. Haman's fate was sealed. Ahasuerus ordered him to be hung on the gallows that Haman had constructed for Mordecai. After Haman was dispatched, Mordecai became Ahasuerus's prime minister, and the king gave all the Jews of the empire the right to carry weapons to defend themselves against any future plots. Ever since, the Jews of Iran have been dubbed "Esther's children."

Once Javad was out of sight, I turned right, ducked around the corner, and headed in the direction of the synagogue. Nothing suggested I was approaching one of Judaism's major pilgrimage sites. On the corner hung a giant poster of a black-turbaned mullah, but in contrast to Khomeini's dagger-like glare, this one was flashing an ear-to-ear grin. For any passing resident the message of the mega-face was clear: we are *everywhere*, and you will not forget that we are *everywhere*.

The tomb was embarrassingly modest, topped with a nondescript dome that could have been mistaken for a neighborhood mosque or, in former times, a local bathhouse. Persian Jews unable to travel to Jerusalem use the tomb of Esther and Mordecai as their own Western Wall, and often leave slips of paper in the twisted, rusty fence that surrounds the compound. But on this day there were no prayer slips in the fence. Only a yarmulke on the head of one of "Esther's children" lingering outside, who told me I was in the right place.

I passed through the gate, but another man, also wearing a yarmulke, gestured for me to wait. He disappeared inside, and a minute later Rabbi Rajad emerged. He was as old as the oldest men at the gate and shabbily dressed, in baggy unwashed pants and a tattered sport coat, and sporting a blue baseball cap that had lost its insignia ages ago. But his smile was bright, revealing a mouthful of yellow, crooked teeth, and his handshake, though as limp as a dishrag, was soft and tender.

In ragged English he asked if I was Jewish—but didn't wait for an answer. He fished in his pocket and brought out a cardboard yarmulke, handed it to me, and led me to the door.

The interior was equally drab. Plain, sand-colored walls were decorated with bits of Jewish memorabilia, and in a tiny side room were a dozen metal chairs with split plastic seats. In the middle, taking up almost the entire room, were two sarcophagi, standing side by side and covered with thick, red velvet cloths fringed with gold—the final resting place of the two biblical figures. Rabbi Rajad pointed with pride to a large ceramic work hanging on the wall near the entrance. It was the Ten Commandments, written in Hebrew.

I asked him if the synagogue still held regular services. This disguised my real question: Were there enough Jews in Hamedan to hold services? According to Jewish law, a service requires the presence of ten adult men. Yes, he said, pointing to the tangle of dilapidated chairs. There were still 150 Jews in the city, and they were all practicing, he added proudly. In 1850, when the global traveler Israel ben Joseph visited Hamedan, the city had an estimated 500 Jewish families and three synagogues. But times had changed. One hundred and fifty years later, the Jewish population in all of Iran had shrunk to 15,000, still the largest in the Middle East outside of Israel, but a flicker of its former presence.

I thanked Rabbi Rajad for the visit and was about to leave when he asked where I was from. I told him, and his eyes brightened, and then he asked if I had a pen I could give him. His hobby was collecting pens from all over the world, and he had accumulated a vast collection, but one still missing was a pen from the United States. Yes, I said, and pulled a plastic ballpoint from my pocket I had been carrying the last few weeks. But it was a German brand, the kind he had probably piled by the hundreds on a dusty shelf at home. As I took it from my pocket I watched his eyes glow, then dim. Still, he managed a weak grin of appreciation before offering another mushy handshake, and led me to the door.

Zigzagging back to the mausoleum, I felt a jab of remorse. I wished I'd packed a boxful of American-made pens he could display beside the Ten Commandments—Bics and Papermates, Crosses, Parkers, and Sheaffers, but it was not to be. I looked forward to the tomb of Avicenna, hoping the medical genius from medieval Persia had a remedy that could offer relief.

Avicenna was one of the leading lights of the Persian golden age. Born in 980 in present-day Uzbekistan, where his father was an official in the regional government, he was quickly recognized as something of a wunderkind. By the age of ten he had memorized the entire Quran, and in his adolescence he learned mathematics, studied Islamic law, and began to dabble in philosophy and the theories of Euclid and Ptolemy. His academic track hit a speed bump when he struggled with Aristotle's *Metaphysics*, but he managed to overcome it and became so immersed in his studies that he would often unravel the solutions to problems in his dreams. By the age of eighteen he was recognized as a qualified physician, and was comfortable enough in his accomplishments to claim that medicine was much easier than the tougher pursuits of math and metaphysics.

Avicenna's life then began a series of twists and turns that kept him always on the move and working under less-than-opportune conditions. His professional breakthrough came when he helped his local emir recover from a serious illness. In gratitude, the emir offered to make him his personal physician, and the post came with a priceless perk—access to the royal library. But disaster soon struck when the library went up in flames. Rivals pointed the finger at Avicenna, claiming he had done the deed so that he alone would be the caretaker of the knowledge he had acquired.

With the benefit of his position also up in flames, Avicenna took to the road after being offered a stipend by the vazir of Urgench, Turkmenistan. But the salary turned out to be too small, so Avicenna was on the road again, this time to Nishapour in Iran, and then Merv, Tabaristan, and Gorgan, on the Caspian Sea. There he acquired a patron—a friend who bought a house near his own so Avicenna would have a suitable place to study and lecture. It was here that he began writing his *Canon of Medicine*.

It wasn't long before Avicenna was on the move again, this time to Rey, part of today's Tehran. There he found an equilibrium and was able to write as many as thirty essays and treatises. It would not last. Eventually he was driven out by the constant bickering between the lady of the house and one of her sons. His next destination was Qazvin, in northwest Iran, but he soon was packing again. This time he headed south, to Hamedan. Avicenna wasn't afflicted with wanderlust or an aversion to put down roots. Economic difficulties in the lives of his patrons usually forced him to uproot himself.

After he had established himself in Hamedan, Avicenna received another offer to become a personal physician, this time from the wife of a local aristocrat, but he was also solicited by the city's new emir, who tried to seduce him with gifts. This new relationship had its ups and downs, and eventually the emir ordered Avicenna banished. At first Avicenna hid in the house of a friend, but, when the emir was stricken with a severe illness, the emir decided to let bygones be bygones and offered Avicenna his position back. Avicenna accepted, but he was not a miracle worker, and the emir ultimately died. Avicenna then hid in the house of a local pharmacist and continued his studies, but eventually he was discovered by the new emir and thrown into jail.

Wars between Hamedan and Esfahan kept Avicenna behind bars until the battles subsided, and then he was allowed to return to his post in Hamedan. But loyalty had its limits. Avicenna finally escaped Hamedan in disguise and headed to Esfahan, where he spent the next ten years as personal physician and scientific consul to the Persian army. A military campaign brought him back to Hamedan, but he contracted colic along the way and died in the city he had fled, in 1037.

Avicenna was a true renaissance man whose vast imagination and intellectual curiosity could never be confined to one area of study. Five hundred years before the European Renaissance, he delved deeply into mathematics and logic, astronomy and philosophy, physics, theology, and poetry. He explored the symptoms of psychological depression, the uses of medicinal herbs, the importance of diet, contagious diseases and the use of quarantine to prevent their spread, and exercise and sleep to maintain good health. Avicenna's most well-known works, *The Book of Healing* and *The Canon of Medicine*, were used as standard texts in European medical schools until the eighteenth century. In *The Canon of Medicine,* he wrote:

> At the conclusion of the first day's exercise, you will know the degree of exercise allowable and when you know the amount of nourishment the person can bear, do not make any change in either on the second day. Arrange that the measure of aliment, and the amount of exercise shall not exceed that limit ascertained on the first day.

Avicenna's tomb stood in a cylindrical anteroom awash in light that spilled down from above. A gaggle of Koreans were milling around the interior, but not a word was spoken above the level of a whisper. Odd though it may have seemed, the scene represented true Persian values—a blending of spiritualism with the logic of science.

I tried to imagine what Avicenna would make of Iranian society today and, if it arrived at his office, what remedies he would recommend for its ills. Iran is certainly youthful—more than 65 percent of the population is under thirty-five—but behind this image of health and vigor hides a long list of ailments. It has vast natural resources aside from oil—natural gas, coal, chromium, copper, iron ore, lead, manganese, zinc, and sulfur—but much of its wealth has been siphoned by corrupt officials. The holdings of Ali Akbar Hashemi Rafsanjani, prominent cleric and former president, include interests in TV stations, mining companies, airlines, and petroleum engineering projects. And much of Iran's wealth has gone to maintain an extensive network of security services whose primary aim is to maintain power by keeping the population in check. To make matter's worse, since the 1979 Islamic Revolution many of Iran's brightest professionals have left to set up new lives in Canada, the United States, and Western Europe. And the clergy's enforced brand of Shiite Islam has alienated an entire generation from religion in any form.

Then there is the utter failure of belief in the government and the Islamic ideology it espouses. International news channels—BBC, CNN, Al Jazeera, Euronews—have become the only reliable conduits of information from the outside world. And there are the radio stations Voice of America and Radio Farda, the Iranian branch of Radio Liberty, both operated by the U.S. State Department. The depth of cynicism is so widespread that Supreme Leader Ayatollah Khamenei finally had to acknowledge it shortly before the 2013 presidential elections. In a desperate attempt to boost turnout, he urged all Iranians to vote "even if they did not support the Islamic regime."

Confronted with such a patient on his examining table, I could imagine Avicenna wringing his hands in despair: Where, oh, where to begin?

In the park outside the mausoleum I heard a voice calling my name. It was Sohrab, fresh from his late-afternoon tryst. He was sprightly and buoyant and said we had one more stop to make before the day was done, so we got in the car and headed out of town.

After we left the city the road crossed neatly tended fields of wheat and barley, and then began a gradual climb into the foothills of the Zagros Mountains. I asked where we were going, but Sohrab kept mum. The heat of the afternoon had broken, and cool evening air was sweeping down into the valley from the swards and gorges tucked in the clefts of the mountains. Sohrab asked me to change the CD in the car stereo, so I fished through the "banned" collection in the door pocket and put on *Chet Baker in Tokyo*. Chet's rhythms suited the hour, with the sun beginning its decline, deepening the hues in the grain fields, allowing the sky to acquire a darker blue. Then Sohrab finally told me where we were headed: Ganjnameh, and he gave me a brief history lesson as Chet's trumpet oozed from the car speakers.

Two cuneiform inscriptions, hammered into the side of a boulder at the base of ten-thousand-foot Mount Alvand, are the focal point of Ganjnameh. The texts, written in three languages—Babylonian, neo-Elamite, and ancient Persian—begin by praising the Zoroastrian god Ahuramazda, but then a bit of megalomania takes over, as Darius II, author of the first inscription, and his son Xerxes, author of the second, proclaim the supremacy of their rule over an empire that at the time was as vast as any the world had ever seen. A few centuries later, more mercenary-minded Persians, unfamiliar with ancient cuneiform, believed the letters contained the directions to a buried treasure. Hence the name of the site—Ganjnameh, or "treasure epistle."

It is an artifact of the Persian Empire, but today Ganjnameh serves the residents of Hamedan in another way. The chiseled boulder is close to a stream that courses through a valley on the side of Mount Alvand. Beyond the gate, walking paths lead along a gradually inclining slope to a rock-lined pool fed by a waterfall. Further on, the paths become hiking trails, transforming the park into another one of those places where Iranians can escape the suffocating presence of the government and imagine what it would be like to enjoy "normal life."

Sohrab dropped me at the entrance, where a row of souvenir stands sold drinks, snacks, and an array of bric-a-brac. With international tourism flattened since the 1979 revolution, internal tourism has taken up some of the slack, as Iranians unable to obtain visas for foreign countries satisfy any itch of wanderlust by traveling in their own country.

As Sohrab had said, it was the "perfect time of day" for Ganjnameh. The shade of the slopes stretched over the valley, and the park was filled with takht sitters, galyoon smokers, sippers of sweet tea, and guzzlers of Istak, a popular brand of nonalcoholic beer. Children romped, vendors hawked cigarettes and chewing gum, and young men sold fresh ears of sweet corn, roasted over small barbecue grills set up on the pavement.

I stopped to study the inscriptions, fifteen feet above the ground, and then walked up the path following the stream as it babbled past groups of eight, ten, and even more taking up entire takhts. Young couples discreetly snuggled, half-hidden by the boulders that lined the path. Even in such a secluded setting, none of the women were bold enough to remove their headscarves. This was not the more liberal Tehran, where bold women may risk challenging the regime with impunity—if they are discreet. Here the message of the roundabout had not been forgotten: We are *everywhere*, and you will not forget that we are *everywhere*.

At the end of the path a slender ribbon of water coursed from a cleft in the rocks and ended in a thunderous splash at the edge of the pool. Children played on the rocks along the water's edge, the colorful veils of the older girls drooping on their heads like wilted flowers.

I perched on a rock and soon struck up a conversation with Mohsen and Nasrin. It was Mohsen who broke the ice, asking the familiar question: "Where are you from?"

Mohsen and Nasrin were also visitors. They had left Iran shortly after the Islamic Revolution and lived in the United States for twenty-eight years, first in Washington DC, then Columbus, Ohio, and finally Nashville, Tennessee, where Mohsen ran a real estate business. Like many Iranian Americans, they returned every year to visit relatives, and each year Nasrin stayed behind a few months so their ten-year-old daughter, Golnaz, could attend an Iranian school to preserve her Farsi and gain firsthand knowledge of her parents' birthplace. For the first few years the arrangement had worked fine, but the parents had begun to have second thoughts.

"God, there's so much brainwashing," Mohsen complained. "We have to reteach half of what she's taught. Everything in our history is now seen through the influence of Islam. Everything begins and ends with Islam. Our society has never been like that. Sure, religion has been an important part, but it was never all of it. And it's getting worse. Those *bastards*, they're afraid of losing control. They know the young people are slipping away. Most of them are already lost—they have no belief in the regime or anything it stands for—so with the much younger ones, they just want to ram religion down their throats."

I had heard this often, that ever since the Islamic Revolution Iranian society had been plagued by what in the Western world might be called an identity crisis. No one could deny that Islam had been the dominant religious force for almost 1,500 years. After the Arab invasion, Zoroastrianism began to wither, and the Arabic alphabet replaced the Pahlavi script in which Farsi had previously been written, but Islam never carried the same cultural and social weight as it did in the Arab world. One could argue that Islam formed the basis of Arab culture, but one could never make this claim in Iran. Here Islam was an import, something forced upon the population, and so, despite its 1,500 years of existence, it still might be equated to a second language. The core of the Persian identity was still drawn from Zoroastrianism and the pre-Islamic social and political philosophies of Cyrus, Darius, and Xerxes. Even in the twenty-first century, Iran still adhered to the ancient Zoroastrian calendar, and the beginning of the year was marked by Noruz, the first day of spring, not the Islamic New Year nor the Gregorian January 1. Today it could even be said that "Persian" and "Iranian" described two conflicting identities, "Iran" becoming the formal name of the nation only in the mid-twentieth century. Yet, thirty-five years of full-throated Shiite Islam—and Shiite Islam as interpreted by the religious institutions in Qom—along with the disregard of the many other influences that shaped the Persian identity, have left many Iranians wondering: Who are we?

Golnaz returned from cavorting in the pool, thoroughly soaked, but in the warm dry air of the summer mountains her jeans and cotton top would be dry in an hour, or less. Mohsen and Nasrin asked me to join them on a takht for a round of Istaks—a sundowner Iranian style—and so we strolled down the path as Golnaz pranced ahead to fetch one of the roasted ears of corn, waving the 10,000-rial note Mohsen had given her.

We settled onto the *takht*, cold cans in hand. Fresh, moist air from the waterfall coursed through the canyon. The evening had cooled, preparing Mohsen and Nasrin for a sensitive question: I asked them if they thought Iran had been trying to build a nuclear weapon.

Mohsen shook his head, not in response but to dismiss the question entirely. "Are these leaders trying to build a bomb? Who knows? No one ever knows what they're thinking about anything. They are so divided and mixed up I'm amazed they can agree on anything."

Mohsen confirmed my suspicions, that the Islamic regime was so faction-ridden—with pragmatists and ideologues, hardliners and a few surviving moderates—that it was hard to see how it could agree on anything as decisive as the development of a nuclear weapon. A *civilian* nuclear program? Throughout Iran support for that was virtually unanimous. A *weapons* program? Expressions of opinion followed the common pattern of Persian debate—elliptical, equivocal, obtuse.

I asked Mohsen if Iran's history of invasions had shaped public opinion. Hamedan was a little too far east to have been ravaged by the Iran-Iraq War, but the martyr's murals were haunting reminders of the half million lives lost. And that war was only the latest installment in a series going back to the invasion of Alexander.

In classic Persian style, Mohsen didn't quite answer the question. "Both India and Pakistan have nuclear weapons, and everyone knows Israel does," he said. "I'm not saying that Iran should have them, but it's a little hard to argue that we shouldn't. The European countries have NATO. What do we have?"

It is not hard getting Iranians to talk. Many welcome the chance to swap views with foreigners, especially Westerners. They have a lot to get off their chests, and Westerners offer a welcome sounding board for all that ails Iran. But Mohsen and Nasrin were a special find: Iranians who had lived most of their lives in the West but still returned, to visit relatives, to ensure that their children acquired some familiarity with their ancestral homeland, to ensure that they themselves didn't lose touch with the social, historical, and cultural forces that had made them who they were. This prompted another question: How were they received when they returned? Was there any lingering friction with longtime friends or relatives who stayed in Iran after the revolution?

"When we get together, sometimes it comes up," Nasrin said, "but it never becomes something to argue about. We all made our decisions years ago and what's the point in bringing it all up, especially when our time together is so short?"

It is also not like Iranians to court conflict, I could have added, not with strangers, and certainly not with friends and family. I had noticed this often in Iranian movies: Situations that one would expect to boil over into open conflict, even violence, in a Western context simply simmered until the story moved on to the next scene. These always rang true as an accurate portrayal of the Iranian culture and one that defied the dictates of an art form that demanded conflict and confrontation in any form. But Mohsen broke with protocol. The conversation had turned to the subject of the regime, one that regularly tests Persian niceties. "Those *bastards* at the airport, sometimes they give us a hard time," he cut in. "When we return to Iran we use only our Iranian passports—that's all they're good for—but the immigration officials can tell that we don't live in Iran, that we're the ones who left and are just back for a visit. Our clothes, our body language, it all gives us away. Once one of those bastards said to me, 'Mr. Sarraf, when you come back you should also show us your *American* passport.' But that's nonsense. I don't have to show them anything but a valid passport—my Iranian one. And they know that. They say this just to intimidate us, to let us know they know that we live in the United States, that even if we think we've escaped, they know it, and they won't let us forget it."

Darkness was settling in, and Golnaz was beginning to nod off, so Mohsen and Nasrin told me it was time to head back to Hamedan, where they were staying with Nasrin's mother. Before they left they wished me a very pleasant stay in Iran and told me I should see some of the real country, not just tourist sites. Of course, I said—that's why I had come to Hamedan.

Hamedan may be a university town, but its choices for dining and nightlife are rather shabby, which means it is on par with most Iranian cities. When the Islamic Revolution banned alcohol, the lively nightlife that thrived in the days of the shah withered. Social life moved largely inside, to the private space of the home, where bootlegged alcohol could be drunk with abandon and the prying eyes of the dress police could not enforce the Islamic dress code. With the pickings for dinner rather slim, I set my sights on a restaurant a block off the central roundabout that a flyer in my hotel promised "authentic Persian cuisine."

After dark, Hamedan's streets don't come alive as much as they carry on the routines of the day. In Avicenna Square around the mausoleum of Avicenna, the leaves of the oak trees glimmered in the dim glow of the streetlights. A few of the book sellers still manned their posts, and one had set up a battery-operated light so passersby could browse his stock in the crisp evening air. Down the side streets some of the merchants kept their doors open, hoping to snag a few shoppers on a late-night prowl for anything from clothing to electronic goods.

Ayatollah Khomeini's face was still lit as I crossed the roundabout looking for "authentic Persian cuisine." The signs on the storefronts, written in Farsi, did not help. I thought I had taken a wrong turn and was heading back to the roundabout when a voice called out, "Can I help you?"

It was another young man about the age of Javad, tall and clean-cut, with the bookish look of the pseudo-intellectual who reads too much philosophy and political science. He crossed the street and asked if I was lost. I asked about the restaurant I was looking for, and he shook his head. It had closed a few months ago, he said, but he knew of another, also off the roundabout, and it had wonderful chicken and fish kebabs. The best in all of Hamedan, in fact, and he was just heading there. He told his name—Hamid. He was a research assistant in biochemistry at Hamedan University, and like many graduate students putting in late hours, he was having a late dinner as well.

All this could have been a setup, or Hamid could have been another tiresome leech looking for a way to hook a Westerner with the hope of snagging a Western visa, but it was getting late and I was hungry, and most important, he showed none of the caginess that reeked from Javad. He had an innocent face that suggested he was anything other than what he seemed—a well-educated Iranian who spoke competent English and had seized an opportunity to converse with a Western visitor.

Hamid led me around the corner and down a flight of stairs into a brightly lit dining room with cheery, canary yellow walls. We found a table, and a waiter took our orders, but Hamid was not going to wait for the food to arrive before serving up questions of his own: Why had I come to Iran? What were my impressions before arriving? What did I think of the country? Had my impressions changed?

My answers were appropriately bland because I still wasn't sure Hamid could be trusted. By the time our plates of fish kebabs arrived I was anxious to move on to questions of my own: What did he think of the state of the country? What could finally bring a change in the government? Would the election of Rouhani make any difference?

In answer, Hamid stabbed at his food, wondering where to begin. Anxiety creased his face. "You said you were here during the 2009 election. Did you see all the celebrations after the last one?"

I had. Crowds of horn-tooting revelers filled the squares in Tehran, and a few brave young women even tore off their veils and waved them in the air. It was the jubilation not of an election win but a homecoming parade, but at the same time it all seemed a little sad. Hassan Rouhani, former member of the Assembly of Experts and the Expediency Council, former head of the Supreme National Security

Council, once Iran's chief nuclear negotiator, had always been a regime man. That he took a softer line on some hardline issues—freedom of speech, Iran's relationship with the West, the loosening of social restrictions—was enough to win popular backing, and the hardest of hardliners were confident enough of their grip on power to allow his victory to stand, to throw this sop to the masses, knowing that they could keep him on a tight leash, and the masses had found such a grudging concession reason for celebration. This was as much of a victory as they could expect.

"They do this every time," an Iranian journalist told me. "Whenever the pressure from the people becomes too great they put a 'moderate' in power to let air out of the balloon. It was the same with Khatami. But whoever it is, he doesn't have any real power."

Even Hamid seemed fooled, not knowing he may have been the victim of another cynical, strategic shuffling of the cards.

"I'm glad," he said, with more resolution than satisfaction. "The whole world once again saw that we don't support this government, that we want real change."

If this had been my first conversation with an Iranian in Iran I would have been surprised that Hamid would express dissent so openly, but I was used to it. Everything he said was a mantra I had heard many times: The regime was stifling Iran. It didn't represent the Persian culture or the Iranian people. We will only find our way again once we get rid of the awful regime. And on and on and on.

The conversation was stirring Hamid's appetite. He asked the waiter for more saffron rice, and a moment later it arrived—an entire dinner plate topped with a smooth dome of rice as large as a basketball. I'd already had my fill of the mahi and salad and aash, so I was content to listen while Hamid picked at the rice mountain and blew off more steam.

"Are Americans really afraid of Iran?" he asked.

"A lot of them see it as a threat," I confessed.

"Why??"

"It all goes back to the hostage crisis, I think."

"But that was over almost forty years ago."

"Americans still haven't gotten over it. It's a wound that hasn't healed. And then came September 11, and Iran being part of the Muslim world hasn't helped. And then there's all the anti-American rhetoric coming from Tehran."

Hamid shook his head in disappointment and stabbed despairingly at his remaining *mahi* and the rice he had loaded onto his plate.

"That's so sad," he said. "They think we're primitive people, like the Taliban, but we're not. We've had a long history of civilization, longer than Western civilization. This may sound strange, but we really admire the U.S. We really do. We want the same things."

His view was not surprising. Many Iranians feel a subliminal connection to the U.S., and favorability ratings of the U.S. among Iranians have long run at 70 to 80 percent, long the highest in the Middle East. But could the U.S. and Iran be brothers in aims, if not arms? I asked Hamid to explain.

"We want freedom, democracy."

Another refrain. Often when Iranians talked about what they wanted for their country it was expressed as a simple wish: "To be a democratic country—like the U.S." or "Freedom—like you have in the U.S." Every time I heard it I thought of the gypsy curse: May you get what you want. There was never any explanation of the kind of democracy they wanted, or a discussion of the headaches that "freedom" brings. Freedom and democracy were stars at the end of a magic wand that when waved would make everything right, and America was the omnipotent wizard who held the wand.

There was still half a dome of rice on the plate, but even Hamid had had his fill. The bill came, and he insisted on paying it, which was expected, and any squabble over it would have been useless. Back out on the street, Hamid continued to plead his case for Iran.

"There are so many talented people in this country," he said. "But look at the condition it is in. We could be as strong as any country in Europe, even as strong as the U.S., if we didn't have this system that holds us back. It doesn't look to the future. It doesn't care about the people. All it cares about is holding on to power."

I agreed, not to be gracious, but because I also believed him. So much of the country's wealth had been diverted to support its sprawling and intrusive security services, so much of the attention of its leaders was focused on suppressing dissent rather than economic development, so many of the educated youth had left the country or were aiming to leave as soon as an opportunity arrived. Did this cause the leaders any loss of sleep? Hardly. Educational standards in Iran were so high that the emigrants—potential troublemakers, in the regime's view—could always be replaced. Any brain drain did not seem to concern them at all. But the way things were going, without any change in sight, it was likely that many of the next generation would follow the example of the present one. The brains would continue to drain from Iran.

It was nearing midnight, but lights still burned in the windows of the sweetshops, and a few late-night customers were on their way home, clutching gift-wrapped boxes of saffron cookies and *gaz*, a toffee-like candy filled with nuts. Hamid and I parted, and like Javad, and Mohsen and Nasrin, he wished me a very pleasant stay in Iran.

I crossed the roundabout and was heading in the direction of the hotel when something felt odd. I looked back and saw that the lights illuminating the grim face of Khomeini on the metal relief had finally gone dark. But still he would not disappear. When cars circled the roundabout their headlights illuminated him, but only for a moment. Then he would retreat into the darkness, only to reemerge, like a persistent flame that refused to be snuffed out. He was still watching, and he would not let me or any of the residents of Hamedan forget it.

Fig. 1. Tower of chocolate at refreshment stand, Saad Abad Palace Complex, North Tehran. A former forested retreat in the days of the shah, the area is now a popular walking area and home to numerous museums.

Fig. 2. (*opposite top*) Tile painting, Golestan Palace, Tehran. Persian art departs from Islamic strictures, which prohibit the depiction of living forms.

Fig. 3. (*opposite bottom*) Courtyard of Imanzadeh Saleh Shrine, North Tehran. The shrine stands next to one of the city's most popular bazaars and the end of one line of the Tehran metro.

Fig. 4. (*above*) Troglodyte village of Kandovan. Residents of the region hid in the rocky hills to escape the Mongol invasion in the thirteenth century, which devastated much of Iran.

Fig. 5. (*above*) Taq-e Bostan, Kermanshah. The rock relief sculptures were carved during the fourth-century Sassanid period to celebrate the glories of the dynasty.

Fig. 6. (*opposite top*) Iwan of the Blue Mosque, Tabriz. An earthquake in 1780 severely damaged the building, under reconstruction since 1973.

Fig. 7. (*opposite bottom*) Entrance to the mausoleum of Ayatollah Khomeini, Tehran. At night the bright green lights illuminate a dark landscape on the highway between Imam Khomeini International Airport and the city.

Fig. 8. (*opposite top*) Fruit vendor, Qazvin. Although Western-style supermarkets abound in every city, the freshest fruits and vegetables are still found the old-fashioned way.

Fig. 9. (*opposite bottom*) Courtyard, Golestan Palace, Tehran. The palace represents a combination of artistic styles, from strict interpretations of Islamic design to nineteenth-century European Romanticism.

Fig. 10. (*above*) Fin Garden, Kashan. Built by Shah Abbas, the site served as his sylvan retreat, but in the nineteenth century it became the spot of the assassination of Amir Kabir, one of Iran's modernizing rulers.

Fig. 11. Entrance to the tomb of Ferdowsi, Tous. Ferdowsi is to Iran what Homer is to the Greeks and Shakespeare to the British: the country's national bard. Ferdowsi arguably saved the Persian language from Arabization when he wrote his epic poem, the *Shahnameh*.

Fig. 12. (*top*) Imam Mosque, Esfahan. The enormous square in front of the mosque is the most pleasant place in the city to relax on a summer evening.

Fig. 13. (*bottom*) Children playing in pool, Naqsh-e Jahan Square, Esfahan. The surrounding square is the second-largest public space in the world, after Tiananmen Square in Beijing.

Fig. 14. Elderly couple, Abyaneh. Abyaneh is one of the traditional villages of rural Iran and a popular weekend getaway destination.

Fig. 15. Dome of Soltaniyeh, Zanjan Province. The third-largest dome in the world, after the Aya Sofya in Istanbul and the Cathedral of Santa Maria del Fiore in Florence, Italy.

Fig. 16. (*above*) Road from Chalous to Tehran through the Alborz Mountains. The area is dotted with ski resorts that Tehranis flock to in the winter.

Fig. 17. (*opposite top*) Carpet merchants, Tabriz carpet bazaar. The city is one of the carpet-making centers of Iran.

Fig. 18. St. (*opposite bottom*) Stepanos Monastery, Aras Valley, on the border with Azerbaijan. The complex is not only a UNESCO World Heritage site but one of the officially designated historic churches of Iran.

Fig. 19.(*above*) Courtyard wall, restored Ameri House, Qajar era, Kashan. Five of these houses are now open to visitors. During the nineteenth century they were owned primarily by wealthy merchants.

Fig. 20. (*opposite top*) Khaju Bridge at sunset, Esfahan. Esfahan's bridges are the city's signature sight. All were built during the rule of Shah Abbas in the sixteenth century, in his effort to unify the sprawling city.

Fig. 21. (*opposite bottom*) Azadi Tower, Tehran. Originally named the Shahyad Tower when it was built in 1971 to commemorate the 2,500th anniversary of the Persian Empire.

Fig. 22. (*top*) Pedestrian shopping street, Rasht. The center of the city is a designated pedestrian zone, which includes a park and promenade in front of the Qajar-era city hall and its signature clock tower.

Fig. 23. (*bottom*) Tomb of Hafez, Shiraz. A copy of the works of Iran's greatest and most popular poet can be found in almost every household.

Fig. 24. (*top*) Imanzadeh Hossein Mausoleum, Qazvin. Shrines to Shiite notables are spread throughout Iran. Many major cities have one.

Fig. 25. (*bottom*) Christmas tree and holiday visitors, Sarkis Cathedral, Tehran. The complex is one of several gathering points of Iran's Armenian community. Beyond its walls the Tehran traffic rushes by on busy Karimkhan Boulevard.

Fig. 26. (*above*) Façade of Sarkis Cathedral, Tehran. Named after Saint Sarkis, the church is the center for the Armenian Diocese of Tehran.

Fig. 27. (*opposite top*) Tabatabaei House, Kashan. Another restored house that was owned by the city's wealthy merchants in the nineteenth century.

Fig. 28. (*opposite bottom*) Restored Sultan Amir Ahmed Bathhouse, Kashan. Like elsewhere in the Middle East, the bathhouse in Iran was the focal point of social life, where business was conducted and gossip exchanged.

Fig. 29. (*above*) Rooftops of Masouleh, Gilan Province. The town was constructed on a steep hillside so that the roof of one house became the aerial terrace of the hill above it.

Fig. 30. (*opposite top*) Farmhouse, Gilan Rural Heritage Museum, Rasht. Eighty structures from various provinces have been relocated to this open-air museum to preserve Iran's rural tradition.

Fig. 31. (*opposite bottom*) Mullah in the courtyard of a madresse (religious school), Esfahan. The city is well known for its centers of Islamic learning, giving it a reputation as one of Iran's more conservative cities.

Fig. 32. Relief sculptures, Persepolis. The processional staircase is one of the highlights of the ancient site, and its relief carvings are some of the finest and most well preserved in Iran.

7 | Kashan

COURT OF THE QAJARS

We need food to maintain life, but exceeding
　　what we need destroys us.
Rose-water pastry when you're not hungry
　　will torture your belly,
but the driest bread after fasting tastes like
　　rose-water pastry.
　　　　　　　—Saadi, *Gulistan*

It felt like a game of peek-a-boo. I was about to take a picture of the entrance of the Borujerdiha, a restored nineteenth-century house tucked into one of the backstreets of Kashan, when a young woman stuck her head out of a doorway halfway down the street. She saw that she had caught my eye, and instantly she knew what I knew—that I had become an object of curiosity, and this so spooked her that she quickly retreated to the protection of the doorway. I turned away, pretended to take a photo, and another, and then she was back again. I faked another photo, lazily turned to look down the street, and aimed my camera in her direction—but not discreetly enough. Again she disappeared. I turned back to the Borujerdiha, faked a few more photos, and again she appeared, but this time with another woman about the same age. Her sister? A cousin? Friend? It didn't matter. They were all smiles and

giggles, struggling to straighten their slipping headscarves as they gig-
gled and ogled from halfway down the street.

After a couple of months in Iran I was used to being the object of
attention in regional cities and highway stops all over the country, but
I had never experienced anything like this. It was all the more unusual
because of Kashan's reputation as a bastion of social, religious, and, of
course, political conservatism. Kashan was not Qom or the southern,
working-class neighborhoods of Tehran, where the sight of women
donning full chadors is not unusual, but nor do the women of Kashan
seek out the most form-fitting manteaux and purposely allow their
scarves to slip off the backs of their heads, like the "liberal elites" of
North Tehran.

The game of peek-a-boo continued. The women emerged from the
doorway, each time more boldly, smiles and giggles bubbling from
their faces, but after a while it was clear that they had had their fun or
were too bashful to take it a step further. And so they disappeared. It
was disappointing, but I was also relieved. It was fascinating to imagine how long this could go on and what it might lead to—an invitation for coffee? But the street was blazing hot and the interior of the
Borujerdiha awaited.

This was my introduction to Kashan, where an air of modest tradi-
tionalism is de rigueur. It might be argued that Kashan's strain of tra-
ditionalism is linked to its reputation as a center for the production of
high-quality arts and crafts. From 1796 to 1925, which marks the reign
of the Qajar dynasty, high-quality pottery and enamelwork, textiles
and carpets, metal products and other handicrafts were churned out
of workshops that filled backstreets like the one I was standing in. This
brought enormous wealth to the city's merchants, who rewarded themselves by constructing grand, spacious homes like the Borujerdiha.
So voluminous was their production that much of it traveled along
the trade routes that passed through central Iran, linking Kashan with
Afghanistan and Asia to the east, and Turkey and Europe to the west.
The name Kashan became synonymous with the highest-quality craftwork produced not only in Iran but the greater Middle East. Enter the

Middle Eastern gallery of almost any art museum in the world, read the name cards identifying the origins of the items in the display cases, and you will find that many of them read, "Kashan, Iran."

The neighborhood of the Borujerdi was the gentrified quarter of nineteenth-century Kashan. Four more merchant houses were a stone's throw away—the Manouchehri, the Attarha, the Tabatabaei, and the Ameri. Eclecticism was not a feature of Qajar-era Kashan. All the houses had been built according to the same plan, making the architect's job easy but shutting down any imaginative flights of fancy. Houses from the Qajar era were not the single-block units one expects today, but quadrangles of rooms circling a central courtyard, where the main feature is a rectangular pool lined with flower beds. This way there would be no squabbling over choice space—every room could boast a poolside view. A salon and reception area lay at one end of the courtyard.

The Qajar house was actually two—a duplex in modern terms. There is the *andaruni*, the inner, private quarters for members of the immediate family, and next to it the more lavish *biruni*, intended to impress visitors and guests. Passageways connect the two, so servants can zip back and forth when needed, and family members can easily move from one side of the complex to the other.

I passed through the entrance of the Borujerdiha, imagining what it would have been like to have visited here 150 or 200 years ago, when Kashan was a buzzing trade center and merchants like Hajj Seyed Jafar Natanzi, who built the Borujerdiha, spent their time schmoozing with business partners and totaling the day's transactions. But I would not have been a potential business partner, client, or supplier. I would have been a visitor from abroad, and in nineteenth-century Qajar Iran, this meant Hajj Natanzi would have pulled out all the stops.

In Iran, hospitality is not a virtue, nor an obligation. It is a first cousin of religious belief, and many Persians would argue that its protocols are far more important than the fatwas read out by high-minded mullahs. And so, in Qajar-era Iran, as I entered the Borujerdiha, a servant would have greeted me in the anteroom with *"Ghodem ru cheshem,"* which loosely translates as "You may step on my eye," which means that the host is so pleased with my visit that I may do the unthinkable. The imagery may not be appealing, but it is the sentiment that is intended to touch the visitor.

Not being a member of the family, I would not have been invited to see the andaruni, but it would not have been a great disappointment, for the living spaces were near mirror images of one another, differing only in extravagance of décor. As a guest, I would see the best of what Hajj Natanzi has to offer. One end of the courtyard is dominated by an iwan, or arched portal, which resembles the proscenium of a theater stage. It is colorful and intricately painted, and on the other side lies the *talar*, or main salon of the entire compound.

This is where the man who greeted me at the door would lead me and where my host would await. Hajj Natanzi welcomes me with an odd combination of formality and warmth, sprinkled with inquiries about my trip to Kashan and how I have enjoyed the city and endless other pleasantries that might seem a bit overdone to a foreigner but all-too-apropos for a fellow Persian, for they are as inherent to the meet-and-greet as a handshake is in the West. Still today a greeting between Iranians may take a few minutes as all the formalities are exchanged.

I have done my homework and have prepared for my arrival with two gifts for Hajj Natanzi—a bouquet of flowers and a box of sweets. They have been carefully chosen, but I remark that they are woefully inadequate and ask my host to accept them nonetheless. As expected, he replies that he is honored, and goes on to excuse the appearance of his house, and hopes that I will find it comfortable enough for as long as I will honor him with a visit. As expected, I reply that it is beautiful and had never set my expectations so high. This is the practice of *taarof*, far more central to Persian social protocol than any smile or hand-shake. It is self-effacing humility doubling as a form of flattery. When Hajj Natanzi offers me tea, of course I must refuse. It is the appropri-ate taarof reply, not because I wouldn't prefer a cup of tea, but I don't want to put him through the trouble. Of course Hajj Natanzi insists, claiming that serving it will bring him great pleasure. Only then will I accept, not because I am eager for a cup of tea, which really makes no difference. What matters is that I do not want to deny him the pleasure of looking after me—another lesson in taarof.

Since I am a guest, and a guest from far away, I am given a place of honor, with the best view of the talar and the five stained-glass windows facing the courtyard. Paintings on the walls of royal princes and sinewy women in swirling white gowns illustrate the influence of European Romanticism that passed into Iran during the Qajar era. There are also hunting scenes, with deer and foxes prancing through forests, birds in full plumage in flight, and perched on tree limbs. In many parts of the Islamic world these paintings would be considered *haram*, or forbidden, because they violate a central tenet of Islam that prohibits the representation of living creatures. But when Islam was brought to Iran, many of its strictures were put aside, or simply ignored, to accommodate Islam into Persian culture, and this more casual approach to visual depiction was one of them.

For commentators on Persian history the Qajar era generally receives mixed reviews. On the one hand, the Qajar rulers were not in any way cultural isolates, and this led to increasing modernization of Iranian society. Throughout the nineteenth century, traders, military experts, and even missionaries were drawn to Iran, bringing with them new technologies, such as the telegraph and railroad service, as well as cultural influences from the European Romantic movement. Landscapes and floral designs became popular subjects for Persian artists, and portrait painting featured commoners rather than royalty, along with women clothed in Western dress. On the downside, spats with Russia led to a series of humiliating wars that began in 1804 and ended in 1820, with Qajar rulers yielding their Caucasian territories—present-day Georgia, Armenia, and Azerbaijan—to the Russian Empire.

Despite the European influence on Qajar art, the interior of the Borujerdiha is quintessentially Persian. The décor of the talar is tasteful but restrained. What is most noticeable is the absence of large pieces of furniture. There are no tables, padded armchairs, crystal lamps, or massive armoires. The room is lined with sofas and cushions for relaxing, and a few low tables to place odds and ends. When the food comes, and it will, in keeping with the requirements of Qajar hospitality, it is laid on a cloth spread over a hand-woven carpet in the middle of the room, and we will sit on the floor around the serving trays. And come it does, and when it does it is enough to feed a caravan. Hajj Natanzi makes a half-hearted apology, expressing the wish that I will find both the quality and quantity sufficient—more taarof. The only utensils we use are a spoon and fork. No knives are needed because—in Persian fashion—the chunks of lamb and chicken have been stewed to a degree of tenderness that they can be pulled apart without being cut.

Today's Iranians may dine at tables and use the occasional knife; men and women will socialize together, comfortably, in public and private; and rare is the house that is home to all the members of an extended family, but it is still surprising the extent to which many of the age-old social habits live on in the present. No Iranian would think of accepting an invitation without bringing a gift to the host. And in any social encounter, the formalities of conversation, which usually include scripted questions and equally scripted responses, can be endless, and expressions of taarof come in ever handy to smooth over the rough spots.

With food still left on my plate, and barely a dent made in the piles on the serving trays, I inform Hajj Natanzi, respectfully, that it is time to leave, but not without an expression of regret that I could not stay longer—more and more taarof. Hajj Natanzi assures me that he will be a much better host the next time, and after a few more expressions of taarof—"I did not even expect this much"—"You are too kind"—one of the servants shows me to the door, but before leaving I make sure to offer Hajj Natanzi a final "*Khoda hafez*" ("May God be with you").

Back on the street in present-day Kashan, the punishing sun burned away the inner cool and hospitality of the Borujerdiha. Sohrab knew of a place to beat the heat, so we piled into the car and headed to Fin Garden, built by Shah Abbas I on the outskirts of Kashan at the beginning of the seventeenth century. Later, a fortress-like wall, complete with watchtowers, was added to further isolate the green preserve from the edge of the city. The garden also had a theological purpose.

Still today, traditional Iranian gardens are divided into quadrants to represent the four gardens of Paradise, referred to in the Quran. But when Islam arrived in Iran in the seventh century, certain elements of the new faith were added to the much older Zoroastrian beliefs, and if we were to follow the origins of the Persian garden all the way back to Cyrus the Great, we'd find that the same four quadrants stood for the holy elements of earth, wind, water, and fire.

All this is moot to any visitor to Fin Garden today. Any past quibbles are dissolved by the beauty of the setting. Tall cypress trees rise high above the garden floor, where flowering plants are bisected by canals (*qanats*) lined with turquoise tiles that both reflect the color of the sky and accent the hue of the water that flows through them. In midsummer the color palette is dominated by deep green, but depending on the time of year the garden may be bursting with the colors of jasmine, violets, tulips, and lilies, irises and roses, persimmons and eglantine. In autumn, apple and cherry trees are heavy with fruit. In every season the aromas of the flowers spill into the air and the cypress boughs sway in the afternoon breeze.

Its history aside, the Fin Garden is the best place in Kashan to escape on a hot summer day. Young women in form-fitting manteaux remove their shoes to bathe their feet in the cool, clear mountain water that enters the qanats from a fountain in the middle of the garden—the final leg of a journey that begins far outside Kashan in the Karkas Mountains. Children barely out of diapers splash and cavort in the qanats and the small pool around the fountain, their laughter mingling with the bubbling of the water.

I walked around the grounds and had a look at the central pavilion and its beautifully painted dome. Then I sat beside one of the qanats, took off my shoes, and plopped my feet in the water. Almost at once my toes were numb. I let them absorb the shock of the cold as I took in the peace of the setting. It didn't take long to realize that the purpose of the garden, with its beauty and geometric harmony, was to fuse the two—artistic beauty and mathematical perfection—and this is what the mind and spirit were meant to find when removed from the cares of the day. The fragility of this private state was reflected in the walls that surrounded the garden and the towers that protected it.

I took a few petals from a nearby rosebush, crumbled them between my fingers, and dropped them in the water. Some rode the mini-rivulet as it ambled along the qanat; others were caught between my toes. I didn't know if the bush I had plucked them from was the special Mohammadi Rose, but if it was, the qanat was now carrying the rose water that has long been a special product of Kashan, continuing a Persian tradition dating back 2,500 years.

Along with its sensory appeal, the medicinal benefits of rose water have been celebrated not only in Persian culture but in India, Pakistan, Malaysia, and the Arab Middle East. For example, if I were having trouble sleeping I could take rose water to ease me into the land of dreams. If my insomnia produced headaches, rose water would help relieve them. If anxiety over headaches and my insomnia gave me heart palpitations, rose water could restore me to a more even keel. In old age, rose water could soothe my rheumatism as well as any depression that rheumatism or old age might bring on. And if my eating habits gave me diarrhea, a regular intake of rose water could restore me to gastrointestinal health. If that weren't enough, a touch of sugar added to rose water would yield rosewater syrup, to sweeten desserts such as rice pudding, nougat cakes, and the Indian favorite, *gulab jamun*.

At the moment I wasn't suffering from any of those ailments, so I had no use for the impromptu rose water running over my feet except to enjoy its cooling effect, which was more than enough. But as I watched it rippling along the qanat, I wondered if I might have grasped some of the essence of Zoroastrianism. The holy elements that Zoroastrianism singles out are all really one, or various manifestations of a Single One. Similarly, the senses of sight and hearing, touch, taste, and smell are different but equal ways of perceiving the world. And to carry this a bit further, both the natural and spiritual worlds are complementary manifestations of a Single One. I pondered this as my toes turned white and concluded that, even if none of these thoughts had anything to do with Zoroastrianism, they were, at the very least, a soothing way to escape the heat, and if some of their soothing effect made it from the mind to the body it was all for the good.

In such a setting, with sunlight dappling through the trees, and cool, clear water rippling over my feet, I almost forgot that Fin Garden was also the site of one of the most infamous crimes in Persian history. It was one that could have been scripted by Shakespeare—the assassination of Amir Kabir, the nineteenth-century prime minister and leading reformer who took bold steps to modernize Iran and suffered the consequences.

The story of Amir Kabir is the kind of rags-to-riches tale that would find a welcome home in American mythology. Born Mirza Taghi Khan Farahani in today's province of Markazi, Amir Kabir's start in life was as modest as modest could be. His father worked as a cook for a local official, Mirza Aboul, but moved to Tabriz when Aboul was reassigned to the northwestern province. There, Amir Kabir was put to work as a domestic helper in Aboul's household. Aboul soon noticed the boy's quickness of mind and decided to educate him alongside his own children. Amir Kabir grabbed the opportunity, continued to excel, and was eventually made the supervisor of Mirza Aboul's stables. He then made the leap to government service, finding a niche as a reliable bureaucrat, first becoming the registrar for the Azerbaijan army and later overseer of the all the army's finances.

Amir Kabir's career then turned to foreign affairs. He spent almost a year in Russia on a diplomatic mission, which gave him the opportunity to see up close the advances in military, economic, and administrative life that had been taking place in the Russian Empire. He then spent four years in Erzurum, Turkey, at a time when the Ottoman Empire was undertaking many reforms in its military and government bureaucracy. His experience in Turkey taught him a lesson he would have great difficulty applying to today's Iran: "The Ottoman government was able to begin reviving its power only after breaking the power of the mullahs," he wrote.

Two hundred years earlier, Peter the Great, imperial Russia's first modernizer, took several trips through Western Europe to study the advances in science, education, engineering, and judicial practices that had been sweeping the continent and returned home intent on pushing a backward, agrarian, peasant-dominated Russia into the modern era, and he imported European expertise back to Russia to speed the path. Amir Kabir followed in Peter's footsteps. In 1851 he founded Dar ul-Funun to teach courses in advanced sciences, with most of the professors imported from the Austro-Hungarian Empire. Long before the era of the internet, he started the newspaper *Vaqaye-ye Ettefaqiyeh* to disseminate information about scientific developments and global events to the people. To increase agricultural production he encouraged the cultivation of sugarcane in the province of Khuzestan. He also encouraged the planting of cotton, one of the world's most profitable cash crops, imported from the United States. He built factories for the production of housewares, carriages, textiles, and other consumer goods, and raised taxes on imports to nurture the growth of the new domestic industries.

The sweep and pace of Amir Kabir's reforms was certain to step on sensitive toes. As part of his economic reforms he reduced the salaries paid to civil servants, who had long enjoyed do-nothing sinecures, but even more challenging was his effort to cut the handouts paid to members of the monarchy. He also sent tax collectors around the country to shake overdue revenues out of local governors and tribal chiefs. Anger mounted. Disempowered elites resented his rapid rise to power and revolutionary approach to change. A cabal of conspirators was formed, headed by the Queen Mother, a collection of grumbly princes, and the royal accountant. The Queen Mother persuaded her teenage son and the current shah, Nasser Al-Din, to clip Amir Kabir's wings. To do his mother's bidding, Nasser Al-Din first stripped Amir Kabir of his powers and later arrested and expelled him from Tehran, to be held in de facto imprisonment in Fin Garden. But Amir Kabir's isolation was not enough to make the royal family feel secure. The Queen Mother convinced her son that Amir Kabir was plotting to regain power, perhaps through connections with the Russian Empire, and so on January 10, 1852, a gang cornered him in the garden's bathhouse—the location of choice for political assassinations—and stabbed him to death.

Fin's bathhouse no longer functions but is open to visitors, so I dried my feet and walked over to have a look. No monument or plaque memorializes the site, an indication of the government's reluctance to lionize a former leader primarily remembered for his attempt to upend the status quo. Only a modest sign at the entrance stated that it was the scene of one of the most infamous events in Iranian political history. The inside of the bathhouse shows no sign of restoration or even minimal upkeep. One is even left to guess where the assassination took place—for fear it might become a place of pilgrimage and revive revolutionary sentiments.

A century and a half after his death, Amir Kabir still remains a threat to the status quo. The proof is in the feeble acknowledgment of what took place in Fin Garden and the impact it had on Iranian history. Many claim that with Amir Kabir's death the pernicious practice of government perks and culture of entitlement that had long strangled Iranian society were allowed to continue, and the fruits of the assassination can be found in the widespread corruption, interweaving of business and political power, and lining of pockets from government coffers that still continues. It is what many Iranians complain about more than the government's repressive laws and the limits on personal freedom—the pilfering of the nation's wealth and culture of cronyism that has hampered Iran's development for nearly four decades. Walk the streets of Tehran or any other city, step over broken pavement that has not been replaced in too many years, pass through parks that receive minimal upkeep, and one gets a mere glimpse into the ways in which Iranian society has been starved of much-needed rials to keep it going. Combined with atrocious economic mismanagement, this has stifled the country more than censorship, gender segregation, and its arcane restrictions on dress.

It was time to go. We would not be staying in Kashan that night, Sohrab told me. He had worked in a diversion to the traditional mountain village of Abyaneh, south of Kashan and nestled at the end of the long, fertile Borzrud Valley. On the way we had one stop to make, the regional center for pottery, ceramics, and other crafts that had made the Kashan region famous.

We hustled out of town along a dusty, two-lane road that cut across the edge of the dry plain that begins where the city of Kashan ends. Sohrab was true to his word. The main street was lined with pottery workshops and showrooms to peddle the wares produced by the local craftsmen. We saw a sign that advertised handmade pottery and pulled up to the door, but inside it was dark and quiet. We guessed that the potter and his crew had taken a long lunch break to beat the heat. But tacked to the wall was a faded campaign poster that showed that Kashan was still Ahmadinejad country: The former president beamed squinty-eyed and raised a fist to rally his faithful. But it was all for naught. In his tumultuous eight years in office the firebrand hardliner had made so many internal enemies, with his grandstanding style, his reckless pronouncements on affairs both domestic and international, that he had been barred from running again in the 2017 elections, and so his gesture fell flat, as political gestures do when changing times render them a relic of a former one.

We cruised the main street and had better luck at the other end of town. Inside another shop the smell of wet clay filled the reception area, which functioned as a combination workshop, showroom, and salesroom. At one of the wheels in the corner of the room the head potter was at work, turning sodden lumps of clay into common bowls and slender vases and pitchers with graceful spouts and handles. The creation of each took a few minutes. As soon as the clay was slapped onto the wheel his hands went to work, guiding the glop of goop into the shape of a pitcher with an S-shaped handle and a beak-like spout. Then he used a wooden stick to coax the clay into decorative whorls and ribs as the wheel spun. As we watched, he made three or four pitchers, each in the span of a minute or two, transforming the hunks of clay into functional objects that could arguably be called works of art, once the finishing touches were applied.

There was more. We went downstairs, to where the clay was subjected to the heat of the furnace and the finishing touches were applied. Wooden skids stacked with newly formed vases awaited the heat, and as we watched, Farhad, the forger and decorator, subjected one of the vases to the 2,000-degree oven and then sat down to add the artistic flourishes to one of the already hardened pieces.

The setting, the grimy basement on a dusty main drag, was unusual for what was taking place: Farhad, both resident Vulcan and Michelangelo, propped one of the vases on his knee to complete the transformation. Fine black outlines delineated the boundaries of flowers and spirals and curves that formed the pattern that circled the vase. These he applied with surgical care. Then came the colors: bright yellow and pale blue, splashes of indigo, and an occasional pink highlight were stroked and dabbed into the carefully sketched outlines.

As Farhad worked on one of the pieces, he asked, with little fanfare, where I was from. I told him, and he beamed—but only slightly. His was not the dumbfounded awe of foreigners, Westerners, and especially Americans, that one often is greeted with. Farhad was not awed. He was used to meeting foreigners. Americans, however, were another matter. Mounted on the wall was a telephone, and scrawled all over the wall were phone numbers with international prefixes, some stretching to nine and ten digits. These were left by visitors, Farhad explained. He had collected numbers from all over the world—Japan and Germany, Brazil and Russia—but he had no phone number from America. He asked me to add mine and said that if I did he would be honored. I didn't have the heart to tell him I hadn't lived in the U.S. for several years and no longer had an American phone number. That would never do. So I took the pen hanging from a string tied to a nail and scribbled the last number I had in the U.S., being sure to include two zeroes and the number 1 country code to show that it was, if anyone doubted, a bona fide American phone number.

Now that Farhad had his American phone number, I asked him when he discovered he had an artist's touch and wanted to pursue pottery painting as a career.

When he was a boy, he said. He loved to paint objects, never images on canvas or a drawing board, only objects, like the ones stacked by the palette-load and awaiting his brush.

Why not paintings, miniatures—Iran had a long history of miniature painting?

He liked the three dimensions, he said, rotating the object and seeing it from different angles. Then there was no front or back, no two views the same.

I asked him how long it would take to finish the vase he was working on. He looked at a paint-spattered clock nearby. It was getting late to finish it by day's end, he said, but by midmorning the next day the once bare shaft of dark orange clay would be transformed into a fine piece of decorative art, or, depending on the admirer, a work of art itself.

I thanked Farhad for his time, the demonstration, and the nugget of insight into his craft, but before I left he had a question: "How can I get a visa to the U.S.?" Farhad had a brother living in Canada, and he had thought of trying to migrate there, but if he chose to leave Iran his sights were set on the U.S.

I didn't want to tell him that his chances of ever being granted even a tourist visa to the U.S. were next to none, so I chose a selective truth: that his talents would be widely admired in the U.S., that there was a great interest in crafts and art from all over the world. And so I danced around the matter, claiming, with semi-honesty, but more than semi-guilt, that I didn't know all that much about American immigration law or any of the arcane regulations of the massive U.S. government bureaucracy, but I could wish him all the best.

This was always one of the most difficult experiences traveling in Iran: listening to the hopes of so many Iranians to migrate to their "dreamland," as one woman told me, while disguising the searing truth—that what they longed for was almost certainly beyond their reach. It was a slight consolation knowing that life in the U.S. would almost never live up to the fairytale that Iranians like Farhad imagined. In their eyes "America" was everything Iran was not and everything they wanted it to be—an open, secular, liberal society that cherished "freedom"—in thought, behavior, and expression—a land unencumbered by the weight of history, invasions, and the insults of geopolitics, a land where opportunities for economic and social mobility were limitless. In many ways this image of what America stood for was little different from those of many others around the world driven by the need to envision an earthly paradise that might provide a release from all their woes. I even often thought it might be better that they never did get to America, that to live with an unfulfilled hope, no matter how illusory, was far better than to face the disillusion of seeing their dreams, so long nurtured, only shattered, like one of Farhad's choice vases.

8 | Abyaneh

HEADING FOR THE HILLS

He who wants a rose must respect the thorn.
—Persian proverb

It was late in the afternoon by the time Sohrab and I headed out of Farhad's workshop. The afternoon heat was beginning to lift and the slanting rays of the sun deepened on the sand-colored façades. We got back in Sohrab's Volvo and after an hour entered a valley to begin a long, slow rise into the foothills of the Zagros Mountains. Willow and poplar trees lined the road as it angled around the curves that clung to the hills on the north side of the valley. I rolled down my window to catch the mountain breeze, beginning to blow fresh and crisp now that the plain was quickly receding behind us. It was time for music, so Sohrab dug into his stash of CDs and popped Dexter Gordon's *Round Midnight* into the dashboard player.

After a series of twists and turns we arrived at a cemetery belonging to a village that had been built on the hillside between the road and the valley below. I had visited cemeteries in other parts of the Muslim world but never a Persian one, so I asked Sohrab to pull over to have a look.

The graves were simple, unadorned slabs of white stone lying almost at ground level, with little more for a marker than another upright stone engraved with the date of birth and death of the deceased, almost always accompanied by a few lines of poetry. Sometimes these were the words of the great poets—Hafez, Saadi, Omar Khayyam—sometimes they were crafted by the family members themselves. In this predominantly Muslim cemetery one stone bore an engraving of Ahura Mazda, the deity of Zoroastrianism, and below this the last words that the loved ones wished to offer to the deceased:

> *I was told that you left and this was not welcome.*
> *You responded that it was fate.*
> *May his soul rest in peace and paradise be his home.*

I was surprised that a Zoroastrian would be permitted to lie beside his Muslim neighbors for all eternity, but Sohrab said that this was not uncommon. Religious minorities usually have their own burial grounds, but in small villages where there aren't enough Zoroastrians, or Christians, or Jews, to warrant a separate cemetery, they will be laid near the neighbors with whom they had shared their entire earthly lives.

We wandered some more. The words on another stone began: "The resting place of my caring father," and then continued with Ali, the father, speaking from the grave:

> *Alas, there is no life in my body anymore.*
> *The only thing I need is forgiveness.*
> *Father and brothers, think of me.*
> *I left life on a long journey from which there is no return.*

The plea for forgiveness was slightly unusual, for in the Persian tradition it is the living who seek forgiveness from the deceased. Perhaps Ali had some things weighing on his soul he wanted to unburden.

Portraits had been chiseled into some of the stones and decorated with flowers or makeshift picture frames. For these the stone was polished black marble rather than the more common white. Some of the engraved texts had been recently refreshed, a sign of the dedication family members extended in looking after the graves of their ancestors.

Another grave showed a family bond continuing into the afterlife. Two brothers, Reza and Hossein, had been buried together, and the epitaph on the polished black stone was meant for both:

May your souls be acquainted with God.
May God shed light on your grave.
The light of our lives, we think of you.
May you be happy in the Garden of Eden.

Within the field of stones one grave stood out, that of Ali Ahmadi, father of Hamid Ahmadi, a *shaheed*, or martyr, of the Iran-Iraq War. The two had been buried together. We were far from the killing grounds of Khuzestan, but Ahmadi's grave was another indication of how far the shadow of the war had stretched, and the black slab was another indication of the depth of the imprint it had left.

Earlier in the day we had passed another martyr's memorial in the center of Kashan. On the side of a roundabout, the entire front of a building had been covered with enlarged photos, all black-and-white headshots, of some of the city's shaheed, inscribed with their names and dates of death. Most of the men were in their twenties or early thirties, but there were many older faces too, men with speckled grey hair and beards, their eyes dulled by the toll of the eight years of war. On the way into Kashan, we had passed another memorial, this time a signboard like the kinds that advertise fast-food outlets or budget motels in other parts of the world. But this one was covered with more headshots, more names, more grim faces, and more dates of birth and death. Beside a mosque that was being renovated on the outskirts of the city was another photo, this one in color. Again, the man was young, and a garland of dried plastic flowers hung from a post on which the photo had been mounted. It was framed in cheap gold laminate and protected by a cover of glass, but, perhaps symbolic of the war's longevity, the photo had faded almost into invisibility from decades of punishing sunlight.

I had visited other memorials honoring victims of war and other human horrors—the siege of Dubrovnik, Pol Pot's reign of terror in Cambodia, the bloody rule of Haile Mengistu in Ethiopia—and the most appropriate were those that made no attempt to glorify the victims but presented them as the simple, unassuming human beings that they were. The martyrs from the Iran-Iraq War were portrayed similarly, human rather than heroic, more victims of geopolitics than the bullets or missiles hurled from the other side. The depictions confirmed a lingering perception—that our popular presentations of heroism destroy the very humanity they aspire to celebrate.

After another tour of the graves, Sohrab and I were back on the road. The cemetery stop had thrown a pall over the afternoon, but with Dexter Gordon again oozing from the CD player, the mood lightened. In less than an hour we pulled into the village of Abyaneh. Choice of accommodation was simple: Abyaneh has only one hotel, unmistakably named, so it could not be missed—the Abyaneh Hotel. It is a bare-bones, clean, three-star affair at the end of town, where the second-floor rooms are fitted with balconies that overlook the town's rooftops and the green valley beyond. I dropped my bag in the room and again looked forward to the luxury of wandering on my own. Sohrab had gone to great lengths to tell me that Abyaneh was best to explore aimlessly and unguided, that the web of winding lanes offered surprises when they were least expected, that the few locals who still lived in town were friendly and welcoming of visitors, and that he did not want to distract from my own personal exploration. All this was probably true, but I guessed that he also was weary from the day's heat and welcomed a predinner snooze.

Rising above the village are the ruins of a Sassanid-era fort that once protected Abyaneh as well as the fertile lands that spread across the valley and the trading caravans that crossed it. Now the pile of broken stone, topped with tufts of grass and weeds, couldn't protect much of anything. But it hardly mattered, because there is little in Abyaneh left to protect. The town's population, once several thousand, has dwindled to a few hundred, mostly elderly men and women who have no reason to leave and who only remain to maintain the age-old traditions that draw weekenders from the cities and curiosity-seeking foreigners.

Abyaneh possesses no magnificent monuments, mosques, or historic sites, and that is precisely its charm. Abyaneh's only attraction is itself—its reputation as one of the oldest villages in Iran, with mud-brick-colored houses arranged like chess pieces on a sloping hillside and the preservation of religious practices that survived the arrival of Islam in the seventh century. In Abyaneh, the fires of Zoroastrianism have never been snuffed out. Elsewhere in Muslim Iran the feet of the dead are washed before burial, but not in Abyaneh, because the practice pollutes the element of water, regarded as holy in Zoroastrianism. And rather than facing Mecca for prayers during religious festivals, residents turn to the East—the direction of the sunrise.

Before heading into town I decided to put the fort to good use. I climbed to the top to get an overview of all that lay below, thinking this would help in navigating the ins and outs of the village. Thinking I had a good lay of the land, I scrambled down and headed into town, but the bird's-eye view proved to be useless. Immediately I was lost, but as Sohrab had said, Abyaneh is best experienced through aimless wandering, and so I wandered, and aimlessly, back and forth through the narrow, brick-colored lanes. In tiny squares where a few of the rugged streets intersected, women wearing the traditional long white scarf splashed with a pattern of red flowers sold fruits and vegetables. Old men, dressed in baggy, billowing pants, gathered in clusters, like old men everywhere, to puff on cigarettes and exchange a few words between heavy, lengthy silences.

Abyaneh has not died completely. Most of the houses may be locked and shuttered, but on this day, a weekend, some of the shutters were drawn back, and windows were open to catch any breeze passing down the knotted lanes. High above, garlands of laundry were draped over latticed balconies. What was noticeably absent was the sound of children—no flocks of giggling schoolgirls playing hopscotch or skipping rope, no boys chasing down a beaten-up football as it caromed off the mud-brick walls. But what had not abandoned the town was the tradition found everywhere in Iran—Persian hospitality.

Rounding a corner, I met an old woman sitting on a rickety chair beside an open doorway. She didn't dart inside, like my peek-a-boo partner outside the Borujerdiha. Her face broke into a wide smile, and her eyes beamed with the fire of youth. I smiled and nodded, and raised my camera as a way of asking for a photo. She didn't dodge into the doorway. She rose from her chair and assumed an elegant, dignified pose, firm and upright, hands clasped behind her back. The shutter snapped, and an even brighter smile spread across her face. I thanked her with another nod and was moving on when she went to the doorway and—waved me inside? I didn't get it. I didn't think she could be inviting me into her home, here in the back streets of Abyaneh, but she was, and, once the message hit home, I swallowed a pang of shame and followed.

Instantly, I was back at the Borujerdiha, in taste and character if not splendor. Only a mud-brick wall and weathered wooden doorway may have been visible on the outside, but within, handwoven carpets were spread across the wooden floor, two small rooms were lined with hand-carved tables and chairs, and a pair of chest-high cabinets were topped with enamelware and glass objects, glazed pottery, and any other knickknacks that could find room on the polished surfaces. But most striking were the photographs. One of the chests was doubling as a display case for a collection of black-and-white photos. Some had turned sepia, but all showed Abyaneh in livelier times—a group of men and women working in a field, anonymous neighbors gathered in a square, sitting on stoops outside their houses. Some of the photos were personal—an old man with a grey mustache and eyes that gazed vacantly into space, two women, much younger, probably the age of the woman now, one of them perhaps the woman now.

She moved to the kitchen, and I knew what was coming. She lit one of the burners on her stove and "put a kettle on." In a minute the water was bubbling, and loose tea leaves were sprinkled into the bottom of a small glass teacup. At the front of the house there was only a door and a single window that faced the narrow street, but at the rear was a wall of windows that overlooked the town and valley beyond.

I sipped slowly while taking in the view, a panorama that made the modest interior immensely rich. All of the valley lay within sight of her window, wide and green and sweeping to the mountains and ridgeline on the other side. After a minute, the woman steered me over to the photos of Abyaneh in decades past, long before the Islamic Revolution, when rural Iran was rural Iran, untouched by decades of changes. One by one she picked them up and indicated through the gaze of her eyes, "This was our town. . . . This is where I shopped. . . . These were my friends and neighbors." As she recounted those times past she showed no pain of loss or air of remorse, and her eyes retained their glow, as though all of the life that she had lived, and what was left of it, captured in these fading photos, was something to be proud of, and to share with any visitor curious enough to have a look.

I finished the tea and handed her the cup, with a smile, as a gesture of appreciation and a signal that I was prepared to leave. She held up a hand, went to the kitchen, and returned with a handful of oranges. I took them, smiled, and nodded again, and, passing through the door, was once again back on the street.

I kept strolling through Abyaneh's lanes, and after a few more turns and dead ends met Mohammad and Sorour. It was clear they were not year-round residents. Mohammad was dressed in jeans, not the baggy, billowing pants of the local men. Sorour donned the flimsiest of head-scarves, pushed back on her head as far as possible without drawing the attention of the dress police, if any dress police could be found in Abyaneh. It was a Tehran habit brought here to the countryside, where the morals police numbered zero, but a habit it was, and hard to shake in a country where guardedness is a fact of life. Mohammad and Sorour were brother and sister, both graduate students in Tehran, and they had come to Abyaneh to look after their grandmother's house, still kept up by the family after Grandmother was unable to live alone here in the village and had to move to Tehran.

Once we had passed the "Where are you from?" introductions, Mohammad and Sorour invited me in to have a look. One glance said the house hadn't been lived in for years. Wall decorations had been removed, and the carpets pulled up. Furniture filled the tiny rooms, but everything was disheveled, orderly enough only for a weekend stay. But for Sorour and Mohammad it was their ancestral home and therefore worthy of a visit to fix whatever needed fixing to prevent it from falling into further decay—and to justify a getaway from Tehran.

The latter may have been the primary purpose of their visit, but ancestral lineage runs deep, along with all its obligations, so their visit was likely a two for one.

We got through the expected follow-ups—Why had I come to Iran? What were my impressions of the country?—and then they invited me up to the roof. The house was not much of a talking point, they said. The best was yet to come. We climbed a narrow, winding staircase that led up through the second level and onto the rooftop deck. They were right. The cramped, musty rooms and tight hallways were behind us. The view from the roof took in the entire village and valley. A plastic table and two plastic deck chairs suggested that Mohammad and Sorour spent their mornings and evenings here, watching the arrival and departure of the sun in its passage across the valley—not a bad way to spend a few days out of Tehran.

As the sun edged westward and the colors deepened across the valley, Sorour and I took seats on the deck chairs, while Mohammad, the gentleman host, perched on a block of concrete. We talked about Hassan Rouhani, the reelected reformist president: Were they supporters? Could Iran have better relations with the West? How long could the regime hold on to power? The future was all a mystery, they concluded—as it always is in Iran. Eventually, and almost inevitably, the conversation landed on the subject of Iran's nuclear program. Did they believe Iran had the right to develop nuclear weapons?

"Every country has the right to develop nuclear energy," Mohammad asserted, a bit reflexively. His answer was safe and noncommittal, and once again showed that, as much as young Iranians may deplore the government and the Islamic regime, national pride is something else. It convinced me, once again, that were Iran to be attacked—by the United States, Israel, it didn't matter—the nation's youth would rally around the government in its defense, but only temporarily, very temporarily.

But did this include nuclear weapons, I asked.

"*No!*" Mohammad exclaimed, with sudden fervency.

No?

"*No!* We don't want war. We do not want conflict with any countries. We want to be friends with everyone."

Anywhere else such statements, which essentially parroted the government line, would have been dismissed as regime propaganda, but in private settings Iranians are not afraid to speak their minds, and it is not uncommon for extremely contentious views to be expressed. I believed that Mohammad was speaking for himself, but, as her brother held the stage, Sorour was shifting uneasily. When I asked her opinion of Iran becoming a nuclear-armed state she was far more pragmatic, and dubious, which translates as quintessentially Persian. "Let's face it," she said, "we are all alone in the world."

Dusk had begun to suffuse the valley with deep shades of purple and brown. It was time for me to find my way back to the hotel. I bid Mohammad and Sorour goodbye and returned to Abyaneh's tangle of lanes. On the way, I stumbled across the remains of the town's *atash-gahdeh,* or fire temple, a 1,500-year-old remnant of its Zoroastrian past. I had been looking for it ever since I entered the town, and suddenly there it was, its flame long extinguished and the temple now succumbing to time as well as the gathering dusk. I managed to find Abyaneh's main street and began the climb out of town, along the way passing a few grocery shops, awaiting the last customers of the day under signs lit by single bulbs, and Abyaneh's only internet café.

Back at the hotel the tables in the dining room were being set for the voluminous, over-the-top buffet that is the central feature of the Persian dining experience. Stainless steel serving bins loaded with roasted lamb and chicken appeared, followed by billowing pillows of saffron rice; white rice laced with spinach and lima beans, green lentils, and raisins; pots of stewed vegetables; flats of steaming loaves of *taftoon* and barbari breads; bowls of lentil and aash soup; and an array of salads. In the days of the shah, the lavish spread would have been accompanied by jugs of smooth, fine Shiraz wine, and no doubt some of the guests had a bootlegged bottle or two stashed away in their rooms. But, for the sake of public appearance, the soft drinks, fruit juices, and nonalcoholic beer would have to do.

Other guests were already starting to take their seats, and soon the room was filled with a cross-section of Iran's middle class—young couples seeking a romantic country getaway, parents with children in tow in need of a few days relief from hectic urban lives, and even a few pensioners, the retired class with enough time on their hands to see the unseen parts of their own country.

I filled a plate and found an inconspicuous part of the room to engage in a bit of people watching. Weary parents were preoccupied correcting the table manners of rambunctious children. Young couples were too preoccupied with each other to be distracted by the rambunctious children or the cornucopia of food. For a moment I was able to enjoy some anonymity. For a moment no one wandered over to say, "Welcome to Iran—where are you from?"

After eating, I stepped outside to take in the cool mountain air. Night had settled in. The sky had darkened, and the ridgeline of the surrounding hills was visible beyond the valley. Outside the hotel entrance a small patio was lined with takhts, and some of the after-dinner crowd had already moved there to nibble on sweets, sip cups of strong coffee, puff on galyoons, and enjoy the night air. I found a spot on the only unoccupied takht and began nursing a pot of mint tea, but it wasn't long before I fell under the gaze of two young couples on a nearby takht. We made eye contact, and I prepared for the inevitable. "Where are you from?" one of the women asked.

I replied, and as expected, in keeping with Persian protocol, they asked me to join them. Then came the introductions. Shapur worked in IT for an Italian company in Tehran. Neda was an accountant for the French energy company Total. Nassim had just returned from Brussels, where she had spent two years studying languages. Navid was an account supervisor for Bank Melli, one of Iran's largest financial institutions. Back in the heady days of the postelection riots of 2009 these would have been Green Movement revolutionaries, and now, since the departure of firebrand and controversial President Mahmoud Ahmadinejad, they were likely ardent supporters of current president and quasi-reformer Hassan Rouhani—or anyone who could inject an inkling of liberalism into Iranian society. Their liberal stripes showed themselves in the postures of Neda and Nassim. Here, in the relative isolation of Abyaneh, far from the ubiquitous eyes of Tehran's morality police, the two women allowed their scarves to slide all the way down the backs of their heads. It was a moment of freedom to be taken whenever the opportunity offered it, and a welcome reminder of normalcy in a country where, for almost forty years, the "new normal," in women's dress and religious restrictions of every kind, may have been accepted as "normal" but never natural.

Everyone in the group was glad to see the end of Ahmadinejad, and his quixotic attempt to return to power in the 2017 election was never taken seriously by anyone but his most ardent backers. Kashan itself was a region where Ahmadinejad had won many followers, primarily by showering it with revenue-generating infrastructure projects and largesse from the national coffers. In American terms, Ahmadinejad was the ultimate pork-barrel politician. As a former mayor of Tehran he knew that political loyalties are easily bought, but his antics during his eight years in power, including Holocaust denial and provocative statements that only stoked unnecessary conflict with the West, earned him the reputation of "loose cannon" among his fellow hardliners, not a reputation to be welcomed in a regime based on top-down, hierarchal control.

"He was an idiot, and a dangerous idiot," said Shapur.

"But he could connect with the common people and those with little education, so the leaders who were out of touch with the people used him for that, to win support for the government," Nassim added.

Navid was a little more glum. "For eight years he was the public face of this country. People all over the world got a very negative impression of Iran, but he never really represented the people."

I agreed with Navid, that Ahmadinejad was grossly out of step with most Iranians, but there was a flaw in his reasoning. The 2009 election was widely regarded as stolen, but Ahmadinejad did win a clear majority to take power in 2005, and so he may not have represented "the Iranian people" as represented by Neda, Shapur, Nassim, and Navid, but there was a swath of Iranian society that did see part of itself in his image.

I thought this might be hard for a group of Green Movement sympathizers to accept, so I kept quiet. But in some respects Iran was not all that different from many countries in the world. There was a large segment of society, urban and educated, eager to embrace liberalism and modernity, and another group that sees those values as a threat to their more conservative, tradition-based lives. Ahmadinejad, like many politicians, was able to exploit the fears of the latter.

Did the rejection of his candidacy in 2017 by the Supreme Guardian Council, the branch of the government charged with approving candidates for the presidential election, mean that the pitchfork army that he represented was also being shown the door? Not at all—it was only being sidelined, and for the moment, Navid explained. "The government has learned how to manipulate us, or how to try. When tensions rise too high, they will allow a reformer to take control, as they did with Mohammad Khatami in 1997, but they won't let him actually make any changes. It's a strategy. It lets air out of the balloon. But when they feel they need to crack down, they will make sure that hardliners are back in power."

For Navid, this partly explained Hassan Rouhani's reelection in 2017.

"The government was never going to play with the vote like they did in 2009," said Neda. "They learned their lesson. They didn't want to see people back in the streets. They weren't going to take that risk. But will they really let him accomplish anything that will improve the situation in Iran? We don't know. If they feel that it's necessary for them to stay in power, they will. To stay in power—that is all that matters to them."

A weighty question hung in the air: Could protestors again take to the streets, demand an overhaul of the entire government, even an end to Islamic rule? Surprisingly, no one could envision Iranians back in the streets again, battling the security forces and incurring martyrs for the liberal cause, like Neda Agha-Soltan, who was gunned down by sniper fire after being stuck in traffic near the site of an antigovernment demonstration. The video of the young woman bleeding to death on the pavement generated sympathy for the Green Movement around the world and stigmatized the government as another brutal dictatorship oppressing its people with bullets. Now, they said, the government was smart enough never to risk such scenes being repeated, and the liberal forces knew better than to risk another violent crackdown. The result was a Mexican standoff: Neither side knew how far the other was willing to go.

One thing was certain: Many Iranians, this group included, explicitly did *not* want to see another revolution, with people out in the streets, even if it would lead to the toppling of the Islamic regime.

"We've been through that once before, and we've seen what can happen," Nassim said, referring to the 1979 Islamic Revolution. "People don't think straight in times like that. Look what that brought us. And look at what is happening all around us—in Syria and Iraq, where society has completely broken down. Do we want to risk that?"

This was a familiar refrain. Many Iranians, even the most fervent opponents of the government, had no appetite for open revolution, and actually preferred not to see the regime removed completely, at least not now. What had changed? Within Iran, nothing. But in Iran's geopolitical neighborhood, everything. The Arab Spring of 2011 saw the tumbling of autocratic regimes in Libya, Egypt, and Yemen. Violent riots broke out on the streets in Bahrain. Syria descended into a bloodbath; competing forces have virtually destroyed the country. Worst of all, from an Iranian point of view, larger external powers— Russia, the U.S., Saudi Arabia, jihadist forces—have filled the void to pursue their own interests, turning the countries in which they are fighting into near failed states. Most Iranians do not fear their country descending into Syria-like carnage if the regime falls, but, for the time being, the uncomfortable and repressive stability that they know is far more preferable to radical, unknown instability. With powerful, self-interested forces all around them, this was not the time for upheaval and the uncertainties it would bring.

Shapur cut in. "Look at all the foreign powers that have gone in there and taken control. You create a—" void, he indicated, with a gesture, but I supplied the word. "Yes, a void, and see what fills it. We've been invaded too many times, and I don't want to see that happen again."

Then how would the political landscape fundamentally change, I asked. Were those wanting change willing to wait forever, for "the right time," however long it would take?

"Maybe something like a 'managed transition' would be best," Neda answered.

Have you ever known anyone to give up power willingly?—I wanted to say, but bit my tongue.

It was time to ask something that seemed facile to many Iranians, yet poignant to outsiders: How did we get here? If Iranian society as a whole wasn't particularly religious, how could the country have been taken over by religious zealots, and how could it stay in power if there was so much opposition to it?

Ask this of one hundred Iranians and you will receive two hundred explanations. None of them are comprehensive, and yet all of them contain a bit of truth. A general consensus reads something like the following: Forty years ago the people had had enough of the shah, his megalomania, his increasing leaning toward dictatorship, the oppression and brutality of his SAVAK security force. They wanted something new, but there was little thought of the consequences. The Ayatollah Khomeini, living in exile in Paris, saw his moment.

"He lied to us," Nassim said. "He said he wasn't going to do anything to change the role of women, that he would only be a caretaker leader until Iran stabilized once again, and so on and so on. We believed it. And he lied. Soon after he took power all the restrictions came. Alcohol was banned. The hijab, even the full chador, became mandatory. All the Western literature disappeared from the bookstores. He totally changed Iranian society."

Shapur picked up on this: "These rulers have been in power so long they've become arrogant. They think that they can control us, that they can run our lives, that they can make us accept their values and live like they think we should."

Neda added: "They want to take our—." She paused, searched for words, and placed her hand over her heart.

Shapur had more to say: "But they really aren't in control anymore. They're struggling to stay in control, but they greatly underestimated the people's reaction in the 2009 election. They thought we were stupid, that we would accept anything they told us, or were far too timid to express our opinions."

I ventured a question I knew couldn't be answered, not in a single sentence, or two, or twenty. I was more interested in the group's reaction than in getting anything like a decisive reply.

"But why are they still in power?"

Neda whispered something to Navid: "She says they wouldn't be if the U.S. would help us."

"In what way?"

Again, Navid translated: "Militarily."

"You mean send in the marines, take over the country?"

"No, just kill all the leaders and leave."

This was wishful thinking, and everyone knew it. As far as this group was concerned, there was no Persian Spring over the horizon and none was sought. If a dramatic change in the government were to occur, it would not come from the streets. Navid proposed another way: "Now there is an enormous amount of debate over government policies, and the pushback by the people against so many restrictive laws is so constant that the leaders have had to open society up, little by little. I don't think the regime will collapse, like what happened in Libya or Egypt. More likely, over time it will just wear away."

Other members of the group nodded in assent, but cautiously rather than convincingly. Trying to predict the political future in Iran was more precarious than storm chasing, but for many Iranians any possible path that would lead Iran out of the morass in which it had been mired for four decades was welcome and worthy of hope. I told them I was skeptical that Iran would ever see such a smooth and seamless transition. Certain changes to the status quo would be so dramatic and symbolic that they would signify the end of the Islamic Revolution— eliminating the mandatory hijab, for example, or loosening the ban on alcohol, if only for non-Muslim tourists in designated hotels. But such changes would open floodgates of reform that the government could never hold back. Incremental changes appease the masses for a while, but in the evolution of any society there comes a tipping point when, I argued, "Islamic democracy" and all the contradictions it stood for would be no more.

There were tentative nods of assent, but in the faces of these young Iranians there was more tentativeness than assent. This was nothing unusual. Any prediction of Iran's future was torturous and had been for decades. Few would go out on a limb to venture any view on what the future held. A painless transition might not be in the cards, but any scenario that would free Iranian society from the stranglehold it has endured since 1979 could not be dismissed. To deny it was to deny hope. But among this group of young Iranians none of them expressed the desire to leave the country for a more fruitful life in the liberal West. They had already been educated in respectable universities—one of the reasons young Iranians want to go West. And likely they had been raised in families that bucked conservative traditions, so social constraints had never cast a shadow over their adult lives—a major concern of many Iranian women. For other Iranians, however, the West came calling. With the U.S. almost closed off as a destination, Canada had become the next-best option, and to a lesser extent the United Kingdom, France, Australia, and New Zealand. But not for this group.

"They aren't going to drive me out of my country," said Nassim.

"They can go to hell," Neda chimed in.

What about the brain drain? This question troubled me, as it should any Iranian. This quiet, creeping ailment had nibbled at the fabric of Iranian society for decades, and it was only getting worse. Many of Iran's best-educated young people had given up expecting any meaningful changes in Iranian society, or hope for its immediate future, and have left to set up new lives abroad. Hard facts are hard to come by, but as many as five million Iranians have left Iran since the Islamic Revolution, and the exodus continues.

"It's a dead country," one friend told me, who eventually migrated to Canada.

I asked this group of young, educated Iranians if the government wasn't concerned about losing them.

"They hope we will leave," Neda responded.

"Fewer of us to bother them," Nassim chimed in.

The conversation had hit rock bottom, as most conversations about politics in Iran eventually do, but then it took a more promising turn. For many years Iranian cinema has been arguably the most accomplished in the Middle East and executed on a level equal to the highest international standards. Politics may be endlessly and depressingly uncertain, but there is no doubt that Iranians are forever proud of their cinema. Near the beginning of Asghar Farhadi's international hit *A Separation*, Simin, the wife of Nader, tells a judge, cryptically, that she wants to emigrate with her daughter because she doesn't want her "to grow up in this situation." Such a loaded remark passed the scrutiny of the government censors because of the ambiguity of the word "situation." Did it refer to politics? Or economic hardship from international sanctions, of course the fault of the West? In art, interpretation is everything. The censors read the comment one way, cinema-savvy audiences another.

With this group of young Iranians, mention of the scene dispelled the gloomy clouds of emigration and threw us into the far more uplifting topic of Iranian cinema. Neda asked if I knew of the directors Majid Majidi and Mohsen Makhmalbaf. That I was not only familiar with them but had seen several of their films surprised her more than the fact that she was talking cinema with a visiting American on a *takht* under the stars in Abyaneh.

Iranian cinema has long been winning accolades around the world through the work of Majidi, Makhmalbaf, Amir Naderi, Bahman Ghobadi, Masoud Kimiai, Parviz Kimiavi, and giant of the cinema Abbas Kiarostami, who passed away in July 2016, plunging Iran's cultural community into deep mourning. But Asghar Farhadi thrust Iranian cinema into Western consciousness with *A Separation*. Perhaps most significant from a sociopolitical viewpoint, it shows that Iranian society grapples with the same commonplace problems that afflict the rest of the world— marital strife, the care of aging parents, class divisions. He followed it with *The Salesman* a year later, about the strains put on a marriage due to a suspected sexual assault, becoming the only director in the history of the Academy Awards to win back-to-back Oscars for Best Foreign Film. But he declined to appear at the ceremony to collect his second statue in protest over U.S. president Donald Trump's proposed immigration ban on several Muslim-majority countries, which only earned Farhadi greater global favor.

International accolades aside, many filmmakers besides Farhadi have used the screen to serve as a window into Iranian society. In *Leila*, by Darius Mehrjui, an otherwise happy marriage is destroyed when in-laws persuade the husband, Reza, to take a second wife because Leila cannot produce a child. Jafar Panahi's *Tehran Taxi* follows the rounds of a nighttime taxi driver, in classic Scorsese fashion, as he encounters drug addiction, suicide, and other social ills. One of my favorites, I told the group, has always been Majidi's *The Color of Paradise*, in which a widower living in the northwest countryside has an opportunity to remarry but worries that his blind son may jeopardize his chances, so he lends him out to a blind carpenter. That a film with the theme of blindness would be filled with images of the lush landscape adds a dark irony. Of course the story ends tragically, as is the case in most great films, but for critics, this gives it the thematic heft that pushes the film into the category of art.

In such a politically charged society like Iran, governed by a theocratic regime, it might seem surprising that overt statements regarding religion or politics are largely absent from Iranian films. But one must remember that this is Iran, where all artistic production is overseen by watchful government censors, and any challenge to the legitimacy of the ruling regime, no matter how sleight-of-hand, may lead to a jail sentence. So the situation of artists in Iran mirrors those in Eastern Europe under communist rule—metaphor, symbolism, and subtext become the means of subversive expression. A recent example is *A Girl Walks Home Alone at Night* by Ana Lily Amirpour, a black-and-white allegorical tale about a female vampire who seeks victims in the industrial neighborhood near her apartment. The metaphor of bloodsucking, and the image of the black cloak being equated to the chador, would fail to resonate with only the most obtuse filmgoers.

A question was biting at me: I wondered to what extent Iranian movies, which must clear the rigorous eyes of censors before they can be released in Iran, truly represented Iranian society. The same could be asked of American films, without the censor factor: Do American films present an honest representation of American life? I knew it wasn't a fair comparison. Saturation coverage of news events beamed around the world reinforce, balance, or counter whatever impressions are gleaned from American movies. But there is no in-depth coverage of daily events in Iran in most of the world's media. The movies are our only window, and few people see them.

For example, I asked these cinemagoers how we were to take most of the scenes in *About Elly*, in which a group of young Iranians rent a beach house for a weekend. All of the women retain their headscarves within the house, even though they are far beyond the ubiquitous eyes of any dress police. Also, no alcohol consumption is shown, when in real life it would be quite conceivable that someone in the group would have brought along a bottle of contraband—or two. Was this "social realism," Iranian style?

"Oh, no," Nassim jumped in. "The directors make these decisions in order to have their films shown in Iran, and to get permission to film in the first place. Whatever is shown in movies, everyone knows that real life is different."

Often one also had to be Iranian, or well versed in Iranian social and political life, to read the subtext that permeates Iranian films. Neda commented on *The Salesman*: "There are scenes where the couples who don't know each other very well are in the same apartment, and the women don't take off their headscarves. That's possible, but it's a delicate matter when meeting anyone. How well do you know them? Are they religious? Would they feel uncomfortable if one of the women removes her scarf? When all the women keep their scarves on there's a tension in the scene that only Iranians would understand."

All of this led to another question: For movies shot in Iran, how difficult was it to get the government's approval? This time the answer had been provided by Asghar Farhadi himself. He appeared at a screening of *A Separation* I attended shortly after it was released, and the question was asked by a member of the audience in the question-and-answer session that followed.

"A shooting script must be submitted to the government before approval to film can be granted," he explained. "But once you get the okay you go ahead and shoot whatever you want."

I felt mischievous and pushed a provocative point: I told them that for the health of the Iranian film industry it would be better that the regime stayed in power. Looks of disbelief swept across previously tired faces. I told them of a statement I once heard by a Czech filmmaker, that the countries of Eastern Europe made far better films when the communists were in control because subversive messages could not be conveyed directly. Good filmmakers became masters of symbolism and metaphor, and audiences became more sophisticated viewers because they had to watch movies more closely and think about their meanings more deeply. Discussions of films were more interesting, since there were greater ranges of interpretation. Conclusion: Creative oppression created a more vibrant creative culture.

"If the choice is between great movies and a better life, I know which one I would take," said Neda.

The hour was late, and any argument for continued artistic repression could hardly receive an honest hearing. One by one, the other *takhts* around us had emptied, as the rest of the hotel guests trudged off to their rooms, where some would undoubtedly finish the night with a few sips from a bottle of bootlegged hooch.

Navid and Shapur, and Neda and Nassim bade me goodnight, but I stayed for a while after the entire patio had cleared and even the lights inside the hotel had gone dark. Now I was alone with the stars, and the darkened sky shimmered with brilliant specks. For the first time I truly felt the cool of the night air, quietly stirred by the breezes that drifted down from the high ridges that encircled the town and the valley below. Talk of politics was swept away by the night breeze, and even the movie screen lost its glimmer and faded into the darkness. All was quiet, and I could imagine myself sitting on the roof of Mohammad and Sorour's grandmother's house on a similar night not so long ago, when national politics was as remote as the stars and the movies were still a distant dream. The village would have been abuzz from daybreak till sunset, with children playing in the lanes and household noises passing through windows habitually left unshuttered. The arrival of dusk meant the dissipation of the day's cares, and one could find sufficient entertainment in the sensations of the night.

9 | Esfahan

BRIDGES TO EVERYWHERE

Whereas the Ottoman genocide against minority populations during and following the First World War is usually depicted as a genocide against Armenians alone, with little recognition of the qualitatively similar genocides against other Christian minorities of the Ottoman Empire; be it resolved that it is the conviction of the International Association of Genocide Scholars that the Ottoman campaign against Christian minorities of the Empire between 1914 and 1923 constituted a genocide against Armenians, Assyrians, and Pontian and Anatolian Greeks.

    —International Association of Genocide Scholars, 2007

Something was brewing. Metal scaffolding was going up on the north end of Imam Square, in prerevolutionary days known as Naqsh-e Jahan (Image of the World) Square, the second-largest public space in the world after Beijing's Tiananmen. The semblance of a stage was beginning to appear, and security checkpoints were being set up in front of the souvenir shops, all of which had been ordered to shut for the following morning.

I stopped into a carpet shop and asked the salesman what all the commotion was about. It looked like the setup for a rock concert, but that would hardly have been possible in conservative Esfahan, to say nothing of the rest of Iran.

"Our president is coming," he said, in a dull voice that radiated little enthusiasm. And he was.

It was late 2009, months after the disputed presidential election. The president was the now disgraced Mahmoud Ahmadinejad, making one of his victory tours of the hardline heartland to whip up nationalistic sentiment among the diehard, the struggling working class he had showered with government largesse during his first term in office to shore up support for his hardline policies. They were ready converts, believing that Ahmadinejad's hardscrabble background would make him sympathetic to their plight. By then he had proven to be a thorn in the side of the clerical establishment with whom he shared the same hardline views, for his freewheeling style had set him at odds with his natural backers.

Well, this was going to be quite a show, I thought. The next morning I wandered over to the square, where all the entrances were now guarded with security booths manned by members of the Revolutionary Guard. I thought that would be as close as I would get, but I passed through after the most cursory of pat-downs and a quick inspection of the belt pack I was carrying, which contained only my guidebook, a pair of sunglasses, and an apple for lunch. The Guard member even nodded and smiled politely before allowing me to move on.

The square was beginning to fill up with regime faithful—women draped in black chadors and civil servants and blue-collar workers who had been bussed in from the surrounding villages and given the day off and a small gratuity for their trouble. Twenty-five dollars and a sack lunch was rumored to be the going rate. But the much greater payoff was the credit they would receive, in perks and favors when needed, for turning out to show their allegiance to the Islamic Revolution.

The rest of the trappings of a presidential visit were in place. Red banners draped from the roof of the square read, "Death to Israel!" and "Death to America!" More Revolutionary Guards were handing out posters bearing the likeness of Ahmadinejad with Ayatollah Khomeini. Sometimes the current supreme leader Ayatollah Khamenei was thrown in for good measure, at times paired with Khomeini, at times alone. Whatever the arrangement, the backdrop was always a field of heavenly clouds, befitting the leaders of the Islamic Revolution. I eased my way through the crowd and eventually made it down to the fourth row of regime boosters. One side was designated for men. The chador-draped women had their own rooting section on the other side of a rope barrier that ran down the middle of the square. A metal barrier circled the stage, where more members of the Guard had been posted to provide a margin of security.

At one o'clock in the afternoon the rally set for ten in the morning had yet to start. Authorities from the regional government mounted the stage to mouth revolutionary slogans—and keep the crowd from thinning. Gathered around me were the representatives of a forgotten Iran—plumbers and electricians, low-level government functionaries, and poorly paid truck drivers and mechanics, none of whom had the connections or capital to slide ahead in a brazenly corrupt system. And among them were likely some true believers in the regime. One of them standing next to me was a young man of about thirty.

"What are you doing here?" he asked in passable English.

"Tourist," I replied, with strategic ease—asserting nothing, confronting nothing.

"No, *here*," he stressed, pointing at the ground.

"Curious," I said. His response was what one would expect from a weekend regime supporter running up against an American tourist at a proregime rally. He rolled his eyes and sighed.

We continued to wait. Finally, at about two o'clock, Ahmadinejad's motorcade rolled into the square. The president was standing through the roof of an SUV, leaning over to shake the hands of followers who darted toward it across the spacious lawn. Onstage he voiced his usual denunciations of the West and claimed the nation's right to develop nuclear power. Cheers erupted at scripted applause lines. The men and women waved their posters in the air. The young man next to me asked where I was from, and I told him. Then word spread that an American was among the fold. Men several rows away nudged each other and smirked. Toward the end of the rally, on cue, chants of "Death to

America!" broke out. The men pumped their fists in the air and did their best to show enthusiasm, but it was all a bit lackluster. The young man eyed me coyly. I extended a hand. It threw him off, but he reached over and shook it. The men around us chuckled. It was all great fun.

All in all, it was a poor showing. Less than half the square was filled, and the three-hour delay drained what enthusiasm the crowd could muster. When it was all over the streets around the square were lined with busses, dozens of them, their engines rumbling, getting ready to ship the rent-a-crowd back to their towns and villages. I strolled around the margins, trying to read anything into the behavior of the crowd now that their job was done, but there was nothing. It was a desultory routine, another day on the job away from the job. Then a voice called out.

"Did you see our president?"

It belonged to a young woman in a black chador, standing beside another young woman still holding one of the posters portraying an ethereal Ahmadinejad surrounded by clouds against a background of powder blue. The faces of the young women glowed, misty-eyed, like teenagers at a 1960s pop concert. I wandered over, asked what they thought of the man they had come to see.

"He's a true global leader," Negar said.

"He wants to reach out to everyone," added Shirin. "It's not his fault if he's refused."

Ahmadinejad had recently made a tour of South America, glad-handing Venezuela's former president Hugo Chávez, Brazil's Lula da Silva, and current president Evo Morales of Bolivia. He had also been chatting up Turkey's Tayyip Erdogan and Bashar al-Assad of Syria. Like many of Ahmadinejad's antics, this trip was all a public relations stunt to show that he, if not the government he represented, had global support, even if not in the most favorable quarters. But, to Negar and Shirin, it was global diplomacy par excellence.

Then a young man appeared, about eighteen years old, another friend of Negar and Shirin. They had all come to Esfahan together on a bus from a village in Esfahan Province and were savoring the last moments before beginning the ride back. His name was Amir, and he was fresh-faced and clean-cut, with a Colgate smile and an innocent face to match. There was none of the growsy look of so many of Iran's male youth who strut the streets of Tehran in silver-studded black belts and kooky haircuts—rebels with a cause but no other way to express it.

"Of course the government is honest," Amir replied when I asked whether the regime's obfuscations over its nuclear program were only cover for a nuclear weapons program. "Our country is based on the principles of Islam, and according to Islam one must tell the truth."

I asked Amir what he thought of Ahmadinejad.

"He's a good man. He cares about the people, but the rest of the world doesn't see any of that. What they see is propaganda, to make Iran look bad."

I had to give Amir credit. Part of what he said was true—the foundation of the Islamic Republic had been based on Islamic principles—but his naivete would have been touching if it weren't so troubling. With obligatory Persian hospitality he wished me a very pleasant stay in Iran and asked for my email address to stay in touch, before making his way over to the busses along with Negar and Shirin. He asked where I was from, and I told him, and without a flinch he again wished me a very good time in Iran. The point was clear but not surprising—the popularity of Americans crosses the starkest ideological lines.

The crowd had thinned further, and back near the stage, which was already being dismantled, I met Mehrad, a graduate student in chemistry at Esfahan University. This time it was he who had spotted me, an out-of-place foreigner, and wandered over. He hadn't attended the rally. He knew nothing about it. He was on his way home from the university and had only stumbled on it by chance. When I told him that I had just seen Ahmadinejad, he shook his head and winced.

"All the politicians in this country are idiots," he said, and went on to add that if he had gotten wind of the rally he would have avoided the square altogether. Our conversation took a few twists and turns and eventually landed on the subject of Mehrad's grandfather, a master textile painter. He had a workshop nearby, within the warrens of the Esfahan bazaar. Would I like to see it? There was little in the square to stick around for now that the rally had broken up, and the specialty souvenir shops were still closed. The choice made itself.

Esfahan's bazaar is almost a thousand years old. The original structure dates to the eleventh century, but most of the current building was constructed six hundred years later, in the seventeenth. It is the largest covered market in the world, wrapping itself around the square in a mile-long arcade that offers everything from tourist souvenirs to household essentials—kitchenware, bed sheets, plastic buckets, and fine fabrics sold by the meter. And then there are the artisans and craftsmen who ply age-old trades despite the encroachment of modernization, like Mehrad's grandfather.

Mehrad led me through a series of winding lanes until we landed at his grandfather's workshop, a grubby space set ablaze by powerful overhead lights that illuminated the table he was hunched over. The old man was certainly a master of the art of textile painting, a traditional craft dating back hundreds of years. A piece of cotton was stretched out on the surface of a table. As I watched, he dipped a wooden block with a linear pattern in ink and pressed it around the edge of the cloth again and again, seamlessly, until it reached the corner, where a different block was needed to make the turn. More wooden blocks with patterns to fill the interior were on hand once the border had been completed. The same pattern could be recreated in an infinite array of colors. An equally infinite array of patterns could fill the interior. The choices were only limited by the imagination of the printer. The blocks acted as the artist's paintbrushes, the final creation the product of his eye.

While Mehrad's grandfather labored under the glow of the high-intensity light, I struck up a conversation with Mohammad, Mehrad's brother, who had operated an internet blog until government authorities "advised" him to shut it down. I asked him what would have happened if he refused. He drew his finger across his throat.

"They control everything here," he said. "They run the economy, the military, the legal system. They've gained so much power. There's no way around them."

Mohammad had firsthand experience with Iran's security services. One day, when he was twenty-two, he was riding his bicycle home, and the police arrested him for attending a violent demonstration. Unknown to him, a few blocks away an explosion had gone off. He tried to reason with them: "If I had planted a bomb would I be running away on a bicycle?" He got nowhere. The police took him in, and he was held for two weeks but finally freed along with a group of men who had been picked up when the investigation went nowhere. But instead of simply opening the jailhouse door and giving the young men a kick in the pants, the police drove them into the remote countryside about thirty-five miles from Tehran and left them there.

"We have to make you pay some way," said the commanding officer as the van pulled away. "After all, we fed you for two weeks."

"When will things change?" I asked Mohammad, aware of the absurdity of the question. The point was only to see what kind of answer I would get. Would it be cynical? Optimistic? Speculative? I knew "optimistic" was out of the question. I also knew the answer was meaningless, because the only thing for certain in Iran is that no one knows anything for certain, not the workings of the government, not the decision-making process behind the decisions, or how the many factions of the government are lining up in their constant tugs-of-war for power. The Iranian government was like a car with many contentious drivers all struggling for control of the wheel, and the people were little more than helpless passengers along for the ride, wherever it may take them. So what was the point of seeking any answer? Only to hear the view of one of the passengers. When will things change? Mehrad's grandfather had been listening in and asked for a translation. Mehrad supplied it. His grandfather offered an answer: "When the U.S. invades."

I had little doubt that the dour mood in the workshop was at least partly due to the presidential visit. The regime casts a long shadow across all parts of Iranian society, and today it had come uncomfortably close. Mehrad's grandfather finished printing the border on the tablecloth and was getting ready to work on the interior, which meant a change of blocks and inks. This put the work on hold, like the change of sets between scenes of a play.

Mehrad led me into the tiny courtyard behind the shop that served as a souvenir stand where the family wares were displayed for sale, stacked on packing crates, old chairs, and every other surface that could bear the weight of bolts of imprinted cotton. If I didn't know better I'd have suspected that Mehrad's sole reason for dragging over to the workshop was to help his grandfather make a sale, that our entire conversation was little more than prelude to a sale's pitch. But no. He was anxious to share his views with a rare foreigner, and he wanted to show off his grandfather's talent. It was a way of saying, "See, we are more than this ugly government and the ridiculous stage show you've just seen." It was his way of lifting the curtain and giving me a glimpse of what was behind the grotesque afternoon spectacle.

His grandfather's work was definitely high quality, featuring painted outlines of birds and flowers and swirling floral patterns that interconnected almost seamlessly, yet there was an unmistakable roughness in the final products, welcome imperfections that indicated that they were made by hand. I had no inclination to buy but felt obligated, so I picked up a couple of sets of table napkins, and Mehrad, following true bazaar practice, haggled with me over the price but finally settled without much of a fight. And as I left, he naturally wished me a very pleasant stay in Iran.

The square was returning to normal, the souvenir shops around the perimeter beginning to reopen. I ran into Reza, a man in his forties sitting beside a rectangular pool and dry fountains that no longer spurted jets of water. No, he had not attended the rally. He had only come to the square for a stroll once he'd heard it was over. For the past twelve years he had worked for an architectural firm in Dubai but shuttled back and forth to visit family members several times a year.

"You know what it is?" he said, when I asked why the rally had been held that day; if it had any purpose other than to whip up government support. "The dam has cracked. It hasn't broken, but it has cracked, and the government knows they have to patch it up."

"And what should the rest of the world do?" I asked.

"The U.S., Israel—forget about military strikes. Cut off the money. If the government was going to fall, those Revolutionary Guards would throw away their uniforms and shave off their beards the next day."

Iranian politics has always functioned within the realm of the opaque, but questions surrounding Iran's nuclear program add another dimension. The drive down from Kashan had bypassed the eastern slopes of the Zagros Mountains. About halfway along, Sohrab and I passed a battery of anti-aircraft guns, their barrels aimed skyward. Their purpose was clear. Not far away was the Natanz nuclear reactor, an underground bunker shielded from attack by concrete walls and a reinforced concrete roof. Where we were headed was the site of an even more important cog in the network of Iran's nuclear research facilities. The site at Esfahan is Iran's largest, employing as many as three thousand scientists before the 2015 nuclear agreement. Watchers of Iran's nuclear program have long claimed that much of the government's research was going on at Esfahan, but, in the murky world of political punditry, any view from outside Iran was no more clear, or less, than any view from within.

Despite the sudden appearance of the anti-aircraft guns, the threat of war seemed far away. The sun was brightly shining in a cloudless sky, and the crisp ridgeline of the Zagros Mountains spread across the horizon.

It was the time and place for a photo op. Up ahead, on cue, appeared a small roadside mosque with a terrace overlooking the valley. It was unusual to come across a mosque, even a small one, out here in the middle of nowhere, but this was no ordinary mosque. It had history to it, described on a signboard so faded by years of punishing sun that even Sohrab couldn't read it. Instead of being bulldozed to be replaced with, perhaps, a gas station, it was being overhauled with a fresh coat of paint. The man in charge of the task was Javad, perched high on a ladder at the base of the dome. Javad wasn't used to having visitors, and even less accustomed to foreign visitors. Nevertheless, he scrambled down to greet us but didn't offer a handshake because his hands, like his overalls, were paint spattered. But he did produce, and proudly, an ID indicating his position as a bona fide restorer of Iran's cultural and historic sites. He had been making the rounds of neglected mosques and other historic places in Esfahan Province, sprucing them up, bringing them back to life. This one wouldn't receive many worshippers because there wasn't a village or house in sight, but it would serve as a showpiece for passing travelers—and the odd American tourist. And Javad liked America. His craggy face brightened when he heard where I was from, his scraggly grey hair waving a little wildly in the wind. As we left, he tried to secure a commission.

"Tell your president I will paint the White House, and for free! It will be my gift to the American people!"

Back at Naqsh-e Jahan Square, I wandered through one of the exits and back onto the street. Most of the busses had left, but a few remained, waiting for the stragglers from the rent-a-crowd to climb aboard. I walked down the street to the National Museum of Contemporary Art, where a sign outside the gate caught my eye: "Remembrance of a Friend: Artworks on the Occasion of Iman Khomeini's Heavenly Departure." It was advertising a special exhibit, and the title was enticing enough to warrant a look. I paid the entrance fee at a booth inside the gate and entered. The grounds were as attractive as any of the artwork could have been: A cluster of sand-colored buildings was surrounded by a rectangular pool that reflected a stand of cypress trees. Like the Qajar houses of Kashan, it was intended to create a garden setting, a haven of peace set apart from the traffic and bustle of the street.

In the hall to the right of the entrance was an exhibit of Persian calligraphy, relatively small works no more than a foot square but exhibiting an astonishing array of color combinations—pink, yellow, and orange; green and blue set on a gold background; browns and reds with flashes of yellow woven into the border designs. The only unifying element among all the works was the delicate, swirling Persian script that swept from right to left, at times in a single line, at others in neatly stacked verses of poetry.

The main event was to be found in the building at the back of the complex. On the ground floor, six rooms were hung with portraits of Ayatollah Khomeini portrayed in ways that interpreted his "heavenly departure," as the sign outside the gate suggested they would. There was the ayatollah surrounded by angels, Ayatollah Khomeini staring into an unknown distance with the visionary gaze of Che Guevara, Ayatollah Khomeini standing on a cloud. The message was as clear as the day's political propaganda: Khomeini was Iran's messiah, the savior who had delivered it from the morbid abyss toward which it was heading under the rule of the shah. But judging the paintings according to strict Islamic doctrine, all of them could be condemned as pure blasphemy. One of Islam's fundamental precepts is "There is no God but Allah," which means there is no divine intermediary between human beings and the Creator himself. Even the Prophet Mohammad is not regarded as a divine being but one divinely inspired, and on these canvases Ayatollah Khomeini was being portrayed with near-godlike status. But when religious principles collide with political propaganda, the latter is usually the winner.

Watching over the exhibit was a team of art students from the nearby academy—young women donning manteaux that hung just far enough down their thighs, and veils that concealed just enough hair to deflect the eyes of the morals police. One sidled over, a little shyly at first, and asked where I was from. One question led to another, and that followed with another, and it soon emerged that I had been a university instructor in the U.S. The rest crowded around. It then emerged that the dream of all was to attend art school in the U.S., but with visas for Iranians almost impossible to obtain they were looking elsewhere—Australia, England, Canada—anywhere but Iran. Since an arts degree offered no possible way out of Iran, like many young, educated Iranians they were all studying English translation as a way of improving their chances of emigrating. Despite the slimness of their chances, the U.S. was still their destination of choice, and for a moment my appearance had revived it, and they were going to make the most of the opportunity. They peppered me with questions: What were the best art schools in the U.S.? Was it better to go to a large university or a smaller one? Did the part of the country matter? How did the U.S. higher education system work? How was it different from Europe? I gave a mini-lecture on American higher education, and American arts education, and the whole time felt twinges of guilt because, sadly, I knew that their chances of ever studying in the U.S. were minimal. If they had degrees in engineering, IT, or business and finance, their chances would be much better, but with arts degrees their overseas choices were probably limited to Canada, Australia, or New Zealand. The sad point was that, across the academic spectrum, many of Iran's "best and brightest" saw no future in Iran. Obtaining a student visa was only the first step. A university degree, better yet a graduate degree, meant a chance of employment, which meant establishing a new life in the land where they had received their education, which meant never returning to Iran.

"Funny, isn't it," Golnaz, one of the students, said as I left, "you've been wanting to come to Iran for such a long time, and we only want to go to America."

Esfahan is one of those cities, like Paris or Madrid, Prague or Saint Petersburg, that is made for exploration by foot. Almost all of the sights are close to the center—the center meaning Naqsh-e Jahan Square—and connected by tree-lined boulevards that bear the pedestrian traffic from early morning until late in the evening. Like Tehran, Esfahan now has a metro, which opened in 2015, but like metros in most cities, it is mainly a commuters' necessity. The best way to experience any city is on foot.

I had a full day ahead of me. I chose to start at the bird market, a mile or two north of the square, head over to the historic bathhouse, now a museum, and then turn south toward Naqsh-e Jahan Square, and from there cross the historic stone bridges that cross the Zayandeh-rud, or Zayandeh River, and end in the Julfa district, home of the largest Armenian community outside of Armenia.

The hotel where I was staying was another *sonnati*, or Qajar-era house converted into a hotel. In several old quarters of Iranian cities, enterprising Iranians saw great promise in these dusty, crumbling relics from the nineteenth century, spruced them up, installed air conditioning, refurbished the rooms with antique furnishings, refitted the courtyard pools, and opened them up for business. In any other part of the world they would have been a developer's dream, with rooms going for $200 to $300 a night. But here in Iran, rooms were almost free for the taking, at around $40, but they were still a flight of fancy for those who believed, "Build it and they will come."

I had breakfast in the open-air courtyard and then made my way up to the bird market, tucked inside a neighborhood bazaar at a busy intersection. Middle Eastern countries may be known for camel markets and the trading of goats, sheep, and donkeys, but, geographically, Iran lies on the eastern fringe of the Middle East. It may border Iraq and the Arab states on the other side of the Persian Gulf, but its eastern border faces Afghanistan, and beyond that Pakistan and central Asia, where the delight in avian wildlife has been celebrated for centuries, in painting and poetry.

Many centuries ago, the Sufi poet Rumi found expression through the image of the bird:

> I want to sing like the birds sing,
> Not worrying about who hears,
> Or what they think.

And the thirteenth-century master Saadi observed:

> A student who learns without desire
> Is a bird without wings.

In Persian literature the bird has also represented freedom and the flight of the soul. In *The Conference of the Birds*, a twelfth-century literary masterpiece of allegory by the poet Farid ud-Din Attar, all of the birds in the world congregate to choose a ruler. Yet each candidate possesses a human shortcoming that has hindered its spiritual progress. To become ruler, each must reach the dwelling of Simorgh, which in Farsi means thirty (*si*) birds (*morgh*). During their journey, many die, and only thirty of the birds eventually reach Simorgh, where they learn a simple but illuminating lesson—that enlightenment resides only in themselves.

Like so much Persian poetry, natural imagery quickly attains spiritual meaning, as though the purpose of the natural world were little more than to serve as a window into the ethereal. In *The Conference of the Birds*, Attar wrote:

> If Simorgh unveils its force to you
> You will find that all the birds,
> Be they thirty or forty or more,
> Are but shadows cast by that unveiling.
> What shadow is ever separated from its maker?
> Do you see?
> The shadow and its maker are one and the same,
> So get over surfaces and delve into mysteries.

The master of verse Hafez connected birds to his favorite subject—love—but a kind of love that embraces both the earthly and the spiritual:

> I saw two birds on a limb this morning
> Laughing with the sun.
> They reminded me of how
> We will one day exist.
> My dear,
> Keep thinking about God,
> Keep thinking about the Beloved
> And soon our nest will be the
> Whole firmament.
> Forget about all your desires for truth,
> We have gone far beyond that.
> For now it is just—
> Pure need.
> Both our hearts are meant to sing.
> Both our souls are destined to touch
> And kiss
> Upon this holy flute
> God carries.

Anywhere in the world such a potent image would rise to the level of myth, and the bird and Iran are no different. In Persian mythology the bird of legend is Simorgh. Simorgh resembles a giant eagle or hawk, but she—and Simorgh is unequivocally female—is anything but a vicious bird of prey. She embodies the values of kindness, empathy, nurturance, and generosity. Simorgh also possesses great wisdom. She has lived so long that she has survived three cycles of the destruction of the world, and in that time absorbed all the knowledge of humanity. Simorgh is also responsible for the fertility of the Earth. She made her nest in the Tree of Life, which rose from the center of the Vourukasha (World Sea). Whenever Simorgh flew from the tree, its leaves shook so violently that it scattered the seeds of every plant on Earth, and this abundant greenery possesses the power to cure the maladies of all humankind.

The powers of Simorgh are most vividly revealed in a tale from Ferdowsi's *Shahnameh.* The grandfather of Rostam was Saam, and, according to the epic poem, Saam was horrified when his wife gave birth to an albino son, whom he named Zal. But Saam believed Zal to be the offspring of demons, so to be rid of him, Saam left him to die on the slopes of the Alborz Mountains. Little did Saam know that the mountaintop was also home to Simorgh. The bird heard Zal's weeping and saved him from certain death, and then raised him as she would one of her own offspring. As time passed, Zal longed to return to the world from which he had come. Parting was difficult, but when the time came Simorgh gave Zal three golden feathers to burn should he ever need her to come to his aid.

Zal returned home and eventually found a wife in Rudaba, one of the kingdom's beauties. Soon they were expecting a child, and when the time came Rudaba's labor was long and painful. Rudaba was about to die when Zal called upon Simorgh by burning the three feathers. True to her word, the bird appeared and taught Zal how to deliver the child by caesarean section. Rudaba survived and gave birth to the legendary hero Rustam.

I found the bazaar and the bird market with relative ease, but neither the spirit of Attar nor of Hafez. But there were birds, by the dozens and hundreds, silent and squawking, flittering and fluttering in metal cages, some still too young for flight. A group of children were gathered around a cardboard box where a collection of young chicks, newly hatched and brightly colored in yellow, pink, blue, and green, flapped their wings and tried to squint through eyes that had yet to see. All were destined to live the rest of their lives in cages in middle-class homes, where they would be watered and fed and occasionally spoken to and played with, but the emotional lift of the spirit inspired by the words of Hafez, Attar, and other poets would be confined to their verses, caged like the birds in the bird market.

I left the market quite downcast. The noise and flutter of feathers, mixed with the stench of the droppings, made it hard to connect this world of birds to Hafez:

> Both our hearts are meant to sing,
> Both our souls are meant to touch.

I left the market behind and headed off to the Ali Gholi Agha Hammam, or traditional bathhouse. It had been built by Ali Gholi Agha, a member of the royal court in the early eighteenth century. Most traditional bathhouses in Iran have been converted either into museums or restaurants, and the Ali Gholi went the historic route.

In the nineteenth century Esfahan was sprinkled with dozens of bathhouses, fed by wells rather than hot springs. They held an important place in both social and religious life. If one wanted to catch up on local gossip, informed citizens went to the bathhouse. If a devout Muslim wanted to maintain bodily purity, he or she went to the bathhouse. If one wanted to kill two birds with one stone, the bathhouse was the place to do it. The bathhouse also functioned as a one-stop medical clinic. If one were suffering from muscle tension, insomnia, bronchitis, anxiety, or any of a list of ailments, a physician might prescribe a trip to the bathhouse.

On the way to the Ali Gholi I imagined a loincloth hanging outside, which in the nineteenth century signaled it was open to men. No loincloth in the morning meant women's hours. In the nineteenth century there also would have been no ticket seller, for the visit would have been provided as a community service. The greeter would have been the *hammami*, who supervised an army of staff whose skills could satisfy every human need. The *dallak* would scrub the client's body with a sponge mitten. A haircut would be given by the *salmani*, a shave by the *challakian*. My clothes would be looked after by a *jamehdar*. An *asignan* would massage my muscles. If I wanted my head shaved, a *sartoashan* would do it. A *sonybandan* would dye my beard, and the *fassandan* would drain any bad blood lurking in my veins.

Let us imagine this is the nineteenth century. I am only here for a simple bath, to wash away the stench of the bird market. I move on to the vaulted hall lined with stone slabs. The light from the ceiling dome passes through imbedded triangles of glass and fills the room with a soft blue-and-white glow. I strip down, wrap myself in a loincloth, and sip sweet tea while the attendant soaps me down. From there I move on to the *garm-khane*, or steam room. After a dip in the pool I stretch out on another slab of stone, and the dallak pours water on the tiles, heated through an underground piping system. Quickly, the air is puffed with clouds of steam. My muscles become limp ribbons. The dallak takes a pumice stone and rubs off the rough, dead skin on my heels and palms. Fully poached and scraped, I am ready to leave.

In the heyday of the *hammam* there would have been stands nearby where clients could refresh themselves with a glass of cherry or pomegranate juice. Nothing like that was waiting when I left, but further up the street I found a juice bar and took some of the edge off with a watermelon-mint combo. With or without the bath it went down cool and smooth, whipped up sparklingly fresh in the blender behind the counter, a recharge just as the afternoon was warming up.

A few minutes later I was back at Naqsh-e Jahan Square. There was no sign of Ahmadinejad's visit of the day before. Not even a torn poster of the hardline duo of Khomeini-Khamenei remained. Like the traveling circus that it was, it had been packed up and carted away. For Esfahanis like Mehrad it was welcome relief. The cleanup crew was sweeping up not discarded trash but the specter of the regime itself.

Naqsh-e Jahan Square was the creation of Shah Abbas after he moved his capital to Esfahan from the northern city of Qazvin, fearing the expansion of the Ottoman Empire. Esfahan was further south but at the time better strategically located, close to the Persian Gulf and the increasingly profitable trade routes for Portuguese and other European merchants. The city also developed a reputation for tolerance and inclusion, which in historical terms dated back to the reign of Cyrus I. Many ethnic and religious groups had made the city their home. Some of the Jews freed from Babylonian captivity settled in Esfahan rather than return to Jerusalem. An account by Ibn Al-Fajah Al-Hamedani, a tenth-century historian, reads:

> When the Jews emigrated from Babylon, fleeing Nebuchadnezzar, they carried with them a sample of the water and soil of Jerusalem. They did not settle down anywhere or in any city without examining the water and soil. They did this everywhere until they reached Esfahan. There they rested, examined the water and soil, and found that both resembled Jerusalem. Then they settled there, and today the name of this settlement is Yahudia.

Many centuries later, Esfahan would receive an inflow of Christians. Throughout the sixteenth century the northern reaches of the empire were populated with Christian Armenian communities under threat from the Turkish Ottomans. In 1606 Shah Abbas ordered a forced resettlement of the Armenians to Esfahan and set aside a section of the city to be their new home. Three hundred thousand Armenians were sent south to populate New Julfa, named after the thriving Armenian city of Julfa, north of Tabriz. The shah's motives are still a little on the sketchy side. Aside from any threat the Turks posed to the Christian minority, he recognized the Armenians' talents in business and commerce, and believed they would provide the economy of his empire with a shot in the arm, and there would be no better place to do this than in the new capital. After much hardship on the part of the Armenians—namely, hunger and disease—those who survived the trek flowed into the Julfa district. For the survivors, it may have been worth it. Quickly, the Armenian merchants became major players in a trading network that stretched from Europe to eastern Asia, laying the foundations of a modern Iranian economy.

The city that Shah Abbas created became a veritable melting pot of cultures from Asia and beyond. Chinese porcelain masters were brought to Esfahan to teach their trade to local craftsmen. The Armenians mingled with Indians, Turks, Georgians, and Christian missionaries. Naqsh-e Jahan Square became the center of civic life. Merchants bought and sold goods that passed through Iran on the camel caravans traveling along the Silk Road. After sunset, the square became Esfahan's entertainment central. Puppeteers and jugglers performed for children, Esfahanis relaxed in coffeehouses, and to provide the needed touch of the risqué, prostitutes combed the crowd in search of clients. The square was also an occasional polo ground, with the shah watching the matches from the third-floor balcony of his Ali Qapu Palace.

Today it would seem ironic that, given its liberal history, Esfahan would become one of Iran's more religiously conservative cities. This is not owing to an abundance of shrines to draw the Shiite faithful, as in Mashhad, or being recognized as an important center of Islamic learning, like Qom. What Esfahan still has are madresses, or teaching centers, where aspiring mullahs cut their teeth on the fine points of Islamic law and Islamic principles. In the medieval period, the golden years of Islamic learning, a student's curriculum included studies in theology, philosophy, natural science, and metaphysics.

In the seventeenth and eighteenth centuries, one of the most prominent madresses was the Chahar-bagh, an expansive complex that had its own mosque, bazaar, and caravansary to accommodate passing traders. Like the monasteries and convents in medieval Europe, the madresses also functioned as business enterprises. Profits from the Chahar-bagh bazaar helped to fund the school, representing the interweaving of religion, politics, and economics that drove civic life not only in Esfahan but in much of Iran. Today the Chahar-bagh is still a functioning madresse, a quiet haven set apart from the urban calamity but residing, quite contentedly, in the middle of it. Shade trees rise over a rectangular pool that connects two brilliant blue-tiled iwans. The dome above the prayer hall is a circle of blue-and-gold-patterned tile work, like other domed ceilings meant to represent the beauty of the heavens.

The way to the mosque follows one of Esfahan's primary shopping streets. At a glance it looks like a commercial thoroughfare from anywhere—DVD outlets and electronics stores adjacent to shops for men's suits and children's toys, mobile phones and furniture, kitchen appliances and jewelry, and somewhere in-between a beauty salon and a one-stop shop for athletic wear. But look a little closer and differences appear. The womenswear boutique has an array of manteaux, or thigh-length jackets to meet the guidelines for proper Islamic wear, and a blizzardy array of headscarves and a wide variety of slacks, slacks being a garment of choice for Iranian women, because for a skirt to be worn in public it must extend to the ankles. None of the DVDs on display promoted American movies—all the latest releases are available, but in pirated form—and the choices of music rule out hip-hop and rap, Eminem and Beyoncé. But what is most striking is the lack of well-known international brands. There is the occasional Samsung store and a Sony outlet, and here and there a sign for Bata and Braun, Mango and Sephora, but they are infrequent waystations on the retail landscape. Strolling along any shopping street in Iran one is tempted to ask, What is wrong with this picture?

The answer is international sanctions. Sanctions have restricted outside investment in Iran, keeping many European retailers waiting at Iran's borders. For several years galloping inflation has made shopping in Iran more like a scavenger's hunt, as penny-pinching consumers flock to bazaars for daily essentials and keep a close eye out for sales on everything else. Consequently, many of the upper-middle class will do their high-end spending in the shopping malls of Dubai and Istanbul, but for Iran's upper crust, who are immune to the impact of sanctions, designer-brand shopping malls in North Tehran serve their needs. Other fashion-conscious Iranians will order favorite items from catalogs and have them delivered to local stores. A friend of mine in Tehran outfitted most of her apartment from Dubai's Ikea outlet. She was the head accountant for the French oil giant Total in its Tehran office, before Total pulled out of Iran entirely following American president Donald's Trump's withdrawal from the 2015 nuclear deal. Till then, she made monthly trips to Dubai to close the accounts for the Dubai office, and used the trips to pick up rugs and kitchenware and do-it-yourself furniture.

If I had been an Esfahani out running my weekly errands, the walk would have been a march of humiliation and frustration. Daily necessities were now priced as luxuries. The rial was snowballing downhill so quickly that many Iranians chose the only option for psychological stability—to stick their heads in the sand.

"We don't even check the exchange rate anymore," one friend told me. "We don't want to know how bad things are."

Fortunately, as I walked, the sun was out to add a bit of lightness to even the wan looks of disgruntled shoppers, and before this stretch became too depressing the street emptied into the grand bazaar.

Esfahan's bazaar sweeps around Naqsh-e Jahan Square in a mile-long arcade where almost anything in the city can be bought and sold, and even the stall keepers do their part to push the boundaries of the regime's Islamic codes. The female mannequins don manteaux that would be too tight for the morals police had they been worn by real women, and other mannequins are given a makeup treatment that puts them in the company of real women who use their faces as counterrevolutionary weapons and thumb their noses at the regime.

The bazaar is also an ideal place to people-watch Iranian expatriates, those who fled the country during the tumultuous years of the revolution and have spent the bulk of their lives in Europe, Canada, or the United States. When they return they visit places like the Esfahan bazaar to pick up souvenirs to retrieve a taste of their former lives, to reclaim a fading identity.

In a stall selling decorative glazed tiles I watched three young women poring over the pieces, moving on to pearl-inlaid jewelry boxes and lacquered pencil cases. They pulled at the corners of their headscarves, tugged at their manteaux wherever they bound up. It was obvious they hadn't learned to move in one smoothly, gracefully, like the local divas with decades of experience. Their facial features were clearly Persian, and I could have been fooled into thinking they had lived in Iran all their lives, but then one called out, in unaccented American English, "Niloo, I think these are marked down!"

Then I was caught at my own game—I had fallen under the gaze of a man on the other side of the corridor.

"Hey, you're an American, aren't you?"

His genuine Nikes and neatly stitched Levis said he hadn't been doing much shopping in Iran.

Masoud had been living in suburban Los Angeles for more than thirty years. He had gone to the U.S. to study physics at Texas A&M University during the Iran-Iraq War and later earned a PhD at the University of Utah. From there he began working on hydrology projects for the State of California. The prospect of his returning to Iran faded with the years. He became an American citizen, but what had not diminished were his views of the Islamic regime.

"I never liked the shah," Masoud told me. "He became too self-centered. He thought he was Iran. But these bastards [referring to the ruling mullahs] I hate everything about them. They've tried to wipe out everything that is important to the Iranian identity, everything that means something to be Iranian, everything except Islam. They've stolen the history and culture of the country."

Being a foreigner, especially an American, serving as a sounding board for passionate denunciations of the ruling order from angry Iranians wasn't at all uncommon, but hearing them so soon in conversation was. I doubted that Masoud spent much time in suburban Los Angeles stewing over the regime. More likely, his return had stirred up long-dormant resentments, and running into a fellow American gave him license to release them. It added a new spin to the tired phrase, "You can't go home again." For an Iranian expatriate, you can't go happily, anyway.

"You know," Masoud went on, "most of the mullahs don't even support the government. You'll never hear it, but probably 80 percent are against it."

A claim like that seemed boggling, but nothing on the Iranian political landscape is impossible. I asked why.

"They see it as betraying true Islamic principles, and they see its hypocrisy, and then there's all the corruption."

Still, Masoud's view clashed with another I'd heard regarding the loyalty of the country's mullahs: "Of course they love the powerful position they hold. Why wouldn't they?"

To be sure, a touch of arrogant self-assurance could be seen in the body language of the mullahs strutting the streets, in Qom, and in Esfahan, and wherever their political power could assert itself. Once newly acquitted, political power was now a part of their role, and one they had gladly settled into. So they carried the air of self-entitlement one sees in the nouveau riches, with little humility and even less concern for the consequences of the power they hold. With so little popular support, their primary interest is not in learning how to use their power for the good of society but to simply preserve it.

Which view was closer to the truth? Did the mullahs on the street see through the ruling mullahs, or did they relish in the power they held by association? There was no reason to haggle over this, for it would have taken the rest of the afternoon and concluded nothing. Instead, Masoud shared a popular joke that had been circulating among the disaffected: "A woman stops at a traffic light and sees a mullah on the corner about to cross the street. She leans out of her window and yells, 'I want to piss on your turban!' 'You'll have to wait your turn,' the mullah replies. 'There's a long line.'"

We both laughed, and, as we parted, Masoud, as expected, wished me a very pleasant stay in Iran and then added, a bit wistfully, "You know, there are a lot of beautiful things to see here."

"I know," I said, with all honesty, and headed out.

Two of Iran's most stunning mosques stand on Naqsh-e Jahan Square—the Imam and Sheikh Lotfollah. Both are masterpieces of both Persian and Islamic architecture. Both were built in the early seventeenth century in the early reign of Shah Abbas. Both had to be constructed at oblique angles to the square so that they could face *qibla*, the direction of Mecca, since the square was aligned on a north-south axis. Today, both are UNESCO World Heritage Sites boasting beautiful blue tile work in their interiors and on their domes, and both are symbols of the Esfahan skyline. And that is where the similarities end.

Shah Abbas intended the Imam Mosque—called the Shah Mosque before the revolution—to be a grand place of prayer for all of Esfahan's faithful. Thus the massive, towering iwan at the entrance, welcoming all who entered, and the massive courtyard beyond. Each side features a large iwan, with the one facing Mecca the largest, though, in true iwan symbolism, all are intended to represent gateways to the spiritual world.

The four-iwan design of the Persian mosque was developed in the eleventh century and soon spread throughout central Asia. But Shah Abbas wanted his mosque to stand for far more than heavenly greatness. Consolidation of his political power was also to be expressed in the plan, so he built four minarets, each 120 feet in height, adding a political statement to his capital's skyline. It may have taken eighteen years to build, but there is nothing grand or monumental about the Sheikh Lotfollah Mosque. It is a dark, gloomy space accessed through an equally gloomy tunnel that takes a few twists and turns before opening into a dimly lit prayer hall decorated with dazzling tile work, and it is topped by a dome with the image of a peacock in the center. The shah didn't build the Sheikh Lotfollah to impress. It has no minarets, because the purpose of the minaret is to call the people to prayer, and the Sheikh Lotfollah was meant for private worship. Its purpose was to be used solely by members of the royal family and the court, and as a place for the women to pray in private. It was not named for any noteworthy Persian but for a traveling Lebanese preacher who happened to be visiting Esfahan.

Despite its modest scale, the mosque's beauty was enough to impress the twentieth-century travel writer Robert Byron, who wrote in *The Road to Oxiana* (1937):

> I have never encountered splendor of this kind before. Other interiors came into my mind as I stood there, to compare it with: Versailles, or the porcelain rooms at Schönbrunn, or the Doge's Palace, or St. Peter's. All are rich; but none so rich.

Curious as to whether I'd be treated to the same magic, I zigzagged down the dimly lit tunnel until it opened up into the prayer hall. It was as dark as a dungeon, but, through the small window grills high near the dome, sharp shafts of light splashed across the blue-and-gold tiles on the opposite walls, recreating the arc of the sun as it passed across the sky. The light was enough to illuminate the rest of the hall with a dim glow that resembled moonlight. The dark blue tiles turned the room into a sanctuary of perpetual nightfall, resembling a forest under a full moon, while the golden tiles were able to catch the light, flickering like distant stars.

The room was as quiet as it was dim. A few more visitors entered. Voices were lowered to a whisper. The only resonant statements came from the verses of the Quran that rose up and down the sides of the mihrab and around the base of the dome in bands of swirling white calligraphy. There was no need for a display of clocks indicating the times for prayer, because the room was a hallowed space set apart from the busy square and the public world it represented. It was an intensely private refuge that even for an unbeliever would encourage a retreat into the realm of the spirit.

Back in the square, I had to pop my sunglasses back on to let my eyes readjust to the afternoon light. I had only been in the mosque for fifteen or twenty minutes, but I felt as though I had been jarred out of a deep sleep. Everywhere life was humming. Shoppers loaded down with bags were leaving the bazaar, and around the pool the fountain spouts were spraying water in parabolic arcs. Sweating locals had removed their shoes and were sitting poolside, cooling their feet.

I strolled over to the Imam Mosque. While the Sheikh Lotfollah provided privacy and seclusion, the Imam provided grandeur. Entering the courtyard, I stumbled into a world of giants. The courtyard stretched into the distance like the surface of the open sea. The tops of the iwans poked the highest heights of the skies. But the most beautiful feature of the mosque was its central dome. It was Persian architects who added the dome to mosque design, beginning in Iran and eventually spreading throughout the Islamic world. Sheikh Bahai Ad-Din Al-Amili, responsible for the creation of Naqsh-e Jahan Square, made sure that the crest of the dome of the Imam Mosque would be the highest point in the city. He covered the interior with the customary gold and blue tiles, but here they were arranged in seven concentric circles, to represent the divisions of the heavens, which embrace the sun, the moon, and all of the stars.

Persian architects also understood that buildings couldn't be all show and no tell. With such a large congregation to preach to and without the aid of amplified sound, acoustics mattered. Consequently, the dome and its supporting walls were constructed so that the preacher could speak at any volume higher than a whisper and his voice would carry to its furthest corners. To test it, I stood beneath the exact peak of the dome and pretended I was blowing out a birthday cake full of candles. I waited. There was a second of silence—and then a hollow "hush" echoed from the back of the hall.

With such stunning settings to send their prayers to the heavens, it might seem surprising that Iranians are the least-frequent mosque-goers in the Muslim world. The BBC has estimated that only 1 to 2 percent of Iranians attend Friday prayers. Only about one-fourth bother to pray at all. The Islamic regime may have only itself to blame. Decades of enforced Islamic dogma have alienated the once moderately religious not only from Islam but religion itself.

Back in the sixteenth century, the square had more than mosques to offer. Across from the Sheikh Lotfollah Mosque was Ali Qapu Palace, the digs that Shah Abbas set up for himself in his new capital. In the ancient world symbolism mattered, so he, too, followed the common practice of building on the ruins of former rulers, as a way of replacing one imperial domination with another. Thus, the foundation of Ali Qapu was constructed on the site of a former Uzbek palace. But Ali Qapu was built in fits and starts, with bits and pieces of the palace cobbled together over seventy years. Nevertheless, Ali Qapu as it stands today is largely the house that Shah Abbas built, with a view of the entire city from its upper floors, which made the entire square his front lawn.

Ali Qapu means "Imperial Gate," but the prime feature of the palace was, again, acoustics. Back in Safavid times Ali Qapu straddled one of the entrances to the square, and the archways were designed to preserve sound as it traveled within its four corners. To give it a try, I stood beside one of the pillars supporting the entrance arch and spoke so quietly that I could hardly hear my own voice, but it could be heard with crisp clarity on the other side. I had tried the same in the Whispering Gallery of St. Paul's Cathedral in London, the balcony that hangs high over the altar, but here at Ali Qapu there were open archways through which the sound could escape while still holding tight, like a balloon with holes that did not leak. Even Sir Christopher Wren would have been impressed.

The acoustic feat for which Ali Qapu is most well known lies much higher up, on the sixth floor, known as the Music Room. During the reign of Shah Abbas it was the setting for music and choral performances when royal guests were on hand to be entertained. I started the climb, up a narrow staircase that wound up through the center of the palace past dim, fusty rooms in need of a sprucing up, and ended where it opened up into an attic-like room that was spacious enough to serve as an intimate salon.

The room was vaguely circular and tapered as it rose to a pinnacle too pointed and angular to be called a dome. The walls were covered with rows of niches that extended to the ceiling. The openings were cut in decorative shapes of vases, flowers, and, of course, musical instruments, which trapped the echoes and allowed the original sounds to swirl through the room, all to the delight of the listeners.

I didn't bother to test the effect by whispering, sneezing, coughing, blowing my nose, or making any other sound, because the purpose of the Music Room wasn't to make sound travel but to preserve its purity. So after a few minutes I left, winding back down the staircase until I reached the third floor, to have a look at the view that Shah Abbas enjoyed when seated on his royal balcony.

The balcony still presents a royal view—the Sheikh Lotfollah Mosque directly across, the dome of the Imam Mosque to the right, the entire square spread out in all its green glory—but what was even more striking were the paintings to the right and left of the entrance. The one to the left showed a tall, willowy woman in a flowing red silken dress, black hair falling down her shoulders. Her figure forms a sweeping curve, passing through her torso from the left and to the right through her long legs. It was painted by Reza Abbasi, Shah Abbas's personal painter. Other paintings by Abbasi throughout the palace depict animals, birds, and floral patterns. Together, they do more than announce a break with the formal dictates of Islam brought by Arab invaders, which prohibited the representation of living creatures. They affirm the Persian appreciation of sensual beauty that both human and natural life can express.

Naqsh-e Jahan Square is, after all, a square, and being a square it has four sides. I had covered three and knew there had to be something worth seeing on its southern end. I left Ali Qapu and crossed the lawn that fills the southern half of the square, climbed another narrow, winding staircase tucked inside the entrance arch, and found the café that in Esfahan is the café of cafés. It has none of the architectural magnificence of the mosques or the palace. As cafés go it is rather drab and dreary, but it does have the most spectacular view of the entire square from its second-floor balcony.

It was time for a break. I had been walking since morning and needed a recharge. I ordered a mint tea from the serving counter and found an empty table with the best view in all of Esfahan, and arguably all of Iran.

If twenty-first-century commercial tourism had swept in on Esfahan, the café would have menus in at least four languages; tour buses would be idling outside the entrance arch from morning till evening;

there would be a half-hour wait for a table among throngs of Russians, Koreans, Chinese, Scandinavians, and other Europeans; and of course the prices would be five times what they are.

But twenty-first-century tourism has yet to hit Esfahan, and so one of the most majestic views in Iran can be had for the cost of a cheap coffee. The serving counter was grubby, and the wobbly tables hadn't been replaced in thirty years, along with the cushions on the seats in the wall niches. Without Asian and European tour groups to hog the tables, they were taken up mostly by Esfahanis and visitors from other parts of Iran. Young couples cozied up in the niche seats while casual customers read newspapers and swapped tales of economic woe—in other words, did what café hounds do as they sip their glasses of sweet tea and cappuccinos.

After the signing of the 2015 nuclear agreement, Iran had hoped for a tourist boom that would give the ailing economy a boost from the euros, yen, and yuan that would come flowing in. Visa restrictions for many European countries were relaxed, and the tourist infrastructure, such as it existed, spruced up.

"We think there is enormous potential here," Aydin, my guide in Tabriz, had told me as we drove through the western edge of the Alborz Mountains. And he was right. The scenery rivals anything that can be found in Europe or the western United States. A ridge of mountain peaks topped with a fringe of snow cuts across the horizon, and tucked within its valleys are waterfalls and alpine pools, cascading streams and meadows laden with wildflowers. Iranian cities, large and small, are peppered with historic sights covering more than two thousand years of history, and within the circuit of globe-trotting adventurers definite bragging rights come with having notched destinations that few have visited. In the few years since the nuclear agreement was signed there has been a trickle of intrepid Europeans venturing to Iran, and almost all have shared glowing reports of their experiences, but the windfall of foreign visitors has yet to arrive. What went wrong?

"I don't think they really know how to promote Iran," Aydin had told me. "The desire is there, both for the economic benefit and to improve the image of the country, but the people in the government don't have any experience competing in the international tourist market. It's all very new to them."

That was true. While the global tourist industry mushroomed in the 1970s, 1980s, and 1990s, the regime was consumed with the Iran-Iraq War and maintaining its grip on power. Other parts of the world—China, India, Southeast Asia, even South America—raced ahead in developing a tourist infrastructure and grabbing their share of the international market. Negative media portrayals of Iran have not helped. But it can't be denied that Iran has also been its own worst enemy. The complete ban on alcohol, even in hotels and tourist locations, kills any possibility of a nightlife scene, and the mandatory hijab alienates many non-Muslim women.

The result is that the souvenir shops that circle the Naqsh-e Jahan Square do a fraction of the business that they could, but, on the bright side, the square, and the rest of Esfahan, has not been turned into a Persian theme park, with locals dressed up in medieval garb to have their photos taken with snap-happy foreigners. So, as the sun began to set, no throng of tourists was roaming around the square. It was almost empty, but as afternoon passed into evening it would fill up. In a few hours the lawn would be filled with picnic blankets. Families would be unpacking elaborate buffets they had carried from home kitchens. Manteau-clad young women would be wading in the pool while more locals lined its sides to cool their feet. Children would splash in the fountain spray and charge up and down the walkways on rollerblades. With few tourists to share it with, the Esfahanis would enjoy the square as their own.

It was time to move on. What lay ahead was the Zayandeh-rud, or the Zayandeh River, and the fourteenth-century bridges that link the northern and southern halves of Esfahan and, beyond the bridges, the Armenian Julfa district. I left the café and headed in the direction of the river along leafy thoroughfares that bypassed parks where young couples were slyly nuzzling on the benches, clusters of old men leaned on their canes as they watched the passersby, and mothers tried to control cantankerous children while pushing another in a stroller. And then there was the river, or part-time river. When I was first here in the summer of 2009 a prolonged drought had dried up the Zayandeh-rud entirely. Nothing but a barren, rocky riverbed cut through Esfahan, but the seven-hundred-year-old bridges were still doing their civic duty, not only holding Esfahan together by day but providing an eye-catching backdrop when brilliantly lit at night.

Esfahan's stone bridges are, after Naqsh-e Jahan Square, the visual signature of the city. They were also part of Shah Abbas's urban renewal project when he aimed to make the city a capital worthy of the name, and unifying the empire meant unifying the city. Eleven bridges cross the river, but those in the city center were designed to offer the strongest architectural, visual—and political—message. There is the Si-o Se Pol, named for the thirty-three arches that form the span. At about a thousand feet, it is also the longest. Then there is the Khaju Pol, the most eye catching, especially at night, when the entire span is lit, including the forty-foot-wide corridor that was designed to accommodate both foot traffic and horse carts. One of the bridges predates the reign of Shah Abbas by a thousand years—the Shahrestan. It was overhauled in both the tenth and eleventh centuries, and the peaceful, dual parabola of the present span adds a touch of modernism in its simplicity.

I chose the Si-o Se Pol to cross the river, for no other reason than I wanted the trek to last the longest. Halfway across I stopped to look upriver. Gently rolling parkland lined both sides of the Zayandeh-rud, with the riverside pathways ready for cyclists and joggers, skaters and power walkers, now that the day was done and the active set of Esfahan was ready to hit the river. The Si-o Se Pol is a double-decker, and at the time of Shah Abbas government officials would select choice spots to watch rowing competitions. The shah did them one better. He constructed a small pavilion in the middle of the span, a prime spot from which to gaze out over the river and admire his capital.

From the end of the bridge I walked westward along the river, and then turned left toward what is arguably the most significant concentration of Armenians outside present-day Armenia.

The Iranian-Armenian connection is one of the oldest between peoples of different cultures and faiths in the Middle East. And it is remarkable considering the two have never shared the same religion or language. Armenia became the first nation in the world to adopt Christianity as the state religion, in 301, more than three centuries before the Arab invasion, when Islam began to usurp Zoroastrianism as the religion of the Persians. Intermarriage between Armenians and Persians was commonplace as far back as the third-century Parthian era. Then the arrival of Christianity pulled Armenia westward, while the arrival of Islam three centuries later drew Iran closer to the Arab world. But the Armenian merchants and craftsmen who dominated many of the cities of Iran's northwest stayed put, and the Persians made no attempt to drive them back to their historic homeland.

Christianity has a long history in Iran, almost as long as Christianity itself. The Acts of the Apostles states that Parthians, Persians, and Medes converted to Christianity at Pentecost, and the Parthian kings allowed the new religion to spread throughout the empire. Christians fleeing Roman persecution found a safe haven in Iran. But, for the next 1,500 years, the fortunes of Persian Christians were beholden to the political conflicts sweeping across Asia.

In the fourth century, the Zoroastrian ruler Shapur II initially allowed religious freedom but then cracked down on both Christians and Jews. Khosro Anushiruwan allowed Christians into the royal court after going to war against the Byzantine emperor Heraclius. Christians enjoyed the status of a protected minority in the early centuries of Islamic rule, but the Crusades revived religious tensions. The early Mongol rulers converted to Christianity after they invaded in the thirteenth century, but when later rulers opted for Islam, persecution resumed.

The invasion of the Uzbeks under Tamerlane in the fourteenth century, the later Turkmen wars, and the even later incursions of the Ottomans had a crippling effect on the Armenian population of northern Iran. Much of the sixteenth century was taken up with wars between the fragmented Persians and the increasingly powerful and expanding Ottoman Empire, with the Christian Armenians caught in the middle. When

Shah Abbas chose to move his capital from the vulnerable northern city of Qazvin to Esfahan, he decided to take the Armenians with him.

For the Armenians, initially, it was not a move up. Over half died from hardship and disease. The remainder settled in the newly created district that Shah Abbas had carved out for them. Then things took a turn for the better. The Armenians were given privileges not accorded to Muslims. Islamic dress was not enforced, and the Armenians were allowed to make wine. In public administration they had their own courts and elected officials and were allowed to operate schools where children were taught in the Armenian language. Harsh punishments were meted out to anyone found harassing the newly arrived minority. Most important, Armenian merchants were given a monopoly over the silk trade. In return, the Julfa district, and therefore the entire city of Esfahan, became fantastically rich. Shah Abbas himself would pay visits to Armenian merchants in their lavishly decorated homes. Through their contacts in the Christian West, the Armenians also brought modern technology to Iran, which was then carried eastward into central Asia and China. The first printed book in Iran, in 1638, was the Book of Psalms, written in Armenian.

When the Armenians arrived in Esfahan and settled in the Julfa district, in 1606, the first thing they could do to make it a home for themselves was build a church. Ground was broken for Vank Cathedral, funded by Armenian merchants. Khajeh Stepanusian footed the bill for the interior decoration. Armenian artists who had studied in Europe added the paintings that cover the walls and dome.

Esfahan still has thirteen Armenian churches, including the Church of Bethlehem and Church of St. Mary, just a short walk from Vank, but the cathedral was where I was headed, and I eventually found it after leaving Julfa's main thoroughfare and zigzagging through its back streets.

Julfa still reflects the buzzing commercial hub of its origins, but, rather than dabbling in silk and other commodities, today's merchants operate high-end boutiques that sell designer fashions—Iranian style—along with cosmetics, handbags, and perfumes for style-conscious Iranian women, in other words, almost all of them.

Vank is much more than a church, or even a cathedral. It is the center of Armenian cultural life in Iran, a building complex behind walls that encircle the entire block. The cathedral may be its centerpiece, but the complex also contains a museum where many of the displays address the 1915 genocide, with archival proof to rebut doubters and an ample collection of grisly photographs to shock visitors first introduced to it. More Armenians poured into Iran fleeing the 1915 genocide, and the newly formed Soviet Union sent more Armenians south to escape communist rule. In a lonely corner of the grounds stands a simple memorial—an elegantly tapered white spire no more than three meters tall that remembers the lost with humble dignity. A memorial honoring patriarchs of the Armenian Church occupies a stone niche beside the cathedral, and more graves can be found within the walls near the entrance, creating a complex impression of celebration, preservation, renewal, and mourning.

The Armenians of Iran long had a dual identity. This is reflected in the cathedral, which displays deferential nods to Persian culture. The domed interior echoes the Persian mosque, and floral paintings above the entrance are reminiscent of Persian miniatures, but all the rest is pure Armenian, with visual reminders of recent Armenian history. Creation is represented on the dome, and a puffy, pudgy cherub flapping white wings greets visitors. The history lesson is saved for a series of murals that wind around the walls, where the abuses of the Ottomans are portrayed in ghoulish detail.

After a look at the cathedral I wandered over to the museum and spent some time eyeing the religious artifacts—Bibles printed in the Armenian language, garments worn by the patriarchs, gilt crosses, jeweled chalices, and other knickknacks from across the Armenian world. But even more intriguing than the objects sealed behind the display cases were the reactions of visitors as they passed through. A reverential silence filled the room, equal to that in the cathedral on the other side of the courtyard. Some of the visitors, mostly Muslim Iranians, were getting their first lesson on the horrors of 1915, while others gained new insight into a singular slice of their own history.

After another look at the cathedral and a stroll around the grounds I headed over to the Church of Bethlehem—or Bedkhem as it is locally known—also tucked behind a nondescript wall within the back lanes of Julfa. I had to bang on the knocker a few times before the caretaker appeared, an old man with a scraggly salt-and-pepper beard and baggy pants cinched to his waist by a belt far too long for his skinny frame. The tail flapped wildly and hung to the tops of his legs. But he was pleased to receive a visitor and led me to the door of the church after collecting the entrance fee. He didn't have any change for the 50,000-rial note I handed him, wagging his head in embarrassment, but grinned in relief when I gestured that he could keep it.

The Church of Bethlehem is surrounded by a cozy, peaceful courtyard shaded by towering trees, making the setting even more of a haven for the spirit than the Vank complex. The late afternoon sun was passing into evening, filling the courtyard with glowing light. The rays cut into the darkness of the church, illuminating a square in the shape of the door on the opposite wall. Outside, a breeze was blowing down the river and into the Julfa district, stirring the leafy branches high overhead and filling the air with the sound of lightly flapping sails.

Bethlehem's interior was another vertical hall taller than it was wide, and this one was covered with seventy-two paintings depicting scenes drawn from the life of Christ. The church was also a gift to the Armenian community by a local merchant, and an inscription across the southern entrance pays him homage:

> Pray for Khaju Petros, who was a good man in the presence of God. He built this church from his own personal expense for the immortality of his name, and his father's name, and his mother's name, in 1077 [Armenian calendar].

As the fate of religious minorities go, the Armenians have done exceptionally well in Iran. A brief setback occurred during the reign of Reza Shah Pahlavi, when his "Persianization" movement in the 1930s restricted the use of the Armenian language in Armenian schools, but the law was later overturned by Mohammad Reza. Since then, the

Armenians have remained significant players in the country's economic and political life.

If I was an Armenian living in Iran today I could send my children to a special school where they would be taught in the Armenian language. For special celebrations, weddings, and birthdays, I could throw parties where men and women would be allowed to mix freely and dance to the tunes of officially "banned" music, providing I kept the volume low. If I had a knack for politics I could run for one of the five seats in the Majlis, or parliament, set aside for religious minorities, and if I were ambitious enough I could seek one of the seats designated for observer status on the powerful Guardian Council, the arm of the Islamic regime charged with interpreting the constitution and approving electoral candidates for the Assembly of Experts, the parliament, and the presidency itself.

When Shah Abbas herded the Armenians to Esfahan he may have had their commercial prowess in mind, but today they are valued by many Muslim Iranians for their access to a special commodity—alcohol. It has been officially banned in Iran ever since the Islamic Revolution, but the Islamic regime turns a blind eye toward its use in the Armenian community. The positive spinoff for nonobservant Muslim Iranians is that the Armenians serve as their bootleggers.

"Oh, sure—my father has his Armenian contact," Shadi, a friend in Tehran, told me. "He'll call him and he'll bring him whatever he wants. He got his name at work. All he had to do was ask around. It's not hard."

The privileges allowed Armenians are not all hush-hush. In any city with a substantial Armenian community, such as Tehran and Esfahan, specially licensed "Armenian clubs" provide a place where the Christian minority can socialize as Christian Armenians. Beyond their doors the constraints of the Islamic Republic are suspended, and they are allowed to welcome non-Muslims. On one of my first nights in Tehran I went to an Armenian club for dinner, just a short walk from the Kosar Hotel. It was not hard to find. Down one of the dimly lit side streets a bright light illuminated an ornately carved wooden door. There was no sign, and it didn't need one. The glowing bulb above the entrance and the brightly painted yellow wall said it wasn't just another house front in another nondescript Tehran neighborhood.

The door opened easily, and I was greeted on the other side by an elegant middle-aged woman in a dark brown silk dress and curly brown hair that tumbled beyond her shoulders. Her English was minimal, but she knew what I was there for and led me into a large dining room that had once been the reception room of a well-to-do house. The menu was printed in Farsi, Armenian, and, of course, English, to accommodate foreign guests. The women had checked their head-scarves and manteaux at the coat rack near the door and were seated at the tables in sleeveless tops and other summer garb common in public before the revolution. An elderly man at a nearby table asked for a tumbler of ice, and when it came he added a double shot of Scotch from a half-pint bottle tucked in the pocket of his sport coat. The fish filet with French fries and salad I ordered was no better or worse than I could have had elsewhere, but the experience was one no Muslim Iranian could share.

I once asked a friend in Tehran if she had ever been to one of the Armenian clubs. She worked for a multinational company, the kind of employer that typically includes members of every conceivable race, religion, and ethnicity among its staff.

"One of my Armenian colleagues told me she would love to invite me but it would be much too risky."

For you? The friend? The club?

"Everyone," she replied.

I found my way back to Julfa's shopping street as the evening dusk was settling over the district. The boutiques and upscale shops were coming to life. Female shoppers were crowded into one selling stylish manteaux and headscarves in a boggling array of patterns. At the cosmetics shop next door more women were picking through the selection of lipsticks, mascara, and choices of hair dye that would add streaks of red or yellow or orange to their dark brown and black locks, to expose beneath their habitually slippery headscarves. In the perpetual battle against the Islamic dress code, the women are at the frontlines.

Julfa is known for having some of the best restaurants in Esfahan, but tonight I was ready to swap quality of cuisine for ambience, so I headed back to Naqsh-e Jahan Square, setting my sights on the Bastani, atop the bazaar beside the Sheikh Lotfollah Mosque. At the Zayandeh River the dusk was passing into darkness. The lights of the bridges had come on, brightening the soft yellow stone and taking Esfahan back to its postmedieval heyday. The Khaju Pol and Si-o Se Pol became shimmering golden necklaces. This time I chose the Khaju Pol to cross, and the series of archways along the lower level. It was more like crossing the river through a tunnel than a bridge, but one that offered nighttime views both up- and downriver, which were blocked by the stone lining the walkway up top.

Halfway across I could hear voices up ahead, men's voices being carried through the underground corridor by the series of archways. They weren't the voices of speech but of song. A group of young men had gathered under one of the domes between the arches and were reciting, or singing, lines of Persian poetry. The Khaju Pol is a popular place for impromptu poetry readings, especially when events on the global political scene generate angst in Iranian society, which is most of the time. This time the occasion was the demise of the 2015 nuclear agreement and the prediction of harsh sanctions and more economic doom for the country's already staggering economy. It is illegal for women to sing in public in Iran, a violation of a most basic human right rarely publicized, so expression of the most recent letdown was left to this group of young men. One of them took his position directly under the arch and sang:

> Life is full of the good and the bad.
> I can laugh at the wind and the sea,
> Because I can tolerate anything . . .

I didn't want to linger, not because I was hungry, which I was, but because listening to the woes of Iranians can become tiring. It's not that they aren't justified, but that they are very justified, and so long-standing, and without any end in sight. So I left the dour chorale and moved on to the square. The warm evening air had kept the square full of loungers and picnickers. The blue domes of the Imam and Sheikh Lotfollah mosques glowed in the beams of the surrounding floodlights. A full moon was rising over the dome of the Sheikh Lotfollah, turning the curved blue surface a haunting purple in the twilight.

I found the tiny staircase leading up to the Bastani and decided to bury myself in a corner table so as not to attract attention and the inevitable litany of questions that would follow: Where are you from? What do you think of Iran? But it was not to be. The Bastani had no corner tables. It favored traditional seating, which meant no tables or chairs but takht platforms, open to the entire room to make dining a social experience—Persian style. But, aesthetics as a recompense, I really couldn't complain. The takht the hostess led me to had a front-row view of the dome of the mosque, brilliantly lit and radiantly blue—and she never asked where I was from.

I had the entire space to myself, a colossal waste of footage with the restaurant beginning to fill up. I had just removed my shoes and squiggled into place when a couple at the takht next to me asked, like friendly new neighbors chatting across a backyard fence, "Where are you—?"

They were Reza and Asfaneh, both licensed tour guides, both managing to make ends meet in a woefully depressed tourist market. Reza spoke near-fluent English and Asfaneh German, but she had also been studying Chinese. As expected, they invited me over to their takht, mainly to hear the uncensored views of Iran from a foreigner who wasn't a client. But this time I was first out of the gate. I asked them what impressions they had of foreign visitors to Iran.

"They are usually better educated than the tourists you find in many other parts of the world," Reza said. "And most of them have a lot of travel experience. Iran isn't the kind of place one goes to for their first trip abroad."

Earlier that day Asfaneh had taken a group of Germans to Esfahan's airport, where they would catch a domestic flight to Tehran and then a Lufthansa flight to Frankfurt. German was a handy language for a tour guide to know in Iran. For Germans, the allure of Iran is the spirit of adventure and the draw of the unique, as it is for many, but also the discovery of a distant historical tie. Ever since the revolution, the drive to emigrate has prompted many Iranians to make new lives for themselves in Germany, also drawn by a distant historical tie. A popular theory claims that the Farsi language, part of the Indo-European family, migrated out of central Europe millennia ago. It traveled southeast across the Balkan peninsula and Asia Minor, and finally settled in present-day Iran. The word *Iran* is derived from *Aryan*. The result is that, among the cultures of Europe, Iran has cultivated more of a "special relationship" with Germany than with any other.

Although Iran officially declared neutrality in both world wars, it tacitly backed Germany, prompting an invasion by British and Soviet forces in 1941 and the seizure of Iran's oil fields, the Allies fearing that the crude would secretly be funneled to the German army.

I asked Reza how many Americans he had guided in the last year.

"We get quite a few," he replied brightly, but numbers are always relative, and I wondered what "quite a few" really meant. I had often traveled for weeks in Iran and never encountered another Western traveler. Many times I wondered if I was the only American in the entire country. I ran into small groups of Chinese, and a few Koreans being led by a Korean-speaking guide, but a European or North American was a rarity. But Reza had led Americans. A few months back he had guided two professors from the Oriental Institute at the University of Chicago, the organization responsible for the excavation of Persepolis after it was discovered in 1931. A mammoth limestone bull's head from the ruins hangs in the institute's museum on the South Side of Chicago.

Asfaneh's rudimentary Chinese had come in handy, not guiding globe-trotting Chinese but leading Iranian tour groups to China. China had become her forte, and I asked how many times she had trooped through the Forbidden City or bussed out to the Great Wall.

"I have no idea—at least forty."

Current geopolitics has caused the Iranian tourist industry to be stymied in both directions. Despite the rosy outlook generated by the 2015 nuclear agreement, and the Iranian government's best efforts to put a better face on the country, the expected boost in tourism is still waiting to happen. And Iranians have long faced towering hurdles in obtaining visas to the world's favorite travel destinations—Western Europe, the United States, the Mediterranean. The fear of the visa refusers is not the threat of terrorism or Islamic fundamentalism. It is unheard of for an Iranian to be implicated in the kind of "soft-terror" attacks that have rocked European and American cities. Instead, the concern is that the "tourist" will use the visa path to gain illegal status and seek a new life outside of Iran. And the fear is justified.

Holiday destinations for many Iranians are limited to countries considered to be at least marginal allies or places so hungry for tourist income that almost any source of revenue will do. I had run into Iranians at Peterhof, the summer getaway of Czar Peter the Great in the suburbs of St. Petersburg, and before the horrifying civil war many Iranians could plan a getaway to Syria. Iranians regularly visit nearby Armenia and Lebanon, and Istanbul has been another favorite destination, but Reza found the experience so unpleasant he refused to lead any more groups to Turkey.

"They aren't interested in what Turkey has to offer at all," he said with a sigh. "Each day they'll go along with the program but just want to get it over with so they can go out drinking at night and hit the nightclubs. Some of the men will ask me where they can find Turkish women."

Then the conversation took an odd turn. It would seem wildly ironic that two people who had spent the better part of their adult lives promoting Iran would have in mind leaving, but that was the case. Reza said that the two had been exploring the prospect of relocating to the U.S., where they could start off guiding groups of Iranians around a country they hardly knew. But they had been boning up on American history and culture to become at least minimally credible authorities in the eyes of newcomers. And they had started laying the groundwork, contacting several tour companies in the U.S. run by Iranian Americans to sell their services.

Reza asked me what their chances were of getting a U.S. work visa, eventually even a green card. I didn't have a clue, but as always when talking to Iranians about migrating to the U.S., I didn't want to burst their balloon. As always, I found a way to preserve a vague sense of hope, and said something about the booming American tourist industry and the number of Iranians aching to inflate it some more. Visa restrictions? Tightening borders? I swept those questions away.

Then the check for our dinners came, but there was no fight over it, just the ritual dance of taarof:

Let me take that.

No, no, why should you?

You're my guest.

But I intruded on you.

Not at all. It was a pleasure.

Then let me return the pleasure.

But you're our guest.

I lost, as I knew I would, and should. After all, in Persian terms I was a guest. The only question was how it would play out, and it did as expected, with Reza paying the bill for the three of us. Then he offered to top the sundae with a cherry. Did I still have room for dessert? He had a special treat in mind, so we left the Bastani and headed down one of the streets leading out of the square. I thought Reza had *gaz* in mind, the soft, chewy chunks of nougat stuffed with pistachios that are the pride of Esfahan, but no. We arrived at what looked like an ice cream parlor, but no. It was a *bastani sonnati* parlor—an appropriate choice after dining at the Bastani restaurant. What is bastani sonnati? Reza told me: a blend of vanilla ice cream mixed with saffron, rose-water, and the mother of all Persian ingredients—pistachios. A line had formed at the counter as the postdinner crowd waited to satisfy their sweet tooths. The scoops were plopped in paper cups or wedged between cookie-like wafers. I tried to pay for the dessert, but lamely, knowing I'd only be beaten down in another battle of taarof. So Reza treated again, and we licked and slurped our bastani sonnatis out on the street as other customers did the same. When it was time to part, both Reza and Asfaneh, predictably, wished me a very pleasant stay in Iran, and Reza handed over one of his business cards.

"Let us know if you need anything, and let us know the next time you're here."

With that we parted, and I watched them vanish under the arches that formed the Ali Qapu Whispering Gallery.

There was still time for a nightcap—Iranian style. The café on the square, with its panoramic view, was closing down, but there was an alternative—the Azadegan, a cave-like, below-ground café near the eastern entrance to the square. I had stumbled on it my first time in Esfahan and was glad to see that, beyond the dingy entrance, illuminated by a single bulb, time had stopped. It still had wobbly tables and beaten-up chairs, and the cushions of the seating that lined the walls hadn't been replaced in at least thirty years. Most important, it still resembled a pack rat's overstuffed attic. Brass serving trays, coffee urns, broken clocks, and every other kind of discarded bric-a-brac lined the walls and dangled from the ceiling. It was frumpy and cluttered and chaotic, but oozed more charm than any chain coffee shop could muster in a century of cappuccinos.

I sat down at one of the tippy tables, and a young man of about twenty brought me a glass of black tea with an accompanying bowl of sugar cubes, to drink tea the Iranian way. It was the Persian way of mainlining sugar—placing a cube between the teeth at the front of the mouth and using it to filter the tea. At the other tables, clusters of men were puffing on water pipes while a few couples snuggled discreetly. A football match was playing on the TV mounted in the corner, but no one was watching. One of the tea sippers caught my eye—a woman of about thirty-five or forty with Western features, peering at a travel guide. Now it was my turn to be curious, receptive, and intrusive, that odd combination of qualities that Iranians managed to blend so well when running into foreigners. I edged over.

"May I ask—where are you from?"

Her name was Alena, and she was half-British, half-Greek, but had been living in the Netherlands for the past twenty years or so, where she ran a vendor's stall at the Waterlooplein open-air market, selling clothing and jewelry and other odds and ends from India, Bangladesh, and the Asian subcontinent. Alena was used to rambling around less-traveled parts of the world. Every year she spent two months touring India, scooping up goods to stock her stall at the Waterlooplein. But the trip to Iran was strictly a holiday. She had set aside a month and was nearing the end of her third week.

I asked what it was like traveling by bus as a single woman, and a foreign single woman. She spoke no Farsi, and almost everyone she encountered spoke no English, Dutch, or Greek.

She bubbled up. "The women keep showing me how to keep my scarf in place. They keep offering me sweets. Wherever we stop, the driver points to his watch to indicate how much time we have before we leave."

It isn't unusual for Western travelers to be met with expressions of disbelief and even dire warnings when they tell friends or family they are planning a trip to Iran. And a single woman? When Alena was back in Amsterdam, what would she tell her friends? Her reply was razor sharp.

"It was like traveling in a sea of gracious gentlemen."

I wasn't surprised. One of the reasons Iranians extend such hospitality to foreigners is to say, "See, *they* are not *us*." *They*, of course, means the regime, *us* means the "real" Iranians, the true Persian character, everyone and anything more than an arm's length from the government.

Then the chat with Alena was cut off. The waiter had overheard two foreigners bantering in English and decided to display some Persian hospitality. The football match on the TV was Brazil versus the U.S. in a World Cup qualifier. He turned up the volume and pumped his fist in the air.

"Go America!" he shouted.

10 | Yazd

LAND OF FIRE AND ICE

Doing good to others is not a duty. It is a joy, for
it increases your own health and happiness.
—Zoroaster

The day was waning, but the heat was not. It was six o'clock, more or
less, and I was watching the sun go down behind the hills to the west
of Yazd, turning the rooftops and *badgirs*, or wind towers, the defining
symbol of the city, a mystifying combination of orange and purple. I
had no thermometer but guessed, by the degree of fatigue that had
overcome me, that the middle of the day must have hit 120 degrees
Fahrenheit. Now I was sitting in the shade on a rooftop terrace of a
restaurant in the center of the city, but the tabletop was still warm to the
touch. A light breeze, blowing across the rooftops, balmy and refreshing
though it was, still carried the residue of the afternoon heat. I heard a
sharp squeal and looked down to see a cat scamper across the terrace,
the baked tile surface singeing its bare paws.

It was the time of day to take pleasure in a sundowner, so I ordered a
beer from the young waiter, who offered me a bowl of crunchy nibbles
after I had plopped myself down. Of course the beer contained no alcohol, the only kind available in Iran—legally, that is. I had tried several of
the alcohol-free brews before, and some were downright undrinkable,
but a few offered a strained resemblance to the real thing, not hard to

achieve after I had been wandering around a desert city like Yazd on a blazing summer afternoon. This one made the grade.

On the Iranian landscape Yazd sits in what might be called the middle of nowhere. One of the few urban outposts in Iran's remote southeast, it is at least four hours north of Kerman and three hours east of Esfahan, on the fringe of Iran's fertile farmland and the beginning of the central desert that spills over into neighboring Afghanistan.

We had driven from Esfahan across two hundred miles of parched and barren landscape that one unfamiliar with the beauty of the desert might describe as sensory depriving and monotonous, but for anyone who has traveled across New Mexico or Arizona at any time of year, the slowly changing palette of colors and shifting shadows as the sun arcs across the sky can delight the eyes, providing a range of stimulation all the more enticing because of its subtlety. The air was growing noticeably warmer each time we emerged from our air-conditioned cocoon, to fill the gas tank or stock up on road snacks, so the breaks became increasingly brief, until we made only mad dashes to and from the car, where the cool air pumped from the vents was matched by the mellow chords of Dave Brubeck's *Take Five* drifting from the CD player.

None of this was surprising, Yazd being one of the hottest cities in Iran in the summertime. But it is also one of the most arid in a country one friend described to me as being "as dry as a potato chip." For four hours I had traipsed around the center of the city in the midday heat, when most of the merchants had either shuttered to take their long lunch break, Mediterranean style, or dropped the blinds in front of their windows to protect against the punishing sun, and all that time I felt not a drop of perspiration. Now, though the intense heat had passed, a wave of exhaustion rolled over me. But not a drop of sweat.

Yazd's remote location has saved it, time and again, from the blood-spilling terror of the many invaders that have swept across the country through the centuries. Arguably, the most ruthless were the Mongols under Genghis Khan, who arrived in the middle of the thirteenth century. But slaughter elsewhere may have been a boon to the city, for many of Iran's elites—scholars, writers, and artists—fled to remote Yazd to escape the carnage to the north and west.

Like so many cities in Iran, Yazd took its turn serving as the capital, but only briefly, under the Muzaffarid dynasty in the fourteenth century. But for centuries it played a role as a welcome stopover on the Silk Road, hosting traveling merchants passing between Afghanistan to the east and Turkey to the west. Marco Polo passed through in 1272 and paid the city polite compliments:

> It is a good and noble city, and has a great amount of trade. They weave there quantities of a certain silk tissue known as Yasdi, which merchants carry into many quarters to dispose of. . . . There are many fine woods producing dates upon the way, such as one can easily ride through; and in them there is great sport to be had in hunting and hawking, there being partridges and quails and abundance of other game, so that the merchants who pass that way have plenty of diversion.

Today, in the raucous world of Iranian politics, Yazd wears no particular political stripes, for it has been home to Iranians from both ends of the spectrum, reformers and hardliners. Mohammad Ali Jafari, the current leader of the Revolutionary Guard, was born in Yazd, but so also was former president Mohammad Khatami, whose attempts at reform were stonewalled by conservative forces in the 1990s, and Mohammad Payandeh, a thorn in the side of the ruling order who was assassinated in 1998. Payandeh was a member of the Writers Association of Iran, a banned organization that has long campaigned for freedom of expression.

The boozeless beer was going down quite easily, thanks to the high-powered fridge in the interior of the café that had kept it ice cold. I ordered another, not having to worry about any debilitating surge of alcohol in the late afternoon heat. Behind me, the rattling of an air conditioner said that cooler and more comfortable seating could be had inside, but the sun had almost set, and the gentle breeze blowing across the rooftops took the edge off the heat, so I decided to stay put on the terrace and reflect on the day.

Hours earlier I had checked into the hotel and was eager to explore the city. Sohrab was content to enjoy the comfort of the hotel's air conditioning, so he left me to wander on my own, dropping me at the looming façade of the Amir Chakhmaq Complex and then skedaddling back to his room. It wasn't a bad idea. The Amir Chakhmaq, and the broad square laid out in front, was the best place to begin a tour of Yazd. Today the mammoth structure, with its two tapered minarets stretching ever skyward, dominates what amounts to Yazd's central square. It was built during the fourteenth-century Teymourian dynasty by the region's governor, Jalal Al-Din Amir Chakhmaq, with the advice and guidance of his wife, Fatemeh Khatoon. In its prime the complex contained a bazaar where passing traders would stock up on much-needed supplies as they made their way along the Silk Road, and there was a caravansary where they could rest their camels, and themselves, before pushing on.

The Amir Chakhmaq Complex started as a mosque, and as it evolved it retained the two towering minarets. Inside one, a circular staircase rises and twists as it gradually narrows, until it reaches a vantage point that looks out on the city and the desert beyond. Never mind the heat— the promise of the view was too tempting—so I began the climb, rising step by step as the cylinder became tighter and narrower but provided a needed buffer from the afternoon heat. Suddenly the steps ended, and the stairway gave way to an uninterrupted view of the city and open desert that swept in all directions.

A view from any height can draw everything around into focus. From the minaret's almost tip-top it was possible to see, in literal terms, the importance of a place like Yazd and what it must have meant to tired traders making their way between the green, fertile provinces of western Iran and the raw, rugged mountains of Afghanistan. Just beyond the longer, broader streets of the newer sections of the city lay the tight, twisting lanes of the original city of Yazd, the pathways and snug mud-and-plaster buildings wrapping around each other to guard against the vast, forbidding, and frightening void that encircled the city on all sides.

Medieval Yazd would have been the Manhattan of Iran, or Persia, as Iran was then known, if prominence was measured by the height of its

buildings and the dramatic skyline that they created. The minarets of
Amir Chakhmaq, as imposing as they appear, are not the tallest structures in Yazd. That honor goes to the minarets of the central mosque,
tucked within the side streets in the center of the city. The mosque dates
to the twelfth century and is still the primary place of prayer for the city's
faithful. In keeping with the spirit of conquest that reigned over Yazd
in medieval times, the mosque was built on the site of a Zoroastrian
fire temple constructed in the fifth century during the Sassanid era of
pre-Islamic Persia. It was constructed by Ala'oddoleh Garshasb at the
beginning of Persia's fertile medieval period, but two hundred years
later the civic powers decided it needed an overhaul, which took forty
years. Over time, which means centuries by Iranian time, three mosques
were constructed on the site, the first dating to the tenth century. Three
hundred years later a second was added, and in the fifteenth century
Rokn-el-din Mohammad Ghazi added a third. But in the nineteenth
century the Qajar rulers decided enough was enough, and rather than
add a fourth, they incorporated them all into one.

It was worth a look. I climbed down from the balcony of the minaret one careful step at a time and left the cooling comfort for Yazd's
blazing streets. I walked slowly, looking for patches of shade under the
shop awnings, but found myself detouring through Yazd's traditional
market. I had been to Yazd before, in the summer of 2009, when the
country was rocked by a widely disputed presidential election. The
U.S. had just been rocked by the election of the country's first Afri-
can American president. I was wearing a T-shirt with "NYC" stitched
in bold letters on the chest, and after I had passed the market stalls,
one of the shopkeepers emerged to shout, "I like your president!" But
no shopkeepers greeted me today, perhaps because my T-shirt didn't
point to any American identity. Or perhaps today was simply hotter.

After some twists and turns through Yazd's back streets I found the
mosque. But the circular, soaring minarets aren't its most impressive
feature, even if they do soar above the skyline of Yazd. No, they are
outdone by the façade, a masterpiece of tile work elaborately decorated in geometric patterns of blues ranging from deep cobalt to tur-

quoise and soft ermine. The designs begin at the base and extend up the front of the entrance, shifting patterns several times all the way to the top of the minaret. Just inside the entrance, Quranic verses in rigid Kufic script decorate the iwan, extending up one side of the enormous archway and down the other. I have always thought this was one of the most attractive features in any mosque, not only in Iran but anywhere in the Islamic world. Whether I could read the text or even grasp its meaning didn't matter. What was important was not what the words said but what they symbolized—the fusion of beauty and thought, artistry and ideas, into a single expression in which each served the other and represented a level of beauty that neither could achieve on its own.

I passed through the portal and entered the *shabestan*, or small foyer, that separated the inner courtyard from the prayer hall. Immediately the temperature dropped ten degrees. The dark gloom was another sharp change from the afternoon sun. It took a moment for the eyes to adjust, and as they did, the mosque's caretaker appeared—an old man in a tattered sport jacket, his head topped with a lace prayer cap. He shuffled so slowly his shoes barely came off the ground. His eyes, accustomed to the dark, widened with a hint of surprise upon greeting a foreigner—or he could have been shocked by seeing anyone around and about in the middle of a summer afternoon. He shuffled closer, raised his eyes, and asked, "Your country?" He made it sound like the answer was a password to gain entrance, or that he collected the nationalities of visitors like some people collect bottle caps.

I told him, and his face dropped a little. He looked almost weary.

"You like Obama?" he asked.

"I like Obama." I told him.

"Obama was good," he added.

I gave a thumbs-up.

"America and Iran—don't have to fight," he continued. "America and Iran—friends."

I gave another thumbs-up.

"Iran doesn't want fight, not anyone, not America. Obama no fight. Obama was good."

Another thumbs-up.

"Friends," I said, and extended a hand. He raised a limp palm and shook, and a little brightness came into his eyes.

Satisfied that Barak Obama's popularity had held up among mosque caretakers, I removed my shoes and padded around the prayer hall. Above the shabestan, a dome was decorated in blue geometric patterns. The *mehrab*, the semicircular niche in the wall pointing toward Mecca, stretched toward the ceiling in the manner of a gothic cathedral. The interior was at least as stunning as the outside, and I thought it a shame that so much beauty had been hidden away. But this could be seen another way—that the architect had so many beautiful plans for the mosque that, once the exterior was wrapped in glittering blue geometric designs, he could afford to discard the leftover, like a dressmaker tossing away useless fabric.

I returned to the sunny streets, where the occasional errand-goer, darting from air-conditioned shop to air-conditioned shop, was the only sign of life. Yazd can be a quiet, sleepy place, especially in the middle of a summer afternoon. But whenever I was about to write it off as nothing more than a quiet, sleepy place, I remembered Sohrab's reply when I asked where in Iran he would prefer to live. We were driving across the desert and had seen many cities, and he knew next to everything about them, the nooks and crannies of their history, both ancient and recent, and what they were all about in the present day. It was only natural to wonder, did he have a favorite? After returning from the U.S., he had settled in Shiraz, where the liberal environment allowed him to keep his extensive wine collection out of view of the authorities. But the city was never his first choice.

"Probably Yazd," he said.

I was surprised, asked him to elaborate.

"It's quiet and a little more traditional. It's far away from the big cities. It has more of the feel of the real Iran."

Yazd is definitely quieter and more "traditional" than Tehran and many of the other major cities, but of course that depends on how one defines "traditional." However this is worked out among the sociologists who try to define contemporary Iran, Yazd does offer an experience that is quintessential in the Middle East—getting lost in the torturous, winding lanes of the Old City.

Yazd dates to Sassanid times, and during the medieval period the centers of towns were purposely designed to create labyrinthine confusion to befuddle invaders who managed to pierce the city's fortifications. In this way the local residents would have a distinct advantage over an invading army, which would inevitably get lost in the illogical array of alleys and lanes.

Fortified by two pleasantly cool but boozeless beers, I felt enough confidence to plunge into Yazd's Old City, if only to see if I could find my way to the main street on the other side. I quickly learned that the scourge of any Old City is uniformity. After a few twists and turns, everything looked alike. The plain, dun-colored walls of the houses that lined the crooked lanes had no distinctive features except for the occasional electrical box or dual door knockers—a larger one for men who came calling, a smaller one for women, to alert the residents of the gender of the guest they were about to receive. The wood-carved front doors showed a hint of individuality, but only for a trained eye, one that can identify a pattern of design from a particular part of the country, not an overheated foreigner trying to find his way through the tanglework of streets.

Centuries ago, Silk Road travelers would rely on the stars to guide them, and so they often traveled at night, when the punishing afternoon heat had abated and the skies were aglow with celestial signposts. But now the sun had yet to set, and so the sky was still a uniform, cloudless blue. For me, it offered little help. I crisscrossed and doubled back over familiar ground and recognized landmarks I had passed several times— the shape of a door knocker, the colors of the flowers in a window box.

Then something changed. I remembered the advice of the Chinese philosopher Lao Tzu: "A good traveler has no fixed plans and is not intent on arriving." Then it became a pleasure to be utterly, completely, and totally lost. I turned right and left, and left and right, without feeling a hint of embarrassment seeing couples zipping by on motorbikes, brazenly sure of their destinations as well as the quickest ways to reach them. Usually the men straddled the driver's seat, while the women, their flowing black chadors flapping in the breeze, held tight from behind as the horn beeped to warn any traffic approaching from the blind corners.

Another realization appeared—that I wasn't lost at all, except in terms of geography. I was beginning to appreciate what Lao Tzu had advised—to dismiss the notion of a destination and appreciate the journey itself. And I was moving closer, deliberately, and without any twists or turns to an important observation—that in the midst of the most maddening disorder, human beings will establish their own patterns to overcome any chaos that threatens them. In American mythology this came to be called "taming the frontier." In today's Iran it means finding a way to live in the Islamic Republic.

I kept winding through the Old City, trying to find the way out to the main street, where I could find a taxi back to my hotel. The stone maze was little different from other "Old Cities" in other parts of the Middle East. Cats skittered across the burning pavement in search of a patch of shade or a few scraps of food. Whenever the alleys converged to form a pint-size square, a group of boys could be found kicking a football against an empty wall while their sisters watched from surrounding front stoops.

I turned down another lane that appeared empty, but then spotted a middle-aged woman shrouded in a full chador and face veil sitting on a plastic chair outside the door of a bungalow. At first I went unnoticed because she was popping the stems off a pile of green beans and dropping the beans into a plastic bowl sitting on a small table. When the sound of my footsteps grew close, she looked up and showed no surprise at the sight of a foreigner traipsing through her neighborhood. As I passed, she nodded politely and extended a soft greeting: "Salaam," she said.

"Salaam," I replied.

It was the simplest of moments, but one that said a great deal about gender relations in Iran and the Arab world. I had traveled to many Arab countries in the Middle East and North Africa, and I could never imagine a local woman extending a greeting to a foreign man, certainly not a woman dressed in conservative garb. One could stretch the imagination to conceive of something like this happening in one of the more cosmopolitan cities, like Cairo, Damascus, or Beirut, where social codes are more relaxed and foreigners abound, but in the back-streets of a remote regional city? Hardly.

It reminded me of another incident that occurred earlier that day. At the intersection in front of the Amir Chakhmaq Complex, a woman crossed the street and approached a taxi driver waiting for a fare. She wasn't looking for a ride, she just needed directions, and after she had posed her question, the driver pointed down the street and then to the left and then to the right and finished with a gesture that indicated stop. The woman thanked him and left. He resumed his chat with another driver. It was a simple interaction that occurs a million times a day all over the world, but here it resonated. In conservative parts of the Arab world I couldn't imagine a local woman casually speaking to a taxi driver, or any strange man, for any reason. If she needed directions, and there were no women in sight, she would have wandered lost before she would have approached an unrelated male. Here, there were many women she could have sought directions from, but she didn't, obviously, and correctly, thinking a taxi driver would have the most reliable answer. That he was a male, and an unrelated male, didn't matter.

Yazd had other surprises. After a few more twists and turns I finally emerged onto the main street and hailed a taxi. Ten minutes later we pulled up to the entrance of the hotel, and I handed the driver a 100,000-rial note, more than enough to cover the fare. I stepped away, and he called after me.

"Too much," he said, in passable English, and gave me 50,000 rials change. At first I was sure the heat had addled my brain, but no, Yazd had a taxi driver who actually handed cash *back* when he was overpaid. He pulled away, and I was left holding a 50,000-rial note.

The hotel where my tour operator had stashed me was a new addition to Yazd, but it had been built to resemble an elaborate residence from the eighteenth or nineteenth century, with the rooms facing a central courtyard and the requisite pool and bubbling fountain. Each morning I had breakfast at one of the courtyard tables with Laurel and Hardy, the names I had given to the two parakeets that spent most of the day perched on the crossbeams of two wooden posts near the breakfast tables. I called them Laurel and Hardy because they spent most of their time fluttering and slapping each other with thickly feathered wings and squawking in what sounded like garbled Farsi, much like the comic duo, without the Farsi, from the early days of cinema. Laurel was colored deep red, with white feathers under his chin. Hardy was pleasingly plump, with a thick cover of ermine blue feathers and a tail that flopped furiously every time he let out a sharp squawk or screech, or whenever the antics of Laurel left him flustered. After a few days, I noticed a pattern in their diurnal rhythms: Hardy was more of an early bird, for he usually won the morning spats, while Laurel came alive in the afternoons, after I had returned from a day's sightseeing and was enjoying a boozeless beer. Then he shrieked more loudly and poked Hardy with his beak because his guard was down. The battles continued the entire time I was in Yazd—Laurel and Hardy, or Hardy and Laurel, sharing the same perch but never at peace. Always they found something to bicker over—a prize morsel scooped off a breakfast plate, or the direction of the wind when there was nothing else to rile their feathers.

Laurel and Hardy's antics aside, the courtyard was an ideal setting for breakfast. In those brief moments when Laurel and Hardy paused in their bickering, the tinkling of the fountain overcame all other sounds, the blue tiles beneath the water reflected the overhead sky, and a light morning breeze, which had yet to bear the blazing heat of day, stirred the branches of the trees that arched overhead.

It would have been easy to never emerge for breakfast at all, but stay in the cool cocoon of my room. It was decorated like a museum, littered with gewgaws that evoked the glories of the Silk Road. Standing on the tables, and tucked into wall niches that served the purpose of shelves, were ceramic vases and pots and metalwork, a specialty of Yazd, in the form of a brass ewer and a serving tray decorated in ornate floral patterns. Standing on the side tables were glass beakers and a pair of brass candlesticks, and lying on the floor was a trio of hand-woven carpets. As beautiful as these items appeared, they were just a sampling of what, over the years, had been loaded onto the backs of camels before beginning the long trek eastward, into neighboring Afghanistan and then Pakistan.

Trade along the Silk Road began in the third century, during the brief Parthian dynasty. Tucked between the Achaemenid and Sassanid dynasties, the Parthian period had rulers who saw the value of the overland trade and placed a tax on all goods entering from the east. The trade was so important to the wealth of both Iran and China that the Chinese dispatched two negotiators to Iran to argue for the free flow of goods. The cities along the road, not only Yazd but Kerman, Islamabad, Tous, Peshawar, Bukhara, Kabul, and Herat, grew into wealthy trading centers with storehouses of valuable goods. In the courtyards of the caravansaries that surrounded the local bazaars, the languages spoken represented the lands that stretched from the Mediterranean to the Pacific—Turkish and Arabic, Farsi and Hindi, Uzbek, Kazakh, and Chinese.

The trade continued for over a thousand years, until improvements in boatbuilding technology made sea travel far safer and faster than the overland caravan routes, constantly vulnerable to sandstorms and plagued with bandits. But almost until the time of the European Renaissance, more goods of greater value were transported by the Silk Road caravans than any other trade route in human history. And more than goods were exchanged. Islam, along with the languages and cultures of the Muslim world, was carried east. Buddhism, along with spices, silk, and precious stones—jade and emeralds, rubies and sapphires—was brought west. On a side table in my room was a small porcelain vase decorated in floral patterns, with a mountain scene and flock of birds that marked it as a product of China.

I could have remained in my room all morning and imagined myself the driver of a caravan sometime back in the first millennium, but the illusion would never have held up, for no camel driver worth a dirham would have wasted precious time admiring his own goods. Also, this was Yazd, and so the day demanded a visit to the place of fire, or temple of fire, formally known as the Yazd Atash Behram, one of the primary places of worship for local Zoroastrians and a place of pilgrimage for the religion's global followers.

If I had expected the Yazd Atash Behram to be a massive chunk of stone trying to mimic the temples of ancient Greece or Rome, I would have been disappointed. But I had no expectations, and so I wasn't. In practice, Zoroastrian fire temples are typically simple affairs. The notion that the scale of the building should reflect the greatness of the deity it is meant to celebrate is a concept alien to Zoroastrianism. The Yazd Atash Behram is no different. Tucked into a sleepy back street lined with cypress and cedar trees, the Atash Behram better resembles a bourgeois manor house from somewhere in southeastern Europe. Built in 1934, its sole reason for being is to house an *atash behram*, or "victorious fire"—a continuously burning flame of which there are only nine in the world. The other eight are in India.

The story of the flame is far more interesting than any building that could house it. If the tale is to be believed, it was first lit by the shah of the Sassanid dynasty in a fire temple in the district of Larestan in 470 CE. It was then moved to the city of Aqda, where it continued to burn for seven hundred years before it was relocated again, in 1173, to the nearby city of Ardakan. This time its stay was relatively brief—only three hundred years—before it was shipped to Yazd, where it is now tended by a Zoroastrian priest.

Because of the number of tourists that traipse through, the Atash Behram breaks with some of the conventions of the traditional fire temple. It has an observation area for non-Zoroastrians to observe the long-burning flame, still alight in a bronze vase behind a curtain of tinted glass. A touch of verisimilitude is preserved, for behind the tinted glass the chamber surrounding the flame is dark except for the glow emanating from the flame itself, all designed to simulate the gloom of the inner sanctum of a Zoroastrian temple, where the flame would normally be burning.

To imagine what it would have been like to have been an ancient follower of Zoroastrianism, I transported myself back a couple thousand years, when the world's first monotheistic religion dominated the Persian Empire. Entering a fire temple, I would be barefoot and dressed in white, with a white cap to cover my head. If my wife was with me, which would have been possible, for there is no segregation of the sexes in Zoroastrian customs, she would also be clad in white, and her head would be covered with a white headscarf. I would hand an offering of sweet-smelling sandalwood to the priest, who would take it to the inner sanctum and place it on the fire using a pair of silver tongs. He would return bearing some of the ashes in a ladle, which I would smudge onto my eyelids and forehead. There would be no sermon, because the role of the priest is not to preach but receive the faithful and tend the sacred fire.

The fire temple itself is something of an anachronism, for the use of a temple to house the sacred flame would have been alien to very early Zoroastrians. The Greek historian Herodotus described Zoroastrians in the fifth century BCE climbing to the tops of small hills to perform their fire ceremonies. The designation of fire to represent the spiritual core of the Zoroastrian belief system developed centuries later, as the imagery of light became associated with the essence of spirituality in many other faiths. "The Lord went in front of them in a pillar of cloud by day to lead them along the way, and in a pillar of fire by night, to give them light," reads the Book of Exodus, recounting the guidance the Israelites received while they wandered in the desert for forty years. The Christian Jesus is often described as "The Light of the World." "The Lord is my light and my salvation," and "In thy light we shall see light," reads the Book of Psalms. "Let us walk in the light of the Lord," said the Prophet Isaiah, for "the Lord shall be unto thee an everlasting light."

The dark-light polarity carried far beyond Zoroastrianism to the traditions of other faiths. Among the ancient Hebrews, the Qumran sect separated its own into the saved ("children of light") and the damned ("children of darkness"). In the Chinese dichotomy of yin and yang, yang is light—ethereal and productive, and therefore a force for good—while yin is the reverse. The Hindu wintertime festival of Diwali celebrates the triumph of light over spiritual darkness. Gnostic thought, which developed in the first and second centuries, saw light and darkness representing spirit and matter, but the two are not equals in any spiritual sense. Evil forces arise from the material world, and there the human being acquires salvation by abandoning it for the world of light.

In many other belief systems light represents enlightenment, or the illumination of the mind as well as the spirit. In the mythology of ancient Egypt, Apophis, the monster of darkness, represented by a serpent, each day threatens to devour Ra, the sun god. Of course he fails, and each day a new day dawns. The Pharaoh Amenhotep IV tried to create a sun cult in Egypt, but his tiptoe into monotheism was quashed by the religious powers. One of the major festivals on the ancient Roman calendar was one that paid homage to Sol Invictus, or the "Invincible Sun." In the Aztec and Mayan belief systems, human sacrifices were needed to preserve a world order that was represented by the continuing life of the sun. Fast-forward to the present day: Let us not forget the Tomb of the Unknown Soldier, where memory of the fallen is symbolized by the eternal flame, never to be extinguished, just like the fire in the Yazd Atash Behram, which has burned much longer.

Almost all religions acquire some of their appeal through a dose of mysticism and mystery, and the origins of Zoroastrianism are a little more mysterious than most. According to the Gathas, seventeen hymns composed by Zoroaster himself and included in the Avesta, Zoroastrianism's primary scripture, the prophet was born somewhere near the border of Iran and present-day Afghanistan, perhaps as far back as 1500 BCE. He had six children, three boys and three girls, and he died around the age of seventy-seven. Most important, he is credited with bringing into the world the belief in a single, universal force from which all spiritual power emanates, in other words, the concept of monotheism. What is also known is that Zoroaster grew disenchanted with the popular polytheism of his time, with its ritual animal sacrifices and use of hallucinogenic plants in religious ceremonies. According to orthodox Zoroastrianism—in keeping with the myths familiar to other religions—Zoroaster retreated into the wilds and received a vision that became the foundation of his theology and a new way of framing the spiritual world. This attributed all of creation to a single source—Ahura Mazda, or the "Wise Lord."

According to the Zoroastrian view, the universe is riven by two competing forces: one that embodies the values of order, creation, and truth, or *Asha*; and one that is reflected in the negative forces of chaos, deceit, disorder, and "uncreation," or *Druj*. Humans are caught up in this cosmic battle with an obligation to defend the forces of Asha against those of Druj. The task, as monumental as it sounds, is relatively simple. The responsibility of the human being is to combat Asha and Druj by promoting, and articulating, the three cardinal principles of Zoroastrianism: good thoughts (*humata*), good words (*hukhta*), and good deeds (*hvarshta*).

Another fundamental principle of Zoroastrianism is the concept of free will. It thoroughly rejects any notion of predestination, common in Indian theology, and also the ancient Greek concept of Fate. The Zoroastrian believes that it is positive actions that quell the dark forces of the universe. Action is a necessary part of human existence and a potential force for good. To take this a step further, asceticism is spurned because it demands the denial of life experiences, even simple pleasure, which can fuel the forces of order. No Zoroastrian priest would think of retreating from the world like a Christian or Buddhist monk, for it is engagement with the world through positive, self-directed action that leads to the supremacy of Asha.

It can't be denied that there is a hint of self-interest in performing good works, for performing them also brings goodness to oneself, and in this respect Zoroastrianism could be seen as dipping into the Hindu notion of karma, or "what goes around comes around."

What is striking about many of the precepts of Zoroastrianism is how they laid the foundation for those of both Christianity and Islam, at the time still invisible on the theological horizon. Zoroastrianism advanced the concept of a dual universe, the individual possessing free will, the notions of heaven and hell as well as Judgment Day and the arrival of a messiah. In the Zoroastrian view, the end of time will be the victory of Ahura Mazda over the dark forces of existence, embodied in Angra Mainyu, which Christians came to call the "evil spirit." Also, a savior will arrive (*Saoshyant*), who will revive the dead spirits, and all the world's souls will then be judged according to their thoughts, words, and actions as they cross over the bridge that leads to the world beyond the earthly one. But humans are not alone throughout their earthly journey. Each is accompanied by a guardian spirit, or *fravashi*, which will be on hand to meet them at the final judgment.

Contrary to both Christianity and Islam, a whiff of animism can be found in Zoroastrianism, for Zoroaster believed that the fundamental spiritual forces of the universe were to be found in the natural elements of earth, wind, water, and fire—wind as opposed to air because wind can be experienced in physical reality, while air remains abstract and ethereal, disconnected from physical, sensory experience. Furthermore, according to Zoroastrianism, fire and water are not opposing forces (there is a limit to duality, even in Zoroastrianism). Both possess purifying qualities and were the last to be created in the birth of the universe. To expand the dualistic view even further, according to Zoroastrianism, fire emerged from water, and it is fire that is the source of wisdom. Consequently, it is at the fire temple where Zoroastrians worship, and the image of fire, or light, has become the symbol of insight or inspiration throughout human history.

Zoroaster had little luck selling his radical theological views to the Persians of eastern Iran. The religious powers saw his attack on ritual and his adherence to the belief in a single deity as an affront to the ruling order. After twelve years of proselytizing, he gained only one convert—his cousin—so he relocated to western Iran, where he had better luck. The king and queen of Bactria favored his views after hearing him debate the local religious authorities and decided to make Zoroastrianism the state religion.

Slowly but surely, Zoroaster's beliefs gained currency and began to spread throughout ancient Persia, so that by the beginning of the Achaemenid era, around 500 BCE, they had become the accepted faith of the Persian people. Zoroastrianism soon spread to the outer reaches of the empire, north to Armenia and Azerbaijan, and even beyond the empire, southeast to India. It suffered a setback in the fourth century BCE, following the invasion of Alexander the Great. The Greek conquerors burned the Avesta, Zoroastrianism's sacred text, which contain the Gathas, poems written by Zoroaster that express his fundamental beliefs.

Still, Zoroastrianism recovered, and all was well for the next thousand years. Then, in the middle of the seventh century, came the Arab invasion and with it the Islamic faith that had already swept the Arabian Peninsula. Defeats in the battles of Qadisiya and Nahavand spelled the end of the Sassanid Empire and sent Zoroastrianism on the run. Fire temples were destroyed or converted into mosques, and many of the faithful fled inland, seeking protection in the greater isolation of the desert cities, such as Yazd.

At first, the Arab-Muslim ruling caliphate in Damascus took a benign attitude toward the Zoroastrian Persians. There was little pressure to convert to Islam, but over time discriminating taxes and other oppressive polices stigmatized the Zoroastrians. Two hundred years later, rule over Persia passed to the Abbasid caliphate operating out of Baghdad, resulting in increasing oppression and even humiliation of the Zoroastrians. In the cities, where the ruling authorities could often persuade the local population to convert by offering economic enticements and other advantages, Islam was able to spread more quickly. The rural areas saw resistance harden, but by the tenth and eleventh centuries, Islam had become the dominant faith of previously Zoroastrian Persia, and the religion that had once spread across the empire was consigned to the hinterlands.

There are few issues in Iran that don't reflect the ever-growing rift between the more secular-minded city dwellers and the theologically driven religious figures in the government, and there is no reason why Zoroastrianism would be an exception. This is fully on display on the last Tuesday before March 21, or Noruz, the Persian New Year. This is the night of Chaharshanbeh-Souri, or the fire-jumping tradition, in which small bonfires are made both in the smallest villages and the residential streets of major cities, and celebrants take turns leaping over the flames so that the purifying element of fire will "burn away" the residue of the passing year and ignite the force of a new beginning.

After the 1979 Islamic Revolution, religious authorities went to great lengths to suppress the tradition. Supreme Leader Ayatollah Khamenei has since called it "irrational," ignoring the fact that few religious beliefs are based on reason, and another ayatollah, Makarem Shirazi, decried it as "unworthy of a Muslim." But in recent years, the government has largely abandoned its attempt to obliterate a three-thousand-year-old tradition and the people's desire to embrace it.

There is little doubt that the newfound popularity of Zoroastrianism has arisen as pushback against the imposition of strict Islamic practices. There is also little doubt that the seventh-century Arab invasion and the repressive policies and persecutions that followed find resonance in the Islamic regime's own policies of repression and imposition of what it believes to be "pure" Islamic practices. To favor Zoroastrianism is therefore not only to respect Iran's ancient culture but to make a political statement.

As he weaved through the Tehran traffic, I listened to the rants of a disillusioned taxi driver: "We have too much of this religion—religion, religion, religion. Too many laws, too much religion in life. What do we really need?"

He added a dramatic pause.

"Good thoughts. Good words. Good deeds," he said, laying out the fundamental principles of Zoroastrianism. "What else is important? Good thoughts. Good words. Good deeds."

Dangling from his rearview mirror was a pendant in the form of the *faravahar*, the universal symbol of Zoroastrianism—a giant pair of wings extending from the profile of a bearded priest. Plastered on his rear window was a sticker with the image of the faravahar, but also hanging from the rearview mirror was a *nazar*, the cobalt-blue talisman believed to ward off the evil eye, found on the ends of key chains and featured on necklaces sold in tourist shops throughout the Middle East.

"There wasn't nearly as much interest in Zoroastrianism before the Islamic Revolution," an Iranian scholar and former professor at Tehran University told me. "Today it's a symbolic form of rebellion. Zoroastrianism is something the government had tried to suppress and even denied its importance in Iran's history. To many hardline clerics, Iran's 'real' history begins with the arrival of Islam, and they want everyone to see Iran the same way. But there was a lot of history before Islam ever arrived, so the Persian identity is much more complex than they want us to believe."

On occasion the fire-jumping tradition has almost abandoned its spiritual meaning entirely and entered into the realm of political expression. During the 2009 postelection demonstrations, antigovernment protestors consigned posters bearing the likenesses of then-president Mahmoud Ahmadinejad and Supreme Leader Ayatollah Khamenei to bonfires set up in the side streets of Tehran and other cities, and then leaped over them with shouts of "Death to the dictator!"

I asked my professor friend if there wasn't a great deal of reflexive rebellion at play.

"Absolutely," he began. "What the government tells us to reject, we embrace. What they say is bad we think must be good. And that holds true in almost every aspect of life—religion, politics, even entertainment. The more they criticize the U.S. and the West, the more popular the U.S. and the West become. The more they warn us of the influence of foreign cultures, the more people want American movies, want to study in the U.S. But there's more than just reflexive rebellion going on. The government wants to define everything about what it means to be Iranian in terms of Islam, so keeping practices like fire-jumping alive is a way of saying there is much more to the Persian identity."

The Yazd fire temple may host the longest-burning flame in the world, but it isn't Zoroastrianism's most commanding monument in the city. That honor would have to go to the two looming *dakhmas,* or "Towers of Silence," just outside Yazd, where the city meets the vast Bafgh Desert. There was just enough time to make a quick tour before the arrival of the searing afternoon heat, so Sohrab and I hopped in the car and headed out to the archaeological park that has put Yazd on Iran's map of religious history.

A Tower of Silence, simply put, is a Zoroastrian cemetery, or, to be more precise, a place for the final resting of the dead. It can't be called a burial ground because, in the Zoroastrian tradition, corpses are not interred in the earth. The reason has to do with Zoroastrian cosmology. A dead body represents decay, or—in Zoroastrian parlance—"uncreation," and is therefore *nasu*, or "unclean." To inter a dead body is to risk the corruption of the earth, one of the four sacred elements. Consequently, Zoroastrians adopted the practice of the "sky burial"—exposing dead bodies to the open air, where the flesh would quickly decompose from its exposure to the sun, and vultures and other carrion birds would pick off the remains. The bones would then be placed in a pit, where they would gradually return to dust.

The structure for the sky burial became the Tower of Silence. Zoroastrians arranged their dead in three concentric circles around the top of a stone tower—men in the outer ring, women in the middle, children in the center. Herodotus observed the practice of sky burial among Zoroastrians in what is now Turkey, but there is no record of towers serving as the platform for the dead until the ninth century CE. The tradition continued without a hitch throughout the gradual but steady Islamization of Iran until the nineteenth century, when the Dar ul-Funun madresse was founded by Amir Kabir in Tehran. Students had no corpses for the study of anatomy because Islamic law forbids dissection, so the towers of silence were regularly robbed of their dead to aid the growing interest in medical research.

In the middle of a summer afternoon the eerie, empty, sun-bleached desert surrounding the towers did evoke the silence of the dead, but the effect was much different from the first time I was here, in 2009. Then there was little silence to be found, not only in Yazd but throughout Iran. The postelection demonstrations had been in full swing, and the upheaval managed to rouse, if not Zoroastrian spirits, the ire of the ticket taker at the entrance booth.

"Where is he from?" he asked Sohrab, after I had paid the entrance fee and was handed my ticket.

Sohrab told him.

"America!" he quipped. "America! Then he knows about elections! What does he think of ours?" Without waiting for a reply, he continued with his own diatribe: "Those bastards at the top think they're going to steal this one from us, that they can step all over us. They aren't going to get away with it! Tell him!"—He nodded toward me.—"Tell him that we can have a democratic system. We can have one here just like there is in America! That's all that we want, fair elections, just like they have in America, but it's not going to happen until we get rid of the whole lot of them!"

The elections were several years in the past, even though their memory had yet to decay, like the ancient corpses. What had gone sour was whatever remaining trust the people had in the government and the ruling clerics. But if today's ticket taker had any gripes, and there could be many—the economy, the irresponsible leadership, runaway inflation, widespread corruption, the international sanctions that had torn at the fabric of day-to-day life—he was as mute as the dead. He handed me my ticket and a map of the site and retreated to his seat in the comforting cool of the entrance booth.

Zoroastrians typically built their towers of silence outside the cities to separate them from ongoing earthly life, just as medieval Europeans created cemeteries beyond the boundaries of the walled town. Often Zoroastrians chose the tops of hills or any rises in the landscape in order to bring the dead closer to the heavenly life where they were bound. The two towers of silence outside Yazd follow this pattern. Perched on top of a pair of hills no more than a few hundred feet apart, they better resemble the ruins of hilltop fortresses, or a pair of watchtowers placed outside the city to warn of an approaching army. I thought it was too late in the day for a climb to the top, without a postage stamp of shade to ease the way, but then I spotted two figures on the horizon line nearing the top of the first tower, and thought—why not?

It was easier than I expected. I was ready for a grinding slog that would only become more grueling as it went on, but I hadn't factored in the sauna-dry Iranian air, and I hadn't counted on a light breeze blowing across the desert to create the illusion that the climb could actually be a refreshing stretch of the legs on a summer afternoon. The trail steepened, and my leg muscles tightened, but again, I felt not a drop of sweat. The breeze picked up, so hot it burned the surfaces of my eyes. Eventually my breath shortened, and it took more work to mount each step. I stopped to rest every forty or fifty feet, looking out to scan the boundless stretch of desert in one direction and Yazd itself, beginning to appear far below, in the other. That was enough to make the final push.

Coming from a longstanding tradition that associates death with darkness and interment in the earth, I found it hard to see the top of the tower as a final resting place for the dead. But that was what made the climb worthwhile, confronting the great differences that exist between cultures in concepts of death and all of its attendant imagery. Death, signifying interment in the earth, had no place in the cosmology of the Zoroastrians. As a sacred element, earth was responsible for generating life and was therefore diametrically opposed to the concept of death, like two magnets with conflicting energies. Death was associated with the sky and the promise of heavenly life, and this necessarily meant the abandonment of the earth. The very concept of the cemetery, or any burial ground, was antithetical to the Zoroastrian concepts of natural law and the order of the universe.

I sat on the tower's crumbling stone wall to reflect on all this, and to look out at the boundless desert, shimmering in the afternoon sun. Centuries ago, a caravan of camels might have been seen on the horizon, vague, indistinct, even inconsequential in relation to the landscape it would have been crossing. The desert became a metaphor for earthly existence, and the tower that once held human bodies at the end of their passage through life, offering them up to the heavens, affirmed the same message.

I could have scrambled down the trail that led to the opposite slope and tried to make it to the top of the second tower, but on this hot summer afternoon, one tower ascent was enough. The second tower would have only duplicated the same experience, and the heat was rising. The breeze blowing across the plain had reached the eyeball-singeing temperature that meant the peak of the day's heat had been reached. Fortunately, the way back to the entrance booth and parking lot was all downhill, and so I scrambled down the trail with the direct rays of the sun now scorching the surfaces of the rocks and raising watery, rippling waves of heat from the sunbaked landscape.

Sohrab and I could have headed back to Yazd and holed up at the hotel for the rest of the day, but there was another way to beat the heat. We got back in the car, careful not to touch any surface that had been exposed to the sun while the car was roasting in the lot, and drove about twenty minutes until we arrived at a tall, beehive-like building that in scale and form could have doubled as a giant Hershey's kiss, with a squat, circular foundation that tapered to a pinpoint top. It was made of brick, and its plain exterior said nothing about its reason for being. Sohrab tugged the door open, and a rush of cool air poured out. We stepped inside, and the inner chill embraced us like a bear hug. But even more stunning than the temperature drop was the enormous, cavernous space and the vital purpose it had once served for the residents of Yazd.

From the ground up, the interior was an enormous cone that narrowed as it rose to a peephole at the tip-top that opened to the blue summer sky. Below ground level was an enormous pit, equal in size to the spacious empty cone that rose above. It would have been the mother-of-all sinkholes if this had been a naturally occurring sinkhole, but it wasn't. The pit had been dug deep into the earth to take advantage of the subterranean cooler temperature for the preservation of ice. Yes, ice. Living in a harsh desert climate like Yazd's taught the Yazdis to appreciate whatever luxuries the punishing environment could offer, and one—when coupled with a bit of ingenuity—was ice. Ice gathered from the nearby mountains in winter could be preserved for the residents of Yazd to provide them with cool drinks in the summer months, and even more ice could be made when the supply ran low. The cone over the pit, and the entire structure, is a *yakhchal*, what many Iranians still call their refrigerators at home. Today, many may be imported from China, South Korea, or Germany, but they remain, in traditional Persian terminology, yakhchals.

The yakhchal was a marvel of Persian engineering that saw its beginning in the fourth century BCE. In the winter months, frigid water from the mountains around Yazd was carried through the *qanats*, or aqueducts, into the yakhchals, where it froze in the subterranean pit. The design of the yakhchal allowed any warm air to rise to the top of the dome and escape through the vents, drawing down the temperature in the space below. The thick walls of the conical dome insulated the interior from the warmer outside air, from winter into spring and on into the summer months, when the ice was ready to make *faloodeh*, a popular frozen dessert made from sugar, rose water, and tiny noodles that is as old as the fifth century BCE.

Similar technology was used to keep Persian houses cool in the summer. Centuries before the arrival of the electrically powered unit, the trusted air conditioner was the badgir, a square chimney-like structure with X-shaped internal baffles. These would catch a breeze blowing from any direction and channel it down through the tower and across a pool of water at the base, cooling the interior. Popular treat though it was, faloodeh couldn't have been made at home because the water in the pool would never have turned to ice, but the room would have easily been kept ten, or fifteen, or maybe even twenty degrees cooler than the outside air.

I had no badgir back in the hotel room, but I didn't need one, because it was equipped with a twenty-first century cooling contraption that pumped out air almost as cool as any badgir could have managed. And so it was a relief to stretch out beneath it at the end of the day and allow the breeze to blow over me, badgir-like. I fixed my eyes on all the craftwork and gewgaws scattered around the room and blocked out the contraption's persistent whir, and for brief moments I could imagine the cool air descending from the tried-and-true, old-form badgir.

Later that night, neither the badgir nor the mellow humming modern unit was needed. After a trip back to the Old City for dinner at another restored bathhouse restaurant, tiled in traditional white and blue, I returned to enjoy the evening breeze in the hotel courtyard, lying on one of the cushioned takhts. The day's heat was a memory, and it would remain so at least until the first appearance of the morning light. For now, the stars overhead sparkled in an inky desert sky.

The only noise was that of the nighttime breeze stirring the fronds of the palm trees high above. Even Laurel and Hardy had quit their antics and settled into sleep. In this moment of peace, I looked into the sky and saw not the familiar outlines of Cygnus and Scorpio, Lyra and Ursa Major, but a caravan of camels bound for the East, parading across the heavenly dome.

11 | Persepolis

SHADOW OF AN EMPIRE

I announce that I will respect the tradition, customs, and religions of my empire and never let any of my governors and subordinates look down on or insult them.... I will never let anyone oppress any others, and if it occurs I will take his or her rights back and penalize the oppressor.
> —Cyrus I, the Cyrus Cylinder

The Shiraz-Esfahan highway, angling northeast out of Shiraz, may not be the most dramatic in Iran, but it is one of the country's most attractive, and arguably its most important in historical terms. Cutting across the fertile plain that surrounds the city, it passes fields of wheat and orchards bursting with berries and citrus fruits. But that is not all. A large proportion of Iran's pistachios, the country's number-one agricultural export, come from the Fars Province, of which Shiraz is the capital. With graceful hills rising above the plain, the view from the road is reminiscent of any of the highways that cross California's San Joaquin Valley, passing the farming towns of Manteca and Modesto before rising into the foothills of the Sierra Nevada Mountains.

Sohrab and I had an early start out of Shiraz, so early that the sun, already rising above the hills, had yet to burn off the morning fog. Despite the rural beauty that lay on both sides of the highway, the glum atmosphere in the hotel's breakfast room still hung in the air, like a fog that would not dissipate. An hour earlier I was watching the guests sip cups of coffee and tea and pick at the shells of hardboiled eggs. What stood out were the wan faces of the women all around the room, many with an abundance of makeup to counter the mandatory headscarves that covered unseen locks of hair. The faces of the women were defiantly "painted," but without breaking the bounds of taste. The men sat hunched over the remains of their morning meal, staring into near-empty plates as they scooped up the last bits, as though attempting to squirrel themselves away from the aura of social repression that daily surrounded them. The Islamic Republic is not a happy place, is what the scene said. An Iranian academic once characterized Iran to me as "a nation held hostage." That was the best way to describe the roomful of hotel guests—as pawns taken prisoner whose only retaliation was to exhibit more grace and dignity than their oppressors.

The Shiraz-Esfahan highway is one of the most heavily traveled in Iran not only because it links two of the country's major cities. Approximately thirty-five miles out of Shiraz it passes Persepolis, the ancient capital of the Achaemenid Empire, where building was begun by Cyrus the Great in the sixth century BCE and finished by his son Darius. Two centuries later it was burned and sacked by Alexander the Great, but it remains one of the most historically significant archaeological sites in the world. The plan for the morning was to pass Persepolis and head up to Pasargadae, the site of Cyrus's first capital and the block of stone that historians generally agree to be his tomb. To add a little more smoothness to the ride, I dug into the Volvo's door pocket, found a collection of Sarah Vaughn recordings, and slid the CD into the dashboard player. In a moment, Sarah's silken voice drifted like an accompanying morning mist through the interior of the Volvo, and it even helped to wipe away the forlorn faces in the hotel breakfast room.

An hour after leaving Shiraz we rolled into the parking lot at the entrance to Pasargadae. By then the mists had cleared, and bright, crisp sunlight was spilling across the plain. Long before the highway put Pasargadae within easy reach of curiosity seekers, many European travelers, enamored with the ancient world, had found their way here. As early as the fifteenth century, the Italian Giosafat Barbaro had passed through, the Dutch sailor Jan Struys arrived another century later, and in the nineteenth century James Morier, a British diplomat. In 1881 and 1882 the Frenchmen Eugène Flandin and Pascal Coste published 350 drawings of the site. Their published accounts fueled interest in the ancient world all across Europe and led to a stream of followers, which means that, on this bright summer morning, my visit was only the most recent in a line that stretched across the centuries.

Despite the many travelers who have trooped through this part of Iran there is little left of Pasargadae to attract them. All that remains is a broad, flat, empty field where a lavish palace once stood, now spotted with the stone stumps of columns that once upheld the roofs and porticos of grand halls and reception rooms—along with the glory of a blossoming empire. Cyrus, the consummate Persian, was a lover of gardens, and so his palace contained a number of interlocking gardens that knitted the sprawling complex together. Giant winged bulls guarded the main gate, symbolism borrowed from Assyrian palaces that were located in what is present-day Iraq. Though they carried no religious meaning in Zoroastrian Persia, they signified Cyrus's aspiration and the power and reach of the empire that he would ultimately create.

We circled the grounds along the roadway that wound through the site, getting out at the few signboards that marked the remnants of individual sections of the palace. Historical evidence suggests that Cyrus began work on Pasargadae about 559 BCE, but he would never live to see its completion, and his successors would not be so attached to it. Cambyses II relocated the Persian capital to Susa, in today's province of Khuzestan, and Darius I would reflect the increasing power of the empire by constructing a far more regal capital at Persepolis. But in his beloved Pasargadae is where Cyrus would be buried, in a plain block tomb that stands atop an apron of stone steps, magnificent in its blandness and modesty.

What is striking about the tomb is not only its slight scale—after all, two thousand years earlier Egypt's pharaohs had themselves buried in monumental pyramids—but its isolation, seemingly out of character for the founder of an empire. With his palace now destroyed by time, the tomb's location evokes an aura of loneliness. Compounding Cyrus's humility is the tomb's self-deprecating epitaph, translated by Plutarch as follows:

> *Oh man, whoever you are and wherever you come from,*
> *. . . I am Cyrus, who won the Persians their empire. Do not*
> *begrudge me this bit of earth that covers my bones.*

Having read of Cyrus's accomplishments in the *Cyropedia* of Xenophon, a student of Socrates, Alexander the Great was so enamored of the Persian ruler that after he had torn through Persepolis he felt obliged to visit the tomb. By then all of its treasures had been carted away by his marauding soldiers, filling him with shame.

It is impossible to overestimate the esteem in which Cyrus is still held in today's Iran, the legacy that he left, and the indelible imprint he made on the Persian identity. In her Nobel Peace Prize acceptance speech, human rights lawyer Shirin Ebadi proudly described herself as "a descendent of Cyrus," referring not to his empire's size but to Cyrus's policy of tolerance and respect for all minorities wherever he had entered as a conqueror. The empire he created would eventually stretch from the eastern Mediterranean to India, becoming the largest in the ancient world and the largest that until then had ever existed. It embraced the kaleidoscope of religious and regional cultures, kingdoms and mini-empires that the ancient Near East comprised. The empire's vast reach provided the basis for the diversity of ethnic groups that are found in Iran today—and the air of chutzpah that occasionally puffs up contemporary Iranians. "We also know what it means to be a superpower," one man told me when I asked him how he might compare Iran to the United States, and he added, lest I forget: "We have seven thousand years of history behind us. You are just getting started."

As might be expected of an emperor, Cyrus was royal born and bred. He was the son of the Achaemenid king Cambyses I and his wife, Mandana, whose father Astyages was the ruler of the nearby Median kingdom. For more than a century Cyrus's family had ruled over the collection of tribes that formed the foundation of what would become the Persian Empire.

Mandana figures prominently in another well-known Persian myth. Not long after she was born, her father had a strange dream in which his daughter's urine was so profuse that it flooded nearly all of Asia. The court interpreters offered a dire reading: that Astyages's grandson would one day overthrow him. To skirt fate, Astyages offered his daughter in marriage to Cambyses I, a vassal prince viewed as no threat to Astyages's reign. Then Astyages had another dream, that a vine sprouting from the womb of his pregnant daughter grew to encircle the entire Earth. This so spooked Astyages that he ordered Harpagus, a loyal court functionary, to kill his grandchild. But Harpagus could not bring himself to fulfill the deed. Instead he handed the boy over to a shepherd, and, years later, the grandson, Cyrus II, would overthrow his grandfather in the battle of Pasargad with the assistance of Harpagus, who would turn against his former sovereign and fulfill the prophecy.

Long before Cyrus took the throne, the expansion of the Achaemenid Empire was underway, if tentatively. As far back as the ninth century BCE the Persian king Achaemenes, for whom the dynasty was named, expanded his territory to the northwest and other neighboring regions. But Cyrus would take empire building to a whole new level, seizing control of the kingdom of Medes, southwest of present-day Tehran, in 553 BCE. As far as Cyrus was concerned, when it came to empire building, family loyalty meant little.

Cyrus then turned westward. In 547 BCE he moved against Croesus, king of Lydia on the Anatolian Peninsula, today's Turkey. Croesus had previously captured Pteria, in today's Cappadocia, in modern Turkey, and turned the Persian residents into slaves. The next year Cyrus defeated Croesus in the Battle of Thymbra and seized the Lydian capital of Sardis. Here Cyrus exhibited the savvy on the battlefield that would become his signature. He took the advice of one of his lieutenants to place his camels in front of his soldiers in the belief that the strange smell would confuse and frighten the enemy's horses. The strategy worked. Cyrus defeated the Lydians handily.

More conquests would come. In 540 BCE Cyrus defeated the Elamites, whose kingdom bordered the Persian Gulf, but the biggest prize would come later in the same year, when the Persian army took control of Babylon, then under the reign of King Nabonidus. This time a little ingenuity figured in the conquest. The path of the Persians was blocked by the Euphrates River, so the army dug a canal that drained the water and lowered the level of the river, enabling the soldiers to wade into the capital in the middle of the night.

The conquest of neighboring Babylon would be Cyrus's coup de grace. He had vanquished his most formidable rival, and in doing so his empire reached its zenith. In Babylon, Nabonidus was already carrying a dubious reputation by preferring to worship the Babylonian god Sin over the principal deity Marduk, angering many of the kingdom's priests. For the Babylonians, capitulation to the Persian Zoroastrians could not have offered much consolation, but Nabonidus's defeat was seen as a comeuppance—a smitten and vengeful Marduk allowing the king to be crushed as payback for his disloyalty.

Most important was how Cyrus responded to his victory. According to the customs of the times, a conqueror would typically destroy the temples and icons of the defeated people, plunder their wealth, and enslave the population in order to establish the supremacy of the new order. Cyrus took a 180-degree turn. In all the lands that he conquered, Cyrus allowed freedom of worship, and in Babylon particularly he guaranteed that his army would not vandalize the people's temples. Equally significant, he declared that all those who had been enslaved by the Babylonians would be free to return to their homelands. This included Babylon's Jews, whom Cyrus permitted to return to Jerusalem to build the Second Temple. And he added to his magnanimity by agreeing to pay for the reconstruction of the temple from the state's coffers. The Old Testament Book of Ezra (6:2–5) states:

> In the first year of King Cyrus, the king issued a decree: concerning the house of god at Jerusalem, let the temple . . . be rebuilt and let its foundations be returned . . . and let the cost be paid

by the royal treasury. Also, let the gold and silver elements of the house of God, which Nebuchadnezzar took from the temple in Jerusalem and brought to Babylon be returned to their palaces.

Cyrus's own words were also recorded in Chronicles (36:23):

All the kingdoms of the Earth hath the Lord God given me, and he has charged me to build a house in Jerusalem. . . . Whomever is among you of his people—the Lord, his God, be with him—let him go there.

In return, the Jewish people dignified Cyrus with the title of "anointed one," the only non-Jew to ever receive the honor.

A natural question arises: Why would Cyrus have expressed such empathy for a people imprisoned in neighboring Babylon? Some historians argue that the concept of monotheism was the tie that bound Cyrus to the Jews. Zoroastrianism, the unofficial religion of the Persians, adhered to the concept of a single deity, which the Jews shared, and this alienated Cyrus from the polytheism of the Babylonians. But Cyrus is not known to have exhibited any firm religious beliefs. As a ruler he appears to have been largely secular, which allowed him to tolerate, if not embrace, all of the faiths within his empire.

Others claim that it was common for conquerors of the era to begin the new phase of rule with a series of reforms. Seen in this light, Cyrus was merely performing to expectations. But the principle of religious tolerance, not to mention its practice, was bold for the time and pushed the concept of reform to an entirely new level. Detractors argue that sheer pragmatism drove Cyrus: The empire had grown far too large to be managed by any central authority. A degree of autonomy was needed to pacify populations in the empire's further reaches, and if this meant allowing a large degree of freedom of faith, it was simply one of the costs of empire building.

The arguments against Cyrus read like more than a little historical nitpicking. Many reasons might explain why he acted as he did, and they may diminish not only his motives but the effects of his actions, but the fact remains that he did enter into history the novel concept of human rights. The claim that the many documents that followed, from the Magna Carta to the American Bill of Rights, owe their existence to the decree of Cyrus is a bit of a stretch. Nevertheless, it can't be disputed that Cyrus's policies redefined the meaning of human existence, and, rather than withering as historical anachronisms, they were perpetuated and refined by many political systems that followed. Thomas Jefferson had studied the Cyrus Cylinder and had its principles in mind when he penned the Declaration of Independence. Jefferson, Benjamin Franklin, and John Adams each owned a copy of Xenophon's *Cyropedia*, which documented the life of Cyrus.

Cyrus's impact on human history will continue to be a subject of debate, but there is even greater disagreement over how he met his end. Xenophon wrote that he died at Pasargadae, calmly and uneventfully. Other theories are far more colorful. Herodotus believed that Cyrus was killed in combat fighting the Massagetae from Central Asia, who were known to eat their dead. The Greek historian Ctesias has Cyrus sacrificing himself while beating back a rebellion by the Derbicae, alongside Scythian and Indian warriors and teams of elephants. But the most salacious account has Cyrus killed and beheaded by the woman he proposed to marry.

To tell this tale we must return to the Massagetae and the Queen Tomyris. Cyrus had set his sights on Massagetae territory for some time and had devised a plan to bring it under his control by marrying Tomyris. He sent her an offer of marriage, which she refused, and this prompted a spurned and humiliated Cyrus to resort to more direct means to subjugate the Massagetae. He prepared an attack, but before it was launched, he received a tip—that the Massagetae knew nothing of wine and the effect that copious amounts have on the senses. He approached with his army and set up a camp but then pulled back, leaving behind many jugs of fine Persian wine. The Massagetae army, led by Tomyris's son Spargapises, raided the camp, killed the remaining soldiers, and discovered the supply of wine. They then drank themselves into a stupor, enabling Cyrus's forces to easily dispatch with the inebriated Massagetae. Tomyris, however, would have the last word. She led a counterattack in which Cyrus was killed, and to avenge her son's death, ordered Cyrus's head chopped off and drowned in a bucket of blood.

All that historians can agree on is that no one really knows how Cyrus died, or where, but most are inclined to believe that the father of ancient Persia received a dramatic sendoff of one kind or another. I like to believe the last colorful and grisly version, because it is the most befitting the founder of an empire. It is also probably far too grisly to be true, but that hardly matters. It emerged in an age when mythology counted far more than history, and ironically had a far greater impact on history than facts.

We left Pasargadae just as the sun was rising toward midday, shortening the shadows left by the stumps of the broken columns. Persepolis was still the destination, but we had another stop to make—Naqsh-e Rustam, a collection of Achaemenid-era tombs dug into a rockface high above the surrounding landscape and decorated with relief sculptures depicting the triumphs of various Persian rulers over invaders. In one relief, victorious Persian leader Shapur I, who defeated the Romans in the third century, is depicted conquering Roman emperors Valerian, Gordian III, and Philip the Arab. Shapur was known for his favorable relationship with the empire's Jews, and he also continued Cyrus's policy of religious tolerance, allowing Christianity to establish a foothold in Zoroastrian Persia.

Naqsh-e Rustam might be described as a Mount Rushmore necropolis. The four tombs carved into the rock face high above the plain contain the graves of those believed to be the most significant kings of the ancient empire. Only one is clearly identified as that of Darius I, whose reign followed Cyrus's. The other three are a guessing game, but a tentative consensus has formed that they belong to Xerxes I, Artaxerxes I, and Darius II.

One characteristic these leaders shared was a superpower rivalry with their only regional rival—the Greeks. Of the three, Xerxes is credited with making the most progress in whittling away at Greek power. He led a campaign that drove deep into Greek territory, but in

480 BCE, his invasion famously imploded when it was met by a much smaller Greek force in the mountain pass at Thermopylae, led by the Spartan king Leonidas. Xerxes was beaten back, but only temporarily. After being led through the mountains by a Greek soldier who jumped sides, Xerxes was able to make his way to Athens, where he conquered the city and then burned it.

The aim of adding Greece to the Persian Empire had to be aborted when upheaval in Babylonia forced Xerxes to return home. Back in the nerve center of his empire, he expanded Persepolis by building the Hall of One Hundred Columns and the Gate of All Nations, and he finished the work started by his father Darius, completing the Treasury and the Apadana, Persepolis's large hypostyle hall, designed for receptions and formal events. It was the grandest palace of the entire complex, supported by seventy-two columns topped with carvings of eagles, lions, and cows—the fertility symbol of the ancient Persians.

Xerxes's death, in 465 BCE, is material for Shakespearean intrigue. Rivalries within the upper ranks of the Persian leadership resulted in a series of murders. According to the records of Aristotle and the Greek historian Ctesias, a series of revenge killings were carried out by Xerxes's sons Darius II and Artaxerxes; Artabanus, the royal bodyguard commander; and Megabyzus, one of Xerxes's generals. But there are so many differences in the versions of the events that the variations exceed the body count. Ctesias claimed that Artabanus coaxed Artaxerxes to seek revenge by killing his brother Darius. This was after he threw the blame for the murder of Xerxes at Darius. Aristotle had a much different theory: that Xerxes was murdered by Artabanus, after he had also done away with Darius. But Artabanus had his comeuppance. According to Aristotle, he and his sons were rubbed out by Artaxerxes, after Artaxerxes found out about the murder of his father. When this knotty intrigue is finally unraveled, all that is agreed is that Artabanus killed Xerxes, but with the assistance of Aspamitres, the court eunuch.

With Xerxes and Darius put to rest, Artaxerxes would emerge as the empire's next ruler. According to biblical records, he allowed Ezra to leave Baghdad and return to Jerusalem to take control of matters both religious and civil for the resurrected Jewish nation. But Artaxerxes's greatest influence on human history is arguably his contribution to the principle of the separation of religion from government affairs, an unheard of notion in the ancient world, and one that has been a difficult practice ever since. It was the founder of the American colony of Rhode Island, Roger Williams, who used the example of Artaxerxes's response to the plight of the Persian Jews to argue that the government should stay out of religious affairs. But Williams added a twist to the argument—claiming that it was the obligation of the government to stay out of religious affairs rather than the reverse.

Blood feuds and the Persian obsession with the Greeks would return when Darius II assumed control of the empire. Darius had been born Ochus, the bastard son of Artaxerxes. After Artaxerxes died, another illegitimate son, Secydianus, took the throne, but only after bumping off his brother Xerxes II, the legitimate heir. Ochus then murdered Secydianus and changed his name to the more dynastically correct Darius II in order to give his reign a veneer of legitimacy. In 413 BCE his attention was directed westward, when a weakening of the Greek forces tempted him to resume the effort to conquer Athens.

While strolling around the grounds, digesting all of these battles and conquests, and rulers and ruled, I started to wonder about the relationship between today's Iranians and their ancient past. Was it the same as the residents of Cairo, who live and work within sight of the Giza Pyramids? Or the Athenians who hawk souvenirs in the backstreets of the Plaka, under the shadow of the Acropolis? And what about the Chinese who crowd smog-filled Beijing or labor in the countryside? Does the philosophy of Confucius still speak to them?

In these cases there seemed to be a significant difference in the connection between the people of the present and their ancient past. By most historians' accounts, the fate of the pharaonic people of the second and third millennium BCE is largely a mystery. Some claim that a long-term disruption of the annual flooding of the Nile, on which the agriculture of the valley depended, forced the pharaonic people to uproot and disperse throughout the region. Other contributing factors were the invasions of the Assyrians in 671 BCE and later the Persians in 525 BCE. In 30 BCE Egypt was absorbed into the Roman Empire, and the spread of Christianity, which led to the adoption of the Greek alphabet and abandonment of hieroglyphics, was the final nail in the coffin.

Whatever theory carries the most weight, it is generally agreed that given the widespread migration that took place across North Africa throughout the centuries, few of today's Egyptians can honestly claim more than a drop of pharaonic blood. Therefore, no Egyptian can state, with a straight face, to borrow from Shirin Ebadi, "I am a descendant of Ramses. . . ." Furthermore, the arrival of Islam in 642 forever severed the Egyptians from the pantheon of pharaonic gods—Isis and Mut, Sekhmet, Horus, and Thoth—and the view of the spiritual world that emanated from them. The result, today, is that for Egyptians and foreign tourists alike the ancient temples and monuments represent an alien if awe-inspiring culture, showpieces of antiquity that bear little relationship to their own worldview and the spiritual tradition that derived from it.

Mention Greece and immediately images arise of the Acropolis rising above Athens, the ancient Agora below, and the Temple of Poseidon, perched on a rock outcropping at Sounion, overlooking the Aegean. And then there is the birthplace of the Olympic Games; the dialogues of Plato and the *Politics* of Aristotle, which formed the basis of Western thought; and the comedies and tragedies of the great dramatists, which became the foundation of modern drama. But one could rightfully ask what direct impact they have on the lives of contemporary Greeks. The growth of the Byzantine Empire, centered in Constantinople, quickly absorbed Greece, tugging it culturally away from its ancient past. Robert D. Kaplan, a former senior fellow at the Center for a New American Security and author of the book *Balkan Ghosts*, described the disparity that exists between the popular image of Greece, promulgated by academics and travel agencies, and the facts of Greece's broader history:

> Greece is where the West both begins and ends. The West—as a humanist ideal—began in ancient Athens where compassion for the individual began to replace the crushing brutality of the

nearby civilizations of Egypt and Mesopotamia. The war that Herodotus chronicles between Greece and Persia in the 5th century BC established a contrast between West and East that has persisted for millennia. Greece is Christian, but it is also Eastern Orthodox, as spiritually close to Russia as it is to the West, and geographically equidistant between Brussels and Moscow. Greece may have invented the West with the democratic innovations of the Age of Pericles, but for more than a thousand years it was a child of Byzantine and Turkish despotism. And while Greece was the northwestern bastion of the anciently civilized Near East, ever since history moved north into colder climates following the collapse of Rome, the inhabitants of Peninsular Greece have found themselves at the poor, southeastern extremity of Europe.

The case of Iran is a little different. The Arab invasion of 651 brought Islam to the opposite side of the Persian Gulf but never really severed Iranians from their Zoroastrian roots, which are still intertwined with the Iranian identity. It is no coincidence that Iran still adheres to the Persian-Zoroastrian calendar, neither the Islamic nor the Gregorian, and that New Year's Eve falls on March 20 (or 21, depending on the cycle of the sun), marking the beginning of Noruz, or "new day" in Farsi. And on the Wednesday preceding Noruz, Iranians of any or no religious affiliation will engage in "fire-jumping." Ask an Iranian abroad where they are from and often they will reply, "I'm Persian." Part of the reason is political, to take a swipe at the ruling regime and all that it stands for, but the response also reveals that beyond the Iranian identity there is another that evokes a more historic, cultural bond to a time long before the term *Iran* became forever interwoven with modern geopolitics. The land of Persia was relabeled "Iran," meaning "land of the Aryans," during World War II, courtesy of Adolf Hitler, to consolidate the historical and linguistic tie between Persia and central Europe.

With the tombs behind us, Sohrab and I climbed back into the Volvo and pulled back onto the highway, heading south. The climax of the day was saved for last. About twenty minutes later we arrived at the parking lot in front of the entrance to Persepolis. In 1979 the ruins were designated a UNESCO World Heritage Site, and in terms of prestige the now crumbled city can hold its own among other great archaeological treasures of the world.

The name *Persepolis* can be attributed to the invading Greeks, who saw it simply as the city (*polis*) of the Persians (*Perse*). Once the Greeks had set their sights on Persepolis the Persian name for the city, Takht-e Jamshid, named for Jamshid, a character from Persian mythology, soon faded from common use. The Greeks turned out to be far more accurate in their nomenclature, for Darius I viewed Persepolis as the crowning jewel of the empire. According to Ernst Herzfeld, the archaeologist appointed in 1931 by the Oriental Institute at the University of Chicago to lead the excavation of Persepolis, it was never intended to be a truly functioning capital. It was meant to be more of a showpiece, to celebrate Noruz and other festivals, and display the usual pomp and circumstance that go hand-in-hand with the running of an empire.

Many of Persepolis's choice artifacts that survived both Alexander's invasion and the toll of time have been carted off to serve as representations of Persian greatness in many of the world's most well-known museums, from the Louvre in Paris to the Metropolitan Museum of Art in New York. But Herzfeld ensured that his own institution would receive an impressive prize for his efforts. One of Persepolis's largest stone-carved bull's heads hangs in the Persian room of the Oriental Institute on the University of Chicago campus.

Alexander's troops went wild in their destruction of Persepolis, but enough of the city remains to give a glimpse into the Persepolis of more than two millennia ago. Still standing are many of the stone doorways of the Tachara, Persepolis's oldest ceremonial palace; the entrance and a few columns of the Gate of All Nations, in its time a palatial reception hall; the Treasury; the Throne Hall; and the Apadana.

The crowning jewel is the grand staircase, and it is the best-preserved feature of the entire complex. It is actually a double staircase, one series of steps leading right and the other left from ground level to wind around the structure and end on a terrace, on which once stood the entire palace complex. When Persepolis was first excavated it was believed that the staircase was designed with unusually long steps and low risers so that visiting nobles, priests, and other members of the elite could climb to the terrace mounted on royal steeds. A revisionist view claims that horses played no part. The notables simply wanted their arrival to take place in the most dignified manner possible, so the staircase, as it was designed, would make them appear to rise effortlessly to the throne, as though gliding on air.

It is not the staircase itself but the relief sculptures carved on its facing that are among Persepolis's most impressive features, along with others on the face of the Apadana, the palace, and the rest of the buildings. In remarkable detail, along the grand staircase, a parade of priests is shown bearing ceremonial gifts accompanied by representatives from every region of the empire. Here and there, twelve-petaled lotus flowers serve as adornments. On the rear of the staircase, a pair of lions are taking a bite out of a horse's hindquarters. The impression these images were intended to project—of power, control, and spiritual transcendence—has carried through the ages.

Dug into a rockface near the top of a ridge behind the ruins of Persepolis are three more tombs like those at Naqsh-e Rustam. The entombed are believed to have been Darius I, Artaxerxes II, and Artaxerxes III. A series of steep stone steps leads up to a panoramic view of the plain and the ruins below. There was no choice but to seek out the view. Thinking it might convey a bit of the long-gone splendor of the place, I began the climb, one aching step at a time, until I had arrived at the entrance to Darius's tomb. Only from such a vantage point is it possible to absorb the scale and sweep of the city that once stretched across the plain, and only from such a vantage point is it also possible to absorb the scale of the loss that resulted from the rampage of Alexander's forces. But even if Alexander hadn't descended on Persepolis, there is little doubt that it would never have survived to the present day. If historical patterns are any guide, either it would have fallen to another invader or been shaken to rubble by one of the earthquakes to which the Persian landscape is forever vulnerable. But most likely Persepolis would have simply succumbed to old age, as all empires do, along with their symbols, if they last long enough. How or when Persepolis would have been destroyed, or simply faded into history, ignores the fact that its demise may have been a little premature.

The Persians do deserve some sympathy, but not all that much. In 480 BCE, when the Persian force led by Xerxes invaded Greece, the Persians showed themselves to be less than magnanimous conquerors. By the time they reached Athens, the city was mostly deserted. Most of the population had fled, giving the Persian army free rein to vandalize and pillage at will, which they did, and to make a lasting impression of their victory they torched the Acropolis and other temples on the mount sacred to the Greeks.

The fall of Persepolis came in 330 BCE, but to fully explain what happened on that date and time we must backtrack. In 334 BCE Alexander began his eastward campaign, entering Asia at the Dardanelles, between the Aegean Sea and the Sea of Marmara, fortified by a massive force. Then emperor Darius III either dismissed Alexander as too young and inexperienced in the art of warfare or never believed the twenty-three-year-old had "the right stuff" to take on his enormous empire. He would soon be proven wrong. Within the year the Macedonian invader had penetrated deep into Persia, and Darius was defeated twice, first in the Battle of Granicus and later in the Battle of Issus, both on the Anatolian Peninsula in modern-day Turkey. At Issus, Alexander's rout of the Persians was so complete it sent Darius and many of his soldiers fleeing the battlefield. Adding to the Persians' humiliation was the fact that they had Alexander's forces greatly outnumbered, by as much as two to one.

Alexander was now almost unstoppable, and Darius started to see the writing on the wall. He offered to cede half of Persia to Alexander in exchange for an alliance with the Greeks, but sensing total victory, Alexander would have none of it. A desperate Darius sweetened the deal, offering Alexander more territory and even his daughter in marriage. Again he was rebuffed. Darius made a third offer, throwing in a pile of silver and even more territory—all of his empire between the

Euphrates River and the Mediterranean Sea. Alexander was tempted, but smelling blood, he chose to press on and routed Darius a third time, at the Battle of Gaugamela. The Persian leadership had had enough of Darius's inept leadership, and the last ruler of the empire was assassinated by one of his own generals.

Alexander conquered Persia, and to the victor go the spoils. The wealth of Persepolis was so massive that, according to Plutarch, 20,000 mules and 5,000 camels were needed to cart it all away. This included 3,500 tons of gold, silver, and other precious metals, so claimed the Greek historian Diodorus Siculus. But more than two thousand years later, it is still unclear what led to the final burning of Persepolis. There are three theories. The first states that the motive was raw revenge for the burning of the Acropolis. The Greek historian Arrian wrote:

> He [Alexander] also set the Persian palace on fire against the advice of Parmenion, who argued that it was ignoble to destroy what was now his own property and that the peoples of Asia would not pay heed to him in the same way if they assumed he had no intention of governing Asia but would merely conquer and move on. But Alexander declared that he wanted to pay back the Persians, who, when they invaded Greece, had razed Athens and burned the temples, and to exact retribution for all the other wrongs they had committed against the Greeks.

According to the second theory, in the middle of a drunken victory banquet, Alexander's troops went wild and began torching the city. The third theory combines the two, claiming that during the victory party the reveling soldiers were goaded on to destroy the city by Thais, believed to have been a mistress of Ptolemy. According to the Greek historian Diodorus:

> While they were feasting and the drinking was far advanced, as they began to be drunken a madness took possession of the minds of the intoxicated guests. At this point one of the women present, Thais by name and Attic by origin, said that for Alexander it would

be the finest of all his feats in Asia if he joined them in a triumphal procession, set fire to the palaces, and permitted women's hands in a minute to extinguish the famed accomplishments of the Persians. This was said to men who were still young and giddy with wine, and so, as would be expected, someone shouted out to form the comus and to light torches, and urged all to take vengeance for the destruction of the Greek temples. Others took up the cry and said that this was a deed worthy of Alexander alone. When the king had caught fire at their words, all leaped up from their couches and passed the word along to form a victory procession in honor of Dionysius.

This is a rare case in which historical accuracy probably means very little. Whether the result of drunken revelry or the spirit of revenge fueled by a drunken revelry doesn't change the fact that Persepolis was destroyed—plain and simple. From the terrace outside the tomb of Darius I it is possible to imagine the enormity of what was lost. The few imposing doorways and columns that remain, along with the grand staircase and the spectacular rows of reliefs, have defied not only a conquering army's worst impulses but the wear of time to remind us of what can be envisioned and achieved, and that ambition tied to will is the marker of human progress. It also reminds us that what took years to build can be destroyed in a flash. But, thankfully, what was not destroyed was the will and desire to build in the first place, and that is what rises again to continue the story of human progress.

Finished with reflections on history, I side-stepped down the steep staircase that had brought me up to the tombs and headed to the Persepolis Museum, standing on the edge of the ruins. It houses a collection of bric-a-brac that had been scoured from the site, mainly second- and third-rate artifacts, none of the prize finds that had long ago been carted off to the first-rate museums of the world.

It sometimes happens that in any museum the main attraction isn't the objects preserved in the climate-controlled display cases but the visitors poring over them, and this was the case here. I circled the room, eyeing the clusters of visitors gathered around the exhibits. They lingered, and pondered, longer than the usual crowd of museumgoers. These were not tourists who had dropped in from other sides of the Earth, like myself, but mostly Iranians—or Persians—peering through a looking glass that took them back to the roots of their own recorded history, and the studied looks on the faces of the observers hinted at questions that only an Iranian—or a Persian—could ask: What does it mean to be Persian? How has the ancient past shaped the Iranian identity? Does it have any influence on the present at all? Is there any purpose in preserving these relics of a far more glorious past than the present could ever live up to? Could such a display only squelch the aspirations of the young generation in today's Iran? If so, maybe the museum should be shut—maybe the entire site. Of course that was nonsensical, but it was where such ruminations took me.

As I circled the room I tried to imagine the thoughts that were spinning through the heads of the visitors. The intrigue became perplexing, and then discouraging, as I knew the answers to these questions were as inaccessible as history itself. Studious, puzzled looks can only reveal so much. Did they feel proud or humbled? Did they see this as their own history or that of a lost people of another time? It was hard to tell. I stepped outside to take a last look at the ragged ruins of the crumbled city. The afternoon was warming up, and many of the visitors, driven away from the midday sun, had gathered in the shade of the museum's portico. But the warm, dry air came with them, making the nearby water cooler the most popular spot on the entire grounds.

Soon I caught the attention of a group of young men, all twenty-somethings, gathered outside the museum entrance. They exchanged a few words, and then one moved toward me—the most emboldened, the one with the most facility with English, leading the way.

He opened with the inevitable: "Where are you from?"

I told him, he translated, and immediately the rest of the group relaxed, the faces brightening. I decided to get ahead of what was to come—the litany of questions that would begin—"Why did you come to Iran?" I asked Mohammad, the English speaker, if this was the first time he had visited Persepolis. Oh no, he replied, he had come here several times, the first with a group from school when he was very young. What did he and his friends think about all they had just seen? Did it make them proud?

The others could manage some English, indicated by the looks of at least vague comprehension that appeared on the young men's faces.

"Oh, no!" Mohammad exclaimed. "We're not proud of *anything!*"

There was a quick translation. Heads nodded in agreement. The bluntness of his answer was surprising.

"What do we have to be proud of?" Mohammad continued. "Our politics? Now that's all we have. Our art and culture, science—that's all in the past."

One of the group translated for the others. There were more nods of agreement.

Mohammad went on: "These leaders talk about the greatness of Iran, but Iran is not important today. You come from a country that is very important, even if it is still very young."

There were more nods of agreement, and I noted the remark of condescension but could not argue with it, because it meant no offense, and it was true. When you're speaking for a civilization seven thousand years old, one with only a couple of centuries behind it seems hardly out of diapers. I asked Mohammad what would make him feel differently about his country.

"We want more freedom," he said, and this time no translation was needed. The nods of assent were more deliberate. I asked what he meant by freedom. A free and fair vote? Iran had that, sometimes, and more often than many countries. Freedom to criticize the government, its policies? The Iranian press was filled with virulent critics who poked at every and any government policy. Nothing was off-limits—except attacks on the legitimacy of the Islamic Revolution itself, and the ruling clerics who struggled to keep it alive despite the virulent streams of criticism of almost every government policy. Is this what Mohammad had in mind?

"We want more social life, places where we can go to meet others, do what other young people do, in other countries. For people our age it's normal. There shouldn't be all these restrictions."

There was another translation. The nods of assent became a chorus.

On any freedom index in the world, the availability of nightclubs hardly ranks alongside press freedom and the right of assembly, but I could not turn up my nose at his definition of freedom, because for those of his generation that is where it all started—today a nightclub, tomorrow an opposition newspaper, and then an opposition government. I asked how many of the group had been supporters of President Hassan Rouhani in the last election. All the hands went up.

"If there was different leadership in this country things would be less strict," Mohammad went on. Heads kept nodding. For a brief moment the hint of a brighter future shone.

I asked about weightier matters, like Iran's relationship with the rest of the world, its image, the willingness of others not to continuously place it in the unwelcome family of "rogue states."

"We don't want all these troubles with other countries, the U.S. What we want is just to be a normal country, for the rest of the world to look at us that way."

The impromptu translator conveyed the more complicated bits of Mohammad's private protest. More heads nodded. The chatter continued, jokes and jabs were exchanged, and suddenly I felt out of the loop, like someone who did not grasp the punch line of a joke. Eventually it emerged that one of the group, Davood, was a member of the basij.

Soon after Ayatollah Khomeini had taken control of Iran he knew that his Islamic Revolution, and the reign of his cabal of clerics, would have to be guarded against all threats, both from without and within. To maintain internal control he recruited a massive army of young enforcers, men and women, drawn mainly from the marginalized lower classes outside the more prosperous urban areas. The arrangement was a simple quid pro quo: in exchange for their service they would receive perks, such as advantages in applying for government jobs, and generous payouts whenever they had to be called to duty. From a less cynical point of view it could be called "leveling the playing field"—offering socioeconomic stepping stones to those who would otherwise have none. For the more critical, the basiji were selling their allegiance to a totalitarian regime. They were the ready-to-be-exploited underclass of Iran. Today there are estimated to be as many as one million "guardians of the revolution," and they played a prominent role in quelling the postelection riots in 2009. It was largely the basij forces that brought "order" to the streets of Tehran and other cities where protests had broken out. Donning crash helmets, waving rubber truncheons, and zipping through the streets on government-supplied motorbikes, the basiji were both loathed and feared.

Ayatollah Khomeini had not stumbled upon anything new. The young had been coopted to support many revolutionary movements in recent history. During the Chinese Cultural Revolution of the 1970s, it was mainly the young and educated who served as the enforcers of Communist Party chairman Mao Tse-tung's purist principles, which led to the purging of all foreign influences from Chinese society and the jailing of their own university professors. The foot soldiers of Pol Pot's Khmer Rouge were mostly teenagers who saw the deranged dictator as an ideological hero who would rid Cambodia of all the forces that wished to destroy it, again from without or within. In 1930s Germany the Hitler Youth was created to instill the Nazi philosophy and guarantee unquestioned obedience to the new order among the country's most impressionable.

However, the creation of the basij and the circumstances that maintain it don't quite adhere to the historical pattern. In all of the previous cases, the driving force was ideological fervor. One could even call it mania, mania bordering on hysteria fueled by paranoia. Ayatollah Khomeini, his senior clerics, and all their successors have struggled to instill the passion for the Islamic Revolution in Iranian society, especially in the early days of the revolution and especially among the youth, but the effort has been largely a failure. They have won over some true believers, but the vast majority of Iranian youth, well aware of the government's notorious corruption and hypocrisy, have become deeply cynical, and in the four decades the regime has held on to power its corruption and hypocrisy has been increasingly exposed, only deepening the cynicism of the youth. The regime leaders, ever pragmatic and ever committed to retaining power, have given up on turning most of the youth into true believers. Instead of trying to win support through ideological commitment they have waved the carrot of pragmatism before the eyes of Iranian society's most disadvantaged: support us, no matter what you think of us, and we will take care of you. It is a cynical bargain for both sides and can be sustained only as long as mutual need exists.

Tall and lanky, and without his black helmet, riot shield, and truncheon, Davood looked more like the captain of a volleyball team than a member of the security police. I asked him why he had joined. Did he believe in the principles of the revolution? Did he believe that Iran needed to be a more devout society? Were there internal enemies that were a threat to the nation's integrity, even its survival?

Davood drew a blank. I half expected a torrent of ideological clap-trap, but he had no ideology to spout. He was just a young man with few ways to move up in a society where proven loyalty to a corrupt regime was often the only step to advancement. His answer was simple, devoid of any moral complications, as decisions often are, and have to be, in any totalitarian state: "It's easier to get into a university. There aren't many opportunities in Iran, and so many of them are controlled by the government." The Islamic regime was simply a fact of life that he had known all his life, and it had to be accommodated, negotiated, and navigated. It was an iceberg that could sink one's chances in life if one wasn't careful.

"Hey, no politics—"

Another member of the group had edged close and spoke quietly but firmly. His words were more caution than warning, one friend looking out for another because they had long learned that unwanted ears could be anywhere. And it had its effect. Davood clammed up, and after an awkward pause the conversation eased into topics that pulled it into a politically safe zone: What had I seen in Iran? Had I met many Iranians? Would I come back?

It was surprising how smoothly but deliberately the change occurred. Almost immediately the demeanor of the young men shifted from gathering interest to awakened fear, as though they had touched an exposed electrical wire and knew enough to retreat. I voiced the scripted replies they expected, and then the group trudged off, after handshakes all around and expressions of heartfelt wishes that I enjoy the rest of my trip. But as they left, the young man who had cut off the discussion edged close. He asked, politely, if I could be his foil for language practice, so we jabbered a bit but soon began conversing on subjects not covered in any English-language textbook. He waited until the rest of the group was out of earshot but still spoke softly.

"You know, it's not possible to talk freely in Iran . . ."

I nodded, not to express agreement but slightly and vaguely, to indicate I grasped not only the truth of what he had said but the sense of shame that accompanied it.

"We do want more freedom," he went on, "but we have to be careful what we say."

And so it ended.

It was late afternoon by the time Sohrab and I were on our way back to Shiraz. The sun had dipped low to the west, almost touching the tops of the faraway hills, deepening the colors of the fields and orchards on both sides of the road. Despite the rural beauty glowing in the light of the late-afternoon sun, a shadow was lengthening across my memory of the day. Not even the smooth strains of Sarah Vaughn could lift the mood. I thought of Davood and felt sad that such cynicism had taken root in someone so young. It was all the more troubling when one considers that 60 percent of the Iranian population is under thirty-five, with no meaningful memory of life before the Islamic Revolution, an event that effectively severed the youth from their own identity and history. Persepolis was a place where they could finally connect to it, stand in the aura of a hint of Persian greatness, and the experience only filled them with shame.

I wondered what reaction Sohrab had to visiting Persepolis. After all, he had been here countless times escorting foreign tourists like myself and witnessed their probing curiosity and awe. Had the novelty of the experience faded? Had it become too routine? I asked him, and rather than answering yes or no, he responded with a story. One day he brought a group of visiting relatives around the site, and that day then-president Mahmoud Ahmadinejad was scheduled to deliver a speech in front of the grand staircase. It was an attempt to wrap himself in the glories of the Persian civilization so that some of the luster might redeem his inglorious and dysfunctional government.

"I told the others that they could listen if they wanted to, but I just walked away. I went back to the parking lot and waited in the car. Everyone knew what he was going to say. I didn't have to hear it."

"Every time you come here, doesn't it give you any sense of pride?" I asked. Sohrab had never been shy about discussing politics, and often in unvarnished terms. "Cockroaches" is how he referred to the clerical leadership, and all of the Iranian leadership. This time he chose to couch his views in a business metaphor.

"We need better management," he said. "Like the Catholic Church a thousand years ago, this government is still in the Dark Ages."

12 | Shiraz

OF SENSES AND SENSIBILITIES

God wants to manhandle us,
Lock us up in a tiny room with Himself
And practice His dropkick.
The Beloved sometimes wants to do us a
    great favor:
Hold us upside down and shake all the
    nonsense out.
                                    —Hafez

A few years ago a Greek friend of mine, well versed in the ups and downs of travel in distant parts of the world, decided to spend a month in Iran. Her starting point was Shiraz, and when she arrived at her hotel, the concierge greeted her with characteristic Persian hospitality: "Welcome to Iran," he said. "You can have *anything* you like!"

"Can I take this off?" she asked, fingering the edge of the headscarf.

He leaned close and whispered, "Maybe in a few months—the bastards will be gone."

That was her introduction to Iran, and it was an appropriate one, for it conveyed the general attitude of Iranians toward the Islamic regime. A few hours later she was riding in a taxi, and the driver started talking politics. The conversation led, as conversations with foreign visitors often do, to the government.

"The shah was bad, but these *fucking bastards* are worse, a *thousand times worse!*" he shouted. The window was open, his words free for all the world to hear. She expected the security forces might appear out of nowhere and haul him off to jail, but no. This was Iran, where the government is well aware of the people's loathing and can only hope that their acts of rebellion are confined to outbursts from car windows. In fact, they may even welcome them, for they let air out of a balloon that might otherwise burst.

Shiraz is an ideal entry point to Iran, and it is also the best place to end a journey, for this city more than any other expresses the love of beauty and the pleasures of the senses that the Persian culture has long embodied. First impressions are lasting ones, but so are final ones, and one could not take away a truer and more accurate impression of the Persian culture and the values it has celebrated for several thousand years than in Shiraz.

"The spring is beautiful in California. The valleys in which the fruit blossoms are fragrant pink. . . . The full green hills are round and soft as breasts," wrote John Steinbeck, describing his native state in *The Grapes of Wrath*. But he could have been just as easily describing the fertile, undulating landscape that surrounds Shiraz.

The world's earliest remnant of wine, dating to 5000 BCE, was discovered here, and by the ninth century BCE the city had become the primary exporter of wine in the Middle East. The semi-arid climate, with its soft spring rains and searing summer heat, could not have been more perfectly designed for the cultivation of the grapes that for seven thousand years have been the prime ingredient of fine Shirazi wine.

> A book of verses underneath the bough
> A flask of wine, a loaf of bread and thou
> Beside me singing in the wilderness
> And wilderness is paradise now.

So wrote Hafez, widely regarded as Iran's greatest poet. Many of his well-known *ghazals*, or love poems in the Persian sonnet form, praise the ruby elixir that made his city famous. Hardly a poem ends without his mention of it, and hardly one neglects to mention his love of it.

For those outside Iran, it might be surprising that, despite the ban on alcohol under the Islamic Republic, the love of wine, and the passions it inspires, have not vanished from Persian life.

"I don't have to go to Dubai to drink. My family makes our own wine in the bathtub at home, and it's better than anything you can buy," a friend in Tehran told me.

Shiraz was home to another of Iran's greatest poets, Abu-Mohammad Mosleh Al-Din Saadi Shirazi, or simply Saadi. His tomb lies in a compound northeast of the city center. The first time I was here I decided to make it my first destination because the peaceful setting would offer a connection to the Persian culture I could carry with me for the succeeding days.

Like Avicenna, Saadi was a bit of a wanderer and lived a life kaleidoscopic in color. He was born in Shiraz near the end of the twelfth century. His father died when he was very young, and a life of relentless poverty forced him to flee to Baghdad, where he studied science, law, theology, and literature. In 1219, the Mongol invasion again sent him on the road, and he would spend the next thirty years of his life wandering through central Asia, Turkey, Egypt, Syria, and Palestine. But the life of a vagabond gave him an education a more settled and comfortable existence never could have equaled. The sources for his work were refugees of war, traveling merchants and thieves, vagrants, farmers, and teahouse philosophers, in other words, common people, who in many cases wove elaborate tapestries of wisdom from their everyday lives.

There is much of the common touch in the works of Persian poets, and many of Saadi's lines read like the drops of two-penny wisdom found in Benjamin Franklin's *Poor Richard's Almanack*:

Whatever is produced in haste goes hastily to waste.

And:

A grateful dog is better than an ungrateful man.

A master of the quip Saadi was, but the hardships he endured early in life were later reshaped into mature wisdom:

> Two things define you:
> Your patience when you have nothing,
> And your attitude when you have everything.

Saadi's marble bier stands in a small, six-sided, tower-like chamber topped with a high dome. Blue tiles, hand-painted with quotes from his works, fill the inner walls. A colonnaded hall extends from the tomb alongside a rectangular pool that stretches beneath a canopy of trees. The setting is quintessentially Persian: elegant but modest, blending air, water, and light into a work of art that ties the creative world to the natural as well as the spiritual.

By the time we got to the tomb it was late afternoon, and the early summer sun was streaming through the arches of the colonnade, deepening the blue of the tiles while sparing us the searing summer heat that was yet to come. In a mark of respect, visitors, one by one, placed the traditional two fingers on the cool stone surface as they passed through the room that held his bier. According to custom, the visitor also prays for the peace of the soul of the deceased by reciting verses from the Fateheh, the first chapter of the Quran. For today's Iranians, the gesture is a way of reaching across the ages to touch, quite literally, the heart of the Persian culture and those who have best expressed it.

Leaving the tomb, I took a stroll around the garden and stumbled on the top of a circular staircase, where a handwritten sign with an arrow pointed downward from the top stair. Down I went, following the twisting spiral deep underground until it touched bottom. There a café had been carved out of the rock, and in the center was a fishpond. Cozy niches had been dug into the walls and lined with thick cushions for seats. Paintings of birds, a favorite image of Saadi, hung on the walls.

I ordered a mint tea and settled into one of the niches to scan the crowd, mostly Shirazis who sought this underground warren to hold on to a bit of Saadi while sipping cappuccinos and watching the fish scuttling around in the pond. But there was a puzzle. How did twenty-first century Iranians come to terms with the works of these literary greats, when so many of their verses paid homage to physical beauty, sensual pleasure, and even drunkenness, facts of human experience that the clerical establishment had spent the better part of forty years trying to deny? How could their poems even be read in schools, when every book had to be approved by religious authorities? I recalled a conversation I'd had with an Iranian American literature professor:

"They tried to tell us that none of those references—to wine, pleasure, beauty—none of them were to be taken literally. The poets were really talking about spiritual beauty, spiritual pleasures, but they had to communicate these to the common people and so they used earthly imagery. Even Hafez—they told us he used wine as an image for spiritual intoxication. But we all knew this was nonsense."

The parents of her generation had attended school during the liberal reign of the Shah Mohammad Reza Pahlavi, when alcohol flowed freely and Tehran teemed with bars and nightclubs. Surely they had to know that the ruling mullahs' attempt at literary interpretation was a bit clouded, and not by drink. Even so, the mullahs were claiming that Hafez, Saadi, and Omar Khayyam were trying to direct their readers' eyes toward heaven, not the wine bottle.

She added: "A lot of young people today are quite confused. They see no alcohol or other pleasures in society and think that maybe it's true, that the poets weren't talking about the pleasures they want to have. But they're young. They want to drink and dance and enjoy themselves."

I was a foreigner with no confusions other than those that come with wandering in a foreign land, so I was content to watch the fish circling in the pond and listen to the clinking of the teacups and the soft sounds of the *ney*, the Persian flute, that drifted from the café's CD player. And there also were the curious gazes of the other customers watching this foreigner listening to the strains of the *ney* and watching the fish circling in the pond and observing the curious gazes of the other customers.

As tranquil as the setting was, I couldn't stay forever because I did have other plans for the evening: to dine at the Sharzeh restaurant, famous for its live Persian music, and then to make it to the tomb of Hafez by closing time. So I left the café and the images of Saadi's beloved birds and headed back to the hotel to relax a bit before going out for the evening.

There was little reason to do so, except to put my feet up. The café on the mezzanine advertised "Happy Hour," but of course there were no drink specials, only tea, coffee, fruit juices, and the usual selection of boozeless beers. I went to my room and tried to find CNN, BBC, or any other satellite news channel but got only the state-run Press TV and its English-fluent anchors bashing Saudi Arabia and reporting cherry-picked stories that reflected negatively on the United States, Europe, and "the West." With gun violence running riot through American society and Brexit problems in the United Kingdom, their job was not hard. After a few minutes I set out for the Sharzeh.

It was close by, and in a few minutes I was at its doors, tucked down a passage just outside the entrance of Shiraz's grand Vakil Bazaar. But the Sharzeh was still shuttered, and a sign indicating eight o'clock in Farsi numerals hung in the window. I had to wait, and if there was any doubt, the owner of a spice stall on the other side of the passage flashed a smile and held up eight fingers.

The Vakil is one of those garishly elegant Middle Eastern bazaars that has fiercely resisted the advances of time. The arched ceiling is cathedral high, and its narrow stone passageways crisscross through densely packed vendors' stalls. True to its timelessness, the Vakil is both luxury boutique and Persian Walmart, with stalls selling everything from precious stones and gold jewelry to underwear and kitchenware and other household goods. The design is part of the genius of the Middle Eastern bazaar: Endless variety means endless choice, and endless choice guarantees a constant stream of customers. So at seven o'clock, at the end of a workday, the aisles were jammed. Office workers on their way home were picking up new wallets and handbags. Housewives finishing the day's shopping were dipping into spice sacks and picking through bins of pistachios. Bolts of colored silk were crammed onto shelves that rose to the ceiling. Brassware dangled from metal hooks, and the scent of olive oil soap and perfumes of lavender and lilac floated from hidden corners.

I wandered right and left and left and right and learned, once again, that the Middle Eastern bazaar doesn't only challenge the senses but all frames of reference. Instead of heading deeper into the Vakil, as I had intended, after a riot of twists and turns I found myself dumped back onto Zand Street. Rather than try again, with still time to kill I headed west, toward a row of contemporary storefronts.

Zand Street is the main boulevard that bisects the center of Shiraz, and it is also the city's primary shopping street—but only after the stores have closed. Its legitimate traders do legitimate business during the day, selling mobile phones and athletic gear and other goods that make up the bulk of the consumer trade, but after 6:00 p.m. the black marketers arrive, spread plastic tarps on the sidewalk, and set cardboard boxes on folding tables. Then the real dealing gets going, for most of the goods for sale are not to be found in the conventional retail market: Western pop music, Hollywood movies, and box sets of pirated American TV series. More commonplace items are also on offer—cheap electronics and kitchenware, household tools and secondhand books—but most of the shoppers are here for the contraband.

I prowled through the stacks of CDs and DVDs, but the pickings were uninspiring—a few Hollywood westerns, more than a few romantic comedies, and troves of CDs by Iranian pop bands, mostly refugees from the Islamic Revolution that have established a Persian counter-culture in Los Angeles. But there were a few finds. I bought copies of *The Strange Case of Benjamin Button* and *Saving Private Ryan* for a dollar each. But I had been taken. Later I learned that that was the "foreigner's price." An Iranian could have had each for fifty cents. But the fault was really my own, because they were so cheap I didn't bother to bargain.

More than a simple contraband bazaar, Zand Street offers insight into the government's failure to repress the liberal inclinations of many Iranians, particularly the urban youth, and the allure of cultural products from the West. Sometime between the liberal presidencies of Hashemi Rafsanjani in the late 1980s and Mohammad Khatami in the 1990s, and after repeated failures to crack down on Western movies and music, the Iranian government made a tacit bargain with the country's youth:

Do what you want behind closed doors but at least pretend to obey us in public. Arbitrary crackdowns used to keep the black marketers looking over their shoulders, but as the underground traffic has risen to street level, even the crackdowns have proven futile.

The blatant openness of the trade, and the hypocrisy it signifies, reminded me of a story told to me by a psychologist friend who has lived outside of Iran for more than thirty years. On a trip back to Shiraz she had to call on one of the city's mullahs at the request of a friend.

"I thought I should dress even more conservatively than I usually would, but when he picked me up at the station he was wearing Levi's and a new pair of Nikes, and when we got to his house he had CD racks full of jazz and pop music. I caught a glance into his daughter's bedroom. There was a poster of Britney Spears on the wall, and lying on the bed was a Barbie doll in a bikini."

All this would have greatly depressed Karim Khan Zand, for whom Zand Street was named. Zand was not a tried-and-true conservative Muslim in the image the ruling regime would like to pretend. Zand was the first ruler of a dynasty that came to power in the middle of the eighteenth century, and he was known for his humble lifestyle and the transparency with which he ran his government. In a gesture of humility, he never assumed the title of shah, preferring to be referred to as a simple *vakil*, or local ruler. But the qualities for which he was most widely known were honesty and personal integrity. He sold the gifts he received from doting admirers and gave the proceeds to the state treasury. Forty years of destructive internal wars preceded his reign, and while the Shiraz was being rebuilt, a group of workers found a pot of gold coins in a pile of rubble. Zand let the workers divide it among themselves.

Having survived decades of war, Zand built the stark, imposing citadel that still stands on Zand Street, just a short walk from the storefronts that line the street that bears his name, and he reconstructed the bazaar, which indirectly bears his name and was largely destroyed during the years of war.

I became so absorbed in the black-market pickings that I lost track of the time. By the time I got back to the Sharzeh the doors were open and the first diners were filing in. Most were from the Persian middle and upper class—men in neat slacks and suits and women trying to outdo themselves in layers of makeup, jewelry, and headscarves with color-coordinated manteaux. The fashion parade was also a political statement, a way for women to thumb their noses at the authorities. It said: You try to suppress us, we will use whatever we have—our faces, our clothing, our figures—to fight back. And these kinds of fashion statements were de rigueur in Shiraz, which leans distinctly liberal on the Iranian social spectrum.

The host showed me to a table on the mezzanine near a railing that overlooked the stage below. The rest of the tables filled up quickly. But there would be a downside to the evening: Any true celebration of Persian culture would be muted, and literally, because all of the performers, singers included, would be limited to men.

Of all the deprivations of human rights suffered by women all over the world, the ban on women singing in public in Iran has long struck me as one of the most odious. At the beginning of the Islamic Revolution, the new ruling mullahs believed that men could be corrupted by the sound of the female voice. Ayatollah Khomeini went even further, linking the influx of all Western music to the incursions of British and Russian forces in the nineteenth and twentieth centuries, calling Western music a form of "cultural colonialism." "Music is said to unsettle the soul," he wrote, "to lead people to indulge in the pure sensuality of the physical expression of their bodies."

Hafez would have taken great exception to Khomeini's puritanism. He wrote:

> Come with your tender mouths moving
> And your beautiful tongues conducting songs
> And with your movements, your magic movements
> Of hands and feet and glands and cells—dancing!
> Know that to God's eye,
> All movement is a wondrous language,
> And music—such exquisite, wild music!

But Hafez was not leading the 1979 Islamic Revolution. Khomeini and his fellow mullahs were, so women's mouths were shut and Tehran's nightclubs were closed. Popular female singers like Marzieh, Homeyra, Hayedeh, and Mahasati were driven underground or into exile. In the years to come, "cultural freedom" would become a political football to be bandied about by would-be moderates seeking popular support. It is hard not to see more than a little misogyny at play. Mahsa Vahdat, who has rendered the verses of Rumi and Hafez into mystical tunes, has said, "Who could be sexually aroused by Hafez's poetry? The government has a political problem with women's voices. Singing will give women power and political influence."

But no Homeyra nor Googoosh would be appearing at the Sharzeh that night. Instead, a group of male musicians and two singers took to the stage, and while the diners dug into their plates of grilled fish and lamb kebabs they pumped out folk tunes that roused the clapping of the crowd and was enough to create the illusion that Iran was, once again, a place where creative expression was not a crime.

Halfway through the first set and my plate of polo-mahi, accompanied by the usual mountain of saffron rice, a young couple nearby used a pause between songs to ask, as if there were any surprise: "Where are you from?" and "Why did you come to Iran?"

They quickly introduced themselves. Jamshid had grown up on a farm near Shiraz where his father grew barley and wheat. He had thick hands and arms, and his girth was another sign of his former athleticism: He had been a champion heavyweight wrestler, winning bronze and silver medals in regional competitions. He graduated from Shiraz University with a degree in biochemical engineering and was working in eco-agriculture. Parisa had a degree in internet technology but had been having a hard time finding a job.

"These days there are none," Parisa lamented. "You can get an advanced degree in an important field but still there are no opportunities."

I asked—Were the sanctions to blame? The rial had lost more than 60 percent of its value, and inflation had propelled the prices of everyday goods into the stratosphere, beyond everyday budgets. Pistachios, a staple snack of rich and poor, had become a luxury.

I expected Parisa to rail against the European Union, the Western powers, and all the other forces in the world that were, in the regime's view, trying to cripple Iran. But no, she didn't know if the sanctions were the prime cause of the country's economic woes. She didn't know if government mismanagement were more to blame. What's more, she didn't care. The hardships of life were painfully simple: Prices were high and rising higher. Money was tight and getting tighter. International politics was an abstraction, alien to the more immediate frustrations of Iran's young professionals and the struggling middle class.

"I don't know why there is so much talk about Iran," she continued. "All we hear about is Iran and Syria, Iran and terrorism, Iran and Saudi Arabia, Iran and the nukes. Everywhere it is Iran, Iran, Iran. Doesn't anybody wonder how such a country can have so much power when it can't even provide jobs for its people?"

For a generation of Iranians whose constant aim was to shut the government out of their lives, it was hard to understand how Iran could command so much global attention. For Parisa and many young Iranians the regime was responsible for so much of the misery that people endured, and it was not going to go away. It couldn't be voted out of office, like an unpopular government in a "normal" country. With no escape at hand, except for those lucky enough to emigrate to Canada, the U.S., or Europe, the regime and its corruption and anti-Western rhetoric had become an inescapable constant, like subzero weather above the Arctic Circle.

The music break ended, the band returned to the stage, and the singing was met with rounds of applause. It was a welcome change from talk of Iran's doldrums. I told Jamshid and Parisa that after dinner I was planning to head to the tomb of Hafez, and then Parisa's eyes brightened. I asked her if it was true, that every household in Iran has a well-worn copy of Hafez's poetry tucked away somewhere in a bookshelf.

"I don't have a Quran," Parisa acknowledged, "but I have three copies of Hafez. One has been in our family for generations. My father gave it to me."

"Do you still read it?"

She smirked. "Sometimes when we have to make an important decision or want to know what will happen in the future we'll take a copy of Hafez off the shelf and open it to any page and read what it says. They say that's the only way to uncover the truth."

"What about all the old female pop stars—Googoosh and Marzieh?" I asked. "Does every household also have a collection of vinyl beside their volume of Hafez?"

"My brother has a collection of all the old pop singers, the women too, and he also has a copy of Hafez," Parisa said.

"When he has to make an important decision, does he open his Hafez or play a track of Googoosh?"

Jamshid cut in: "I don't know about Googoosh, but I bought an entire collection of Elvis Presley off the internet. I only paid a dollar for it. A friend downloaded it for me."

"Does Elvis tell your future?"

"Now that's silly," Parisa concluded.

"So is letting Hafez do it," Jamshid added.

"Who cares? We still do it," Parisa concluded.

It was time to go. The band was still running through its repertoire of pop tunes and folk melodies, hopping neatly from one to the other to keep the crowd happy, but Hafez was waiting. My bill came, but Jamshid and Parisa insisted on paying it, and I let them, but only after the expected and customary exchanges of taarof:

"Of course you mustn't . . ."

"Don't be silly, it's nothing . . ."

It was a battle I was sure to lose, but one that had to be waged. I was a visitor, a guest at their table, and a foreigner, three reasons why it would have been an inexcusable breach of Persian hospitality for them to allow me to pay, as it would have been a breach of Persian hospitality for me to refuse. So I thanked them profusely, which was also expected, and then made my way to the door and hopped into a taxi.

Ten minutes later I was at the entrance to the resting place of Iran's most revered poet. Call these the Big Five, the voice of each occupies a special place in Persian literature: Ferdowsi, the historian; Rumi, the mystic; Saadi, the wise advisor; Omar Khayyam, the philosopher-scientist; and Hafez, the voice of the commoner—humble, flawed, and self-effacing, but also longing and searching, a victim of human frailties and self-indulgence, but always joyful, always hopeful—a Persian Everyman:

> Look inside my playful verse,
> For Hafez is barefoot and dancing
> And in such a grand and generous,
> In such a fantastic mood.

A biography of Hafez would be one of the shortest Persian books because almost nothing is known about his life. Scholars claim he was born in Shiraz in 1315, maybe 1317, and he died there, probably in 1390. And that is where the facts of his life begin and end, and the mystery is partly what makes him so mythic.

It is not hard to understand Hafez's grip on Persian culture. If there is any word that appears more often in Hafez's poetry than *wine*, it is *love*, and throughout his poetry it is continually shapeshifting, at times representing physical beauty, at others sensual emotions, sometimes the deeply spiritual or profoundly mystical. Whatever its source, for Hafez it was the force that drives all existence:

> We are people who need to love,
> Because love is the soul's life,
> Love is simply creation's greatest joy.

If Hafez were nothing more than a gauzy sentimentalist, his works would be gathering dust in some literary archive, but he could also be the gadfly of entrenched government elites and religious pretenders, a role far more useful in Iran today than in its medieval past, and this is one of the reasons his works resonate so loudly in contemporary Iran:

> The dregs of society are godly compared to you pompous
>   poseurs.

I would rather frequent infamous hovels
Such as a tavern or a cabaret
Than places infested with you hypocrites.
I would rather choose an abject wine seller or a debauchee
As my spiritual guide than any one of you liars and cheats.

It was after ten o'clock, but the gates were still open and dozens of visitors were wandering around the grounds. At the entrance a handful of vendors were selling steaming bowls of aash and warm slices of barbari bread. A late-night chill had settled in, hinting that winter had yet to fully yield to spring. Women with delicately made-up faces and displaying carefully groomed locks of hair pulled their veils more snugly over their heads.

It is no accident that the tombs of both Saadi and Hafez have gardens as their settings. Gardens are as central to Persian culture as they are to all the great civilizations of the East—China, Japan, and Mughal India—and the glory of the natural world spills out of Persian poetry. And like the transcendentalist philosophers Ralph Waldo Emerson and Henry David Thoreau, Hafez saw nature as a gateway to eternal truths:

How did the rose ever open its heart,
And give to this world all its beauty?
It felt the encouragement of light against its being,
Otherwise we all remain too frightened.

The modernist design of Saadi's tomb would never have been fitting for the burial place of Hafez. His is a modest, walled enclosure. Beside the garden stands a grove of orange trees, surrounded by reflecting pools and flowerbeds. In the middle of it all, under a circle of columns that support a stone gazebo, stands a marble bier. As at the tomb of Saadi, visitors approach and place a finger or hand on the surface. With a simple touch, those who have been nurtured on the verses of Hafez, which means almost the entire Iranian population, are able to touch the beauty of his simplicity, and the simple beauty of his wisdom.

I wandered the grounds for an hour or so, taking in the delicate strains of the *santour* and *dutar* as they tinkled from the speakers. The site seemed designed so that love, the emotion Hafez prized most, could never leave him. With no bars or nightclubs or any of the usual places where young people meet, Iran's parks and gardens have become venues where young couples may sit and discreetly nuzzle, taking inspiration from Hafez's lines in ways the ruling mullahs would frown upon. Toward the end of my walk, the music was cut and replaced with an announcement stating that the gates would be closing. It was time to leave. On the way to the exit, I met three young women, and one threw out a question: "Where are you from?"

"Oh, we just love America!" one tittered, after I responded.

"What do you like about it?"

"Everything!" the third said.

"The freedom!" the first one threw in.

I asked what they meant by freedom.

"From this!" the second girl chirped, fingering the edge of her veil.

The girls rattled off more reasons for their love of the U.S.—the culture! democracy! everything about it!—and then, of course, they wanted to know: Why had I come to Iran? What did I think of Iran?

I answered with my timeworn script—that the country had always interested me, that I always knew it was much different from the Arab world but wanted to see it firsthand. One of the women concluded: "Isn't it strange, as long as you've wanted to come to Iran, we've only wanted to go to the U.S."

It was all a little sad. For all the affection for America among young people, there is still very little understanding of what "America" is all about. For some it is everything that Iran isn't, but to actually articulate its appeal is a tougher task. None of the girls had been to the U.S., but all were dying to go. One had cousins living in suburban Los Angeles, and the brother of another was studying at the University of Miami. The women were art students and had set their sights on doing graduate studies at an American university. I admired their dreams but didn't have the heart to tell them that their chances of receiving a student visa were almost nil. Back in the pro-American days of the shah, fifty thousand Iranians were studying at American universities. Now there are only about eleven thousand. The girls might be accepted at any of a number of graduate art programs, but the odds of a young, single Iranian woman being granted a student visa were, as the saying goes, worse than hitting the lottery.

I wished them all the best and caught a taxi outside the gate and was soon back at the hotel. It was late. The Happy Hour café had closed for the night, so I checked my email at the computer set up in the lobby. The connection had become ornery, though it had been working fine earlier in the day. I asked Mahmoud, the night clerk, for help. He fiddled with the connections and restarted the terminal but could not cajole it into cooperation.

"No freedom!" he sighed. "They do this"—by "they" he could only mean the government—"to let us live a normal life, for a while, but then they turn it off. It's a way of reminding us that they control our lives, that they can do whatever they want."

"What about your guests?" I asked. "Don't they ever complain?" I knew it was a stupid question, and he replied as expected.

"It wouldn't matter. The guests from Iran, they know there's nothing we can do. We say anything, they will put us in jail, kill us, torture us."

I knew that nothing like that would happen over a fluky internet connection, but his point was made.

Like hotel night clerks everywhere in the world, Mahmoud's constant battle was how to pass the hours of interminable boredom, and there was no better relief than a late-night chat with a night-crawling guest. With no guests to pander to ("Welcome to Iran! You can have *anything* you like!"), he could drop his professional pose. We moved to the sitting area in the lobby and dropped into two overstuffed chairs.

"You know what we want?" Mahmoud began, leaning forward. "We just want to be a normal country. So many countries *want* to be important in the world. We'd like to be completely *un*important for a change, for no one to care about us at all. These leaders talk about Iran being a power in this part of the world, but the power they want, they only want it for themselves. They don't care about the people. You're from America?"

I nodded, but Mahmoud kept going.

"You know what we *don't* want? We don't want to compete with anyone, not even America. Power only brings trouble. Everywhere in the world, they hear 'Iran' and we know what they think: 'Iran wants a nuclear weapon, Iran supports terrorism, Iran does this, Iran does that.'"

I listened to Mahmoud's gripes with much empathy, but he was only repeating the chorus of a song I had heard too many times, and it always came down to complaints about the government. A sullen Mahmoud, sitting alone in the gloom of the lobby with a fitful internet connection, was the entire situation's sad but fitting representation.

The next morning Sohrab and I drove to Bagh-e Eram, or Eram Garden. It was a relief to get out of the hotel. Mahmoud's lament still hung in the lobby area like the stench of burnt coffee. The other guests in the breakfast room, daintily eating their croissants and jam, sipping from teacups with the practiced elegance of Victorian aristocrats, again seemed like a group of dinner guests who had been taken hostage and had no choice but to defy their captors with all the dignity they could muster.

Day-to-day reality in Iran may be as glum as Mahmoud described, but Iran's gardens, dating to Achaemenid times, have always served as a representation of *paradise*, originally a Farsi word meaning "enhanced space."

In the Persian view, paradise, as represented on Earth, is an expanse of green neatly divided into linear water channels and pathways, with a rectangular pool to reflect the sunlight and provide cooling relief in the heat of summer, but at this time of year to serve as a launching pad for the burst of spring. It is a setting that represents natural beauty as a mystical arrangement of balance and order, where geometric symmetry expresses balance and harmony, a concept that dates to the ancient Greeks and found resonance in the Christian world in the design of its massive cathedrals and the altarpieces that decorated them.

The Bagh-e Eram is more than a garden. Situated in the center is the Qavam House, a rambling thirty-two-room villa decorated with painted tiles inscribed with lines of verse by the only Persian who could honor such a place—Hafez. The house was built by the *ilkhanate*, or leader of the Qashqai tribes that inhabited the Shiraz region in the middle of the nineteenth century. Cultural influences from eastern and central Europe were filtering into Iran at the time, and the result was a building that borrowed heavily from Bulgarian and Turkish design.

It had rained in the night. Not much, just enough to dampen the grass and turn the leafy canopy into a latticework through which the hanging droplets could fall. I was lucky enough to get to the Bagh-e Eram before the sun had risen high enough to burn off the moisture from the overnight rain, so the grass was still glistening in the sunlight and the flowers were freshly aromatic, as flowers should be in the morning, and as any Persian poet, classic or modern, would agree.

I had circled the Qavam House and was crossing in front of the rectangular pool below the façade when a voice called out from a short distance away in smooth, unaccented English: "Hey, are you an American?"

The man looked about fifty and had the same stocky build as the wrestler Jamshid. Before I could reply, he strode over with very un-Persian-like nonchalance.

"I can tell. I just love Americans."

A little stunned by his forwardness, all I could reply was "have you been there?"

"Have I been to America?!" he replied.

His name was Arash, and as we stood under the drooping fronds of the palm trees he told me the story of his life in America. He had one to tell, and he wanted to unburden it to the only person in the Bagh-e Eram, or probably all of Shiraz, or all of Iran, who might understand.

Arash had gone to the U.S. in 1976 on a student visa, when Shah Mohammad Reza Pahlavi still held a firm grip on power and the U.S. and Iran were at least nominal allies. In 1980 Arash graduated from the University of Texas into a different world. The exiled shah was dying of cancer in Egypt, and Ayatollah Khomeini had become the Supreme Leader of the new Islamic Republic of Iran. Despite the turmoil back home, Arash's life continued relatively unruffled. He married and had a son. I didn't ask him what kind of work he did because it didn't matter. Years passed, and then came the terrorist attacks of September 11, 2001.

"To be honest, the year before I got in a little trouble with the IRS," he said. "My bank accounts were audited, and I thought that was the end of it. But then my house was raided. They came at about four o'clock in the morning. An FBI SWAT team broke the door down, took my computer and all my files, and they arrested me. A couple of days later they charged me with supporting a terrorist organization—Al-Qaeda. I couldn't believe it. Didn't they know, Al-Qaeda is Sunni and almost all Iranians are Shiites?

"The next few months were a nightmare. They took everything I had. My son had just gotten out of college and had a couple of job offers from the federal government, but they were withdrawn. My wife was a high school principal and up for a promotion, but she was passed over.

"That wasn't the worst. For a year I was held in a federal prison in Texas, and then they moved me to another one in Louisiana. A couple of months later I was moved again, this time to the CIA prison in Big Springs, Tennessee. I was there four and a half years. They tortured me, but whatever they wanted to know I don't have any idea. After a while I think they didn't know what to do with me, so they said they would drop all the charges if I agreed to return to Iran and give up any chance of returning to the U.S. I had lived in the U.S. for twenty-eight years, and my wife and son are still there, but what was I going to do, sit in prison the rest of my life? So I came back here. It's not over though. I have a lawyer who works in human rights, and we're trying to take this to the International Criminal Court."

What he'd said thus far wasn't all that surprising. What followed, though, was.

"You know," he said, with surprising ease, "I've got nothing against the American people. I can't say much for the government, but the American people, they're the best in the world. I just love Americans." A grin appeared on Arash's face. "You know, I still follow the Dallas Cowboys."

Arash wished me a very pleasant stay in Iran—"I hope you like it here, this is a great country, you know." And then he turned away, and as he retreated under the canopy of tree limbs, the blooming flowers, the morning sunlight, the decorated façade of the pavilion, and even the water in the reflecting pool left with him. I didn't know if Arash's story was more startling, sad, or admirable, or an odd mixture of all three. I was finally able to sort it out this way: The pitiful treatment he received from the country where he had made his home spoke for itself. It was surprising that it didn't color his entire view of America and Americans, and that he was still able to feel affection for the people he had lived among helped to prove the power of human relationships to overcome the divisive world of geopolitics.

After the encounter with Arash I needed something to brighten the day and knew where to find it—the Shah Cheragh Mosque.

According to Persian folklore, sometime in the early fourteenth century the cleric Ayatollah Dastghaib saw a light from the top of a hill and followed it to a nearby cemetery. A newly dug grave was discovered, and a body was unearthed wearing a coat of arms. A ring identified the body as that of the warrior Ahmad Ibn Musa. He and his brother Mohammad were the sons of the seventh of the Twelve Holy Imams, Musa Al-Khadim. The two holed up in Shiraz while on the run from Abbasid persecution at the end of the eighth century. It was in Shiraz where the two met their end. Many mosques in Iran are grand edifices with a history behind them to match, but the Shah Cheragh is relatively small and has no historical significance whatsoever. This is all to its credit, for it celebrates the beauty of light and color and nothing more. It is a poem in architectural form. It is also called the Pink Mosque because of the pink tiles that cover the interior, but the most brilliant color is found in the prayer hall facing the courtyard. Lined with arched windows of colored glass that catch the sunlight early in the morning, they transform the interior into a shimmering, kaleidoscopic display. Mirza Hassan Ali, the ruler of Shiraz at the time, built the mosque to create the unusual light effect and configured the design so that it would be strongest in the morning.

The beauty of light often finds expression in Persian poetry, and when it does it is usually linked to the spiritual world. In his *Rubaiyat,* Omar Khayyam wrote:

Wake! For the Sun, who scattered into flight
The stars before him from the field of night,
Drives night along with them from Heaven,
And strikes the sultan's turret with a shaft of light.

I was a little late getting to the Shah Cheragh. The sun had risen so high that the light in the prayer hall had dimmed, though flickers were still streaming through the windows and dancing off the carpet and the vaulted ceiling, enough to resemble the last glimpse of the sun at evening.

Back at the hotel, the diversions to round off a day of sightseeing were the same as the day before: the room TV offered nothing in English except predictable Press TV, and the "Happy Hour" crowd consisted of a handful of couples sipping fruit juices and munching on tasteless snacks.

Instead of returning to the Sharzeh for dinner I decided to try its satellite branch across the Roodkhaneye Khoshk, the dry river that cuts through the heart of the city. The Sharzeh II was located in an upscale neighborhood where the young were known to frolic, and therefore a good place to witness what passes for Iranian nightlife.

But Sharzeh II was no match for Sharzeh I. The plastic-coated menus displaying photos of each dish gave it a coffee shop feel, and the two musicians—again both male—were crowded onto a tiny stage in a corner of the dining room. The only touch of cultural flavor was the open-mouthed oven at the entrance, where arriving guests could watch flat slabs of dough being slapped against the inner walls and quickly transforming into steaming, sweet-scented *taftoon* loaves.

There wasn't much reason to linger once I had finished my dinner, so I paid the bill and returned to the street. It was Wednesday night, the beginning of the Iranian weekend. The stores were open, and moneyed Shirazis were out on the town: Top-end BMWs and Mercedes backed up the traffic, and women in form-fitting manteaux and hair-revealing headscarves paraded, catwalk-style, between the jewelry stores and cosmetic boutiques as they attempted to stretch their greatly devalued rials.

Not only women expressed resistance to the regime through their appearance. A few young men sported odd haircuts that the religious authorities had condemned as "un-Islamic" and added thick black belts embellished with metal studs to bell-bottom jeans that had disappeared from the global fashion scene in the 1970s. All this was simply to irk government hardliners, who viewed such things as symbols of "corrupt" Western fashion. At a pizzeria down the street from the Sharzeh a throng of young Shirazis filled its two levels to do what they could to create a nightclub atmosphere. Pop tunes—banned, tolerated, officially sanctioned, it made no difference—blasted into the night.

Around the corner from the pizzeria was a small supermarket, so I ducked in to see what goods could be had in a sanctions-afflicted country. American laws may prohibit any commercial relationship with Iran, but the shelves were stocked with Heinz ketchup and Breck shampoo, Kellogg's cereals, Revlon cosmetics, and Johnson & Johnson bandages. In the soft-drink coolers the Pepsi cans were curiously printed in Farsi.

The store was a tribute to the Iranian entrepreneurs who had set up shop in Dubai and other cities on the other side of the Persian Gulf. Sanctions may drain the bank accounts of most of the population where they are applied and pinch some of the ruling, moneyed elite, but they are almost always a boon to black marketers, smugglers, and anyone else who thrives on illegal trade. In Dubai, for example, they typically ordered more than they could ever deliver to the local markets and shipped the surplus to Iran. International sanctions may have halted the sale of airplane parts, medical equipment, and other goods easy to monitor, but the flow of consumer items continued, ready to be snapped up by Iranians hankering for a taste of America.

"Sanctions? All they are is good for business—for *Iranians* doing business," a correspondent for Radio Farda, the Iranian branch of Radio Free Europe/Radio Liberty, told me.

It was after midnight, but still the traffic hadn't thinned. The streets had become a parade route for late-model cars inching their way between the lights. With no taxis in sight, I began walking along the line of cars, when a large suv pulled up beside me. A young woman poked her head out of the window and asked, in clear, crisp English, where I was trying to go.

Looking for a taxi on a Wednesday night in Shiraz was a fool's errand, she said, though not in those exact words. But she knew of a taxi stand about a mile away and offered to take me there. She opened the back door, and I got in. Her name was Fereshteh, and piloting the enormous rig was her brother, Saeed. Saeed had lived in Los Angeles for two years, working in public relations, but had returned to Iran to get married. Fereshteh had spent six months in California and had wanted to stay longer, but her visa had been about to expire, and hiding from American immigration officials among family members with American citizenship was not an appealing option, as attractive as a new life in America appeared. So she, too, returned to Iran.

"You're American, aren't you?" she asked, in smooth, unaccented English, echoing Arash from the Bagh-e Eram.

Answering without answering, I asked how she could tell.

"The way you were walking," Saeed cut in. "We saw you from the end of the street. Ferri did. She said, 'Look, there's an American.'"

I asked them how Americans walk.

"Like you . . ." Saeed equivocated.

"How do I walk?"

". . . Like an American."

I asked Saeed about his life in LA and living in the U.S.

"Once you get past the politics and religion there are a lot of similarities to Iran," he began. "We are also a society with a lot of different cultures. You have all the Spanish-speakers and everyone else who came before, the Europeans. We aren't much different. My father is Azeri, but his father was part Kurdish. My mother is Persian—mostly. She thinks there's also some Turkish in there somewhere. You line up a group of Iranians and there's no one you can say that looks 'Iranian.' There are Azeris, Baluchis, Arabs, Uzbeks, Persians, Armenians . . ."

I felt like prodding a little. "So multiculturalism and diversity link the two?"

"No, that's not all. We also know what it means to be a superpower. We were also a superpower once."

"Once" was more than two thousand years in the past, but in the Persian mind, when seeking respect and affirmation, two thousand years may as well be yesterday. But there was no point in quibbling. There was a subtext here, and I knew what it said—that Iran didn't feel inferior to the U.S., that it believed its seven thousand years of civilization, while not outweighing America's military and economic power, at least put Iran on an equal footing. In economic terms, Iran was "old money," slightly faded but still holding its regal air; America was nouveau riche—young, glossy, even promising, but still quite "young," naive, and inexperienced. Seen in this light, the Iranian position in the nearly four-decade-old standoff could be summarized as follows: "You have global economic, military, and political power beyond anything the world has ever seen. We have seven thousand years of history and artistic development and cultural achievements, and we don't need an empire anymore. We've 'been there and done that.' See us as an equal and we can do business."

We never found the taxi stand, so Saeed and Ferri offered to take me back to my hotel. In expected, obligatory taarof, I told them they didn't have to put themselves out, and in expected, obligatory taarof, they said it was no problem at all, that it was on their way—more or less—but the last part wasn't expressed directly, it was what I inferred. Where Persian protocols are concerned, little to nothing is directly expressed. The subtext is all that matters, but sometimes the subtext is as transparent as waxed paper.

Zigzagging through the empty streets of Shiraz's residential neighborhoods, we continued to dissect the American-Iranian impasse. It was self-defeating and foolish, we concluded. If the Russians and Americans could maintain diplomatic relations all through the Cold War, and in doing so avoided a nuclear holocaust, why couldn't the Americans and Iranians?

Back at the hotel, there was still a little life left in the "Happy Hour Café." The sleepy waiter was tending to his last customers, so I ordered a mint tea and settled back to ponder the relationship between the United States and Iran. Forty years of Cold War diplomacy, as much as they avoided nuclear holocaust, never improved relations between the Soviet Union and the United States to a significant degree. The two continued to talk past each other but learned to agree to disagree. Nevertheless, the relationship did foster a degree of understanding, if not agreement.

The lesson from all this was that better relations between countries, even the most adversarial, do not need diplomatic relations to improve. In fact, relationships might have a better chance of improving if the diplomats simply got out of the way.

The following morning offered an affirmation of my view. I had just returned to my room from breakfast when the maid rapped on the door, but a little hastily, as hotel maids do. Once she saw me she started to back out, but I waved her in. As she puttered around the room, she finally got up the courage to ask, in practiced but pidgin English, "Where—are—you—from?"

I told her.

"Oooh . . ." she oozed, her eyes widening. I sensed surprise, admiration, envy, possibly a combination of all three.

The next morning I was heading to breakfast when a voice at the end of the hall called out: "Good—morn—ing!" she cooed, as smooth and as sweet as any of the birds portrayed in Saadi's garden.